# MODERN SOCIOLOGY

# MODERN SOCIOLOGY

(In 2 Volumes)

## Volume 2
## (Cultural Sociology)

*Editor*

**G.S. Mohanty**

ISHA

**ISHA BOOKS**

**Delhi-110033**

**Modern Sociology**
*(Cultural Sociology)*

Rs. 1800 (Set)
Rs. 900 (Each Volume)

ISBN : 81-8205-207-6 (Set)
ISBN : 81-8205-280-7 (Vol. 2)



Published in 2005 in India by
Isha Books
D-43, Prithviraj Road,
Adarsh Nagar, Delhi - 110033
e-mail : ishabooks@hotmail.com

Laser Typesetting at : Global Printers, New Delhi
Printed at : Chawla Offset Press, Delhi

# Contents

# Preface

The word culture comes from the Latin root *colere* (to inhabit, to cultivate, or to honour). In general, it refers to human activity; different definitions of culture reflect different theories for understanding, or criteria for valuing, human activity. Culture is traditionally the oldest human character, its significant traces separating *Homo* from *australopithecines*, and Man from the Animals, though new discoveries are blurring these edges in our day.

Culture is one of the most interesting and widely used concepts in sociology. It is central to the humanities, the social sciences, and the fine and performing arts, where it is understood in a variety of ways. It is also used colloquially in everyday life, where it takes on a myriad of meanings. But while the tremendous range of definitions and usage makes the concept interesting, this same multiplicity of meanings makes culture confusing and ambiguous.

The present book is a concise introduction to the burgeoning field of cultural sociology. It focuses upon the cultural processes and meanings that are central to every sphere of contemporary life. Readers will be exposed to the basic issues and frameworks used for understanding culture and to some of the significant research in the field. It is designed to facilitate awareness, identification and analysis of cultural processes and meanings, in order to allow readers to become more effective in the increasingly multi-cultural environments of the contemporary world.

***Editor***

# 1

# Introducton

A culture is a human group which shares a number of essential aspects of daily life. Language, customs, traditions, religion and values are some of the shared products that define each cultural group. Each human group creates both material and non- material culture. Material culture for example includes physical objects (money, homes, cars) while non-material culture addresses the beliefs, values and behavior share by a particular group. Taken together, this material and non-material culture shapes the emotional, cognitive, spiritual, and social experiences of individuals within the group.

Sociologists are interested not only in the specific things that define a culture but also in how that particular culture impacts both the individuals within it and the larger society around it. Sociology is 'about' people. Sociology is the study of humanity. However this description of sociology is only partially correct. To say that sociology is about people and humanity is not enough to distinguish it from the other subjects in the human sciences. For it is equally the case that Psychology, Social Policy, Economics and Social History, amongst others, are all in some sense about people and humanity. Thus the fact that sociology is about people and humanity gets us only part way along the road to a full definition of the subject.

Sociology is also concerned with human culture. A provisional definition of culture used by sociologists is that of

' a way of life'. Sociology has always concerned itself with the study of culture and this would fit in with what we already know about sociology; namely it the study of people in society. Sociology is characterised by the fact that it examines the informal and formal social relationships engaged in by individuals. Sociologists might typically observe and explain types of interactions which take place between individuals. So to include this idea of social interaction in any definition of sociology is helpful.

However the inclusion of social interaction does not establish sociology's distinctiveness when it is considered alongside, for example psychology. Psychology, just like sociology, also involves the study of human interaction. There may be a way of differentiating sociology.

Linton defines the concept of a non-material culture as:

> "The way of life of its members; the collection of ideas and habits which they learn, share and transmit from generation to generation".

The ideas of sharing, teaching and learning are crucial here for understanding the process whereby people learn to become human beings. This is because people are born into an existing cultural system. In order to learn how to behave in society, therefore, arrangements have to be made for people to fit-into existing patterns of behaviour and we call this a process of socialisation.

## The Socialisation Process

Learning how to become human and to behave in ways that accord with the general expectations of others is a process that begins at birth and continues throughout our life. We never stop learning how to behave, mainly because our society is always changing and we are continually faced with learning how to behave in new and different situations. When starting to look at the socialisation process, therefore, we can begin by identifying two basic types of socialisation:

a. *Primary socialisation:* Primary socialisation occurs between the individual and those people in their life with whom they have primary relationships. A primary relationship is one in which the individual has a close, personal, intimate and face-to-face relationship with the people that are responsible for the socialisation process. For most of us, the first primary relationship we form is with our parent(s) or guardians - the people who are charged with the initial socialisation process. As we grow older and start to develop as human beings, we start to form primary attachments with friends and eventually with other adults.

Agencies of Socialisation

The first agency that takes responsibility for primary socialisation is the family, and the main agents of socialisation are a child's parents and relations. In a family group, for example, we learn many of the basic characteristics of being human in terms of our particular society. For example, we learn how to:

— Walk

— Talk

— Use various tools, such as knives and forks and so forth.

The family group doesn't just teach us the physical characteristics of being human, however. Our parents use their values to try to teach us things like:

— The difference between right and wrong behaviour and

— How to relate appropriately to others (family, friends, strangers, etc.).

Although this socialisation process is lengthy and complicated, it is important not to see it just as a situation in which an agent of socialisation, such as a parent, simply teaches behaviour that is then copied without question by the child. Although part of a child's socialisation does involve copying the behaviour they see around them, the child is also actively involved in the socialisation process. Children do not always obey their parents and even at an early age, conflicts occur. In addition, while the child is learning how to adapt to their environment they are changing the way the people around them behave, in a variety of different ways. Finally, perhaps, as we start to get a little older we start to make decisions for ourselves, based upon our experience in the world. We start to try to manipulate our world and the people in it. In this respect, we start to learn how to deal with other people by understanding the type of behaviour that others expect of us.

Many of the things we learn through our primary socialisation stay with us for life. This is because, as human beings, we learn the basic principles involved with "being human", rather than simply a set of things we must or must not do. This is important to us, because it means that we can apply these principles to new and different situations. For example, we don't just learn how to relate to adults, we learn how to distinguish between different types of adult on the basis of their status and their relationship to us. For example, we don't behave towards a parent in the same way that we behave towards an adult who is not familiar to us.

If you watch very young children, just as they are starting to be introduced to adults who not are familiar to them, you frequently find they become quiet and shy. This is because the child is unsure about how to behave appropriately towards the stranger. The same process happens in any new situation. Teenage men and women, for example, tend to be initially shy and awkward in each others company. This embarrassment is simply part of not being sure about how they are expected to behave appropriately in this new situation.

Finally, one of the main things socialised into us during this particular period of primary socialisation is a knowledge of gender roles; that is, what it means, in our society to be either masculine or feminine.

## Secondary Socialisation

Secondary socialisation occurs between the individual and those people in their life with whom they have secondary relationships. A secondary relationship is one in which the individual does not have a close, personal, intimate or face-to-face relationship with the people that are responsible for the socialisation process.

Secondary socialisation is necessary because it represents the way that we start to learn about the nature of the social world beyond our primary contacts. We have to learn to deal with people who are not emotionally close to us, mainly because the vast majority of the people we will come into contact with in our adult lives will be dealt with unemotionally. We have to learn how to cope with this, which is why this second type of socialisation is necessary.

Agents of socialisation will consequently be teachers, priests, television personalities, rock stars and so forth. In some cases, such as school and teachers, we are in daily, face-to-face contact with the people who are socialising us without ever developing a primary attachment to them. In other cases, such as admiring a particular film or rock star, we may never meet them, yet we can still be influenced by what they look like, what they do and how they do it.

## Structure of Social Life: Values, Norms, Roles and Status

So far, we have looked at the ideas of society, culture and socialisation in very general terms. The next stage in our development of sociological understanding is to look at the significance of these ideas in more specific terms. To help us do this, we need to look at a number of related ideas that give substance to the sociological argument that human social behaviour is learned. The main ideas we need to explore in greater depth, therefore, are those of:

— Social Role.

— Social Status.

— Values and

— Norms.

These ideas to show some of the basic ways that social behaviour is structured.

***Values***

All human societies have certain problems that have to be solved if life is to be maintained. There are a variety of ways, that people can decide to solve these problems and the choices we make concerning such solutions are based upon what sociologists call values. Values are beliefs that we have about what is important, both to us and to society as a whole. A value, therefore, is a belief about the way something should be.

Some values are very personal to us as individuals, whilst others are much more widely-held by large groups of people. In this case, values become morals - things that we consider to be of such absolute and fundamental importance that we believe everyone should hold such ideas as a personal value. A good example of a moral value in our society might be that it is wrong to kill another human being.

Finally, for the moment, it should be apparent that values, by definition, always involve judgements. In short, the values we hold are general behavioural guidelines. They tell us what we believe is right or wrong, for example, but that do not tell us how we should behave appropriately in any given social situation. This is the part played by norms in the overall structure of our social behaviour.

### *Norms*

Every value that we hold has a number of associated ideas called norms. Norms are expected, socially-acceptable, ways of behaving in any given social situation. Like values they differ from individual to individual and society to society.

The second example noted above expresses a mixture of values. In Britain, the "alcohol norm" reflects the value that we, as a society, place on concepts of childhood and adulthood. An adult is considered to be someone over the age of 18; drinking alcohol in a pub is a pastime we associate with adults, therefore, anyone under the age of 18 should not be allowed to drink alcohol in a pub because they are not legally an adult. In Saudi Arabia, the ban on drinking alcohol - whether you are considered to be a child or an adult - is related to religious values.

The idea of norms is not only useful as a means of showing the various ways that human behaviour is structured. It also helps to illustrate one of the ideas noted earlier concerning the subject matter of Sociology. You will recall that one of the problems we identified was that society does not have a physical existence, yet sociologists argue that it affects our behaviour because it is a force. We can demonstrate the existence of this force using the concept of norms.

Although we cannot see norms, sociologists argue that they act on us in various ways because they represent expected and acceptable ways of behaving in society. If this is the case, we should be able to experiment with norms of behaviour to see the possible effect of disrupting normative expectations.

## Disrupting Norms of Behaviour

The American sociologist Harold Garfinkel decided to show how norms exist by asking his students, in a series of experiments, to deliberately break some expected norms.

Such experiments show how important norms are and how easy it is to disrupt norms - with frequently alarming results. Because there are thousands of norms that we recognise, it is easy to construct simple everyday experiments to test the existence of norms in your life.

Although it is not advisable if you value your sanity and freedom, you could:

— Ignore your friends.

— Talk to a complete stranger as if they were your closest friend.

— Walk around wearing a dress (if you are male).

— Drive your car on the right-hand side of the road.

*Sub-Cultures*

Of more interest to us is the way this sense of belonging to the same culture can be broken down into more specific values and norms since, although we share many things with others in our society, not everyone has exactly the same values and norms. Some groups of people share a particular way of life and we term these smaller groups sub-cultures. Some examples that show the wide range of sub-cultural groups in our society might be:

— Football supporters,

— Trainspotters,

— Orthodox Jews,

— Travellers,

— College students.

Although we will be looking in much more detail at the idea of sub-cultural groups in various parts of the course, we can use the last example, that of being part of a "College student sub-culture", to illustrate a couple of other sociological ideas.

Firstly, by becoming a College student you have chosen to join a particular subcultural group with its own particular "way of life". However, just because you are part of this sub-culture doesn't mean that you cannot be part of other sub-cultural groups or, indeed, the culture of our society as a whole. While some of the values of this sub-culture and the norms associated with these values may be different to the values and norms of other sub-cultures, they can still be part of the wider culture in our society. Indeed, the reason you might value an educational qualification is precisely because this qualification has a value in wider society. A prospective employer, might offer you a job on the basis of your educational qualifications, whereas they wouldn't consider you for the job if you didn't have the qualifications.

Secondly, we have started to introduce the idea that an individual's place in society can be looked at on two basic levels:

— In terms of a general sense of culture - what it means to people, for example, to be English, French, American and so forth.

— In terms of a specific sense of sub-cultures. That is, the various groups we belong to that involve particular sets of norms that apply only when we participate in these groups.

Every individual participates in numerous sub-cultural groups. The norms that apply in one group may be different to the norms that apply in another. The problem, here, is that the potential for normative confusion is huge - and we have seen that the penalties for not behaving in accordance with social norms can be very great. As people, therefore, we have to constantly consider how we can manage our lives to produce a sense of order and basic predictability. How, in short, do we establish a structure of rules governing behaviour that we can immediately recognise and conform to in a variety of different situations?

### Social Roles

An initial definition of a role is that it represents the way that someone is expected to behave in a particular social situation. Roles, therefore, are the parts that we play in our relationships with others and this idea is similar to that of an actor playing a part in a play. Each individual plays many roles in society, some examples being:

— Teacher,

— Student,

— Mother,

— Son,

— Employer,

— Employee and so forth.

Each role has a number of associated characteristics. It involves:

— *Norms of behaviour*: A person playing the role of a student is expected to behave in a particular way.

— A group of other roles that relate specifically to the role we are playing.

This is called a role-set and examples of the College student's role set might be:

— Other students.

— Your class teacher.

— Other teachers.

— College caretakers.

— College Administration staff.

— College librarians and so on.

The main reason for mentioning the idea of a role set is to impress on you the idea that we can only play a role in relation to other people. There would be little point, for example, of my trying to play the role of teacher if I had no students to teach.

Status is important in our society and the way that we feel about our status in relation to others will affect the way that we behave in certain situations. This is because status is closely related to the idea of power - the ability to get people to do things, regardless of their ability to resist.

A teacher, for example, may believe that their status is greater than that of their students; therefore, he or she might feel justified in:

— Setting students work do outside their class.

— Telling a noisy student to be quiet.

— Making an unruly student leave the class.

Having noted that our life consists of playing out a wide variety of roles, we can note two further aspects to role play:

— There are some roles that we choose to play. These are called achieved roles precisely because we have to chosen to play them; we have done something to achieve them. Your role as a College student is an achieved one because you have chosen to play it.

— There are some roles we are forced to play. These are called ascribed roles because they are roles that are given to us by other, more powerful, people. For example, between the ages of 5 and 16 in our society, everyone is given the ascribed role of schoolchild. The government has decided that everyone must play this role, whether they want to or not.

Similarly, status can also be achieved or ascribed. A teacher has a higher status than a student because they have achieved the level of qualification and training necessary to qualify for this role. On the other hand, your status as male or female is an ascribed status - it is something that derives from your biological status.

Roles have two further dimensions that are worth noting here:

— *What is called the prescibed aspect of a role:* Each role you adopt, whether achieved or ascribed, contains a set of normative expectations about how you should behave when you are in that role. The norms associated with the role tell us and others how to play the role successfully. For example, you have all adopted the role of student and you understand many of the prescriptions that go with this role. An A-level student is expected to:

  — Attend classes.

  — Do homework.

  — Take notes.

  — Listen attentively etc.

— *What we term role performance:* This relates to how successfully you play your prescribed role. If you think about it, all students play the same basic role, but their performance - success or failure in that role, for example - will vary dramatically. Alternatively, there may be more than one way to perform a role successfully.

This distinction is useful because it tells us something about role play. The prescribed element in any role provides a basic structure governing the way people are generally supposed to interact. Thus, the teacher - student relationship will always be based on a set of norms particular to the culture in which the roles exist. However, the actual relationship between teacher and student (role performance) can be modified by a range of other relevant factors. For example, the age of the individual playing the student role may alter the way the role is performed.

For sociologists, the idea that human beings do not have instincts means that we have to develop a sense of how to behave towards each other. The fact that we have to develop and learn role play is, in this respect, strong evidence against the existence of instincts.

In addition, by playing roles we introduce two things into our life:

— A sense of order.

Each role we play is associated with a set of norms.

These rules give us a sense of routine. Once we have learnt the rules associated with a particular role we can then play that role easily and successfully, whatever the actual situation we find ourselves in.

— A sense of predictability.

This is because we know, when playing a particular role in relation to other people, they will behave in roughly predictable ways. When we know what role someone is playing in relation to us, it gives us a set of guidelines for our own behaviour. A student, for example, knows roughly the kinds of things that a teacher expects because the student has learnt how to play their role.

Order and predictability are important to us, since without them the social world would be a very dangerous and confusing place. For example, consider the idea that if we didn't play certain roles how impossible life would be. Imagine, for example, a situation in which you could not remember what your relationship to everyone around you was supposed to be.

Each time the teacher came into the classroom they would have to patiently explain who they were and what they were going to do with you. As students, each time you came into the classroom you would have to learn exactly what a student was supposed to do. This would be extremely time-consuming - people would spend so much time learning who they were and how they were supposed to behave that nothing would ever get done.

If you now think about all of the relationships you have with people - and the roles you play - the scale of the problem should be apparent. One great benefit of role play, therefore, is that once we have learnt what is expected of us in one role, we can use that knowledge whenever we have to play that role.

By playing roles, therefore, we organise our behaviour so that we can deal appropriately with other people. Role play helps us to regulate our behaviour and that of others. The adoption of roles is a way of controlling people's behaviour, mainly because the norms associated with each role give us boundary markers against which to judge acceptable and unacceptable behaviour.

One of the great advantages of role play is that it helps us to accomplish certain tasks easily and effectively. For example, the teaching and learning process is made easier if both teacher and student are behaving towards each other in ways that are considered appropriate for their roles.

One final idea we have to note is that, for all the advantages they give us in the organisation of our lives, the wide number and variety of roles that we play occasionally causes us problems. One major problem is called role conflict and this occurs when the norms that are consistent with one role that we play prevent us from behaving in accordance with the norms consistent with another role. Imagine that you play two different roles in your life.

**Social Control**

All the ideas we've looked at so far have been implicitly concerned with the various ways that people attempt to create order, stability and predictability in their own and other people's behaviour. In this respect, we have been indirectly talking about the various ways that any society attempts to control the behaviour of its members. These controls affect not just the way people actually behave, but also the way they think about the nature of the social world.

Therefore, we can start to bring all of these ideas together under the general heading of social control and look a little more closely at the various forms of social control that exist in any society. At its most basic, social control involves all of the things that we do or have done to us that are designed to maintain or change people's behaviour. The socialisation process, involves social control because it represents an attempt by people to shape the way in which a child develops. When we develop certain values and adopt particular norms, this too is a form of social control since we are placing limits on what we consider to be acceptable or normal behaviour.

Role play is again a form of social control because we are trying to act in ways that are considered orderly and predictable in certain situations. Social life, in this respect, is a life-long process of learning rules. We may not always agree with those rules, nor do we always obey them, but the fact remains that they exist and we have to take note of their existence.

People, therefore, create rules of behaviour that are the basis for social organisation and since we always have a choice as to whether or not we obey these rules, they are supported by social sanctions. These are the things we do in order to try to make people conform to our expectations. Sanctions can be one of two types:

— Positive sanctions (or rewards) are pleasant things we can do to try to make people conform and behave in a routine, predictable, fashion.

— Negative sanctions (or punishments) are basically the not very nice things we can do to try to make people conform and behave in a routine, predictable, fashion. There are a vast range of negative sanctions we can use in our society, ranging from not talking to people if they annoy us, through beating them up to putting them in prison.

The ultimate negative sanction, perhaps, is to kill someone.

— *Formal social controls:* Control here is based around the idea of formal, legal, norms (or laws) of behaviour. That is, rules of behaviour that are written down and, in societies such as our own, that apply equally to everyone (not all societies apply formal rules equally). Where laws are involved, it is usual to find a group of people, normally employed by the government, whose job it is to enforce the law. In our society, for example, the main agency of formal social control is the police and the judiciary (courts), although the armed forces can, on occasions, be used to perform this role.

  — Not all formal norms are laws, however. When you are accepted into College, for example, you agree to abide by the formal rules governing behaviour in this institution. For example, if you do not attend classes then you will be punished in some way.

  — In general terms, formal rules and social controls exist to tell everyone within a society or social group what is and is not acceptable in terms of behaviour. Such formal controls usually exist where a group is very large and its members are not in day-to-day contact with each other.

— *Informal Social Controls:* Like their formal counterpart, informal controls exist to reward or punish people for unacceptable behaviour (what sociologists call deviance). Informal controls cover a vast array of possible sanctions and tend to differ from individual to individual, group to group and society to society. Informal controls apply to informal norms of behaviour and they include things like ridicule, sarcasm, disapproving looks, punching people in the face and so forth.

Most, if not all, A-level Sociology students begin their course with a fairly vague idea about what is involved in the "study of society". A copy of the syllabus is an initial starting point because it maps-out for you the areas you will be studying during your course. However, it doesn't tell you a great deal about what Sociology is. This Introduction, therefore, is designed to help you identify the subject matter of Sociology and, to help us do this we will be looking at four main ideas:

— An initial definition of Sociology as a subject.

— The types of questions that sociologists ask.

— The Sociological Perspective.

— The difference between Naturalistic and sociological ideas and explanations.

Sociology is the study of human societies. It is usually classed as one of the social sciences and was established as a subject in the late 18th century.

However, the subject has only really gained acceptance as an academic subject in the 20th century through the work of writers such as Emile Durkheim, Max Weber and Talcott Parsons. One name that you may have heard of - Karl Marx - has probably done more to stimulate people's interest in the subject than anyone else, even though he lived and wrote in a period before Sociology became fully established as an academic discipline.

Sociology, therefore, has a reasonably long history of development although in Britain it has only been in the last 30 - 40 years that Sociology as an examined subject in the education system has achieved a level of prominence equivalent to or above most of the other subjects it is possible to study. At present, approximately 40,000 students sit an A-level Sociology exam, making it one of the most popular A-levels in our society.

Sociology is the study of the social world. It involves studying human beings and their patterns of behaviour. In order to do this, we focus on the way people form relationships and how these relationships, considered in their totality, are represented by the concept of a "society". In this respect, the focus of the sociologist's attention is group behaviour. That is, the effect that the groups people join or are born into have upon people's social behaviour.

***How sociologists study the social world.***

The definitions included words like "scientific", "systematic" and "objective" - ideas that tell us something about the both the way sociologists study social behaviour and the kind of knowledge they are trying to produce about social life. While we will develop these ideas in much greater detail in another part of the course, we need to note a couple of things about them now.

Objective basically means that sociologists try to create knowledge that is factual, rather than simply based on opinion. In simple terms, sociologists try to avoid personal bias intruding into their research. To do this, they use:

— *Systematic ways of studying social behaviour:* By this is meant that sociologists try to use methods of research that are governed by certain rules of evidence. For example, a sociologist will try to test his or her ideas in some way. We will see an example of this in a moment when we look at the difference between Naturalistic and sociological explanations of human behaviour.

Sociology is a social science concerned with the study of human social relationships and the various ways these relationships are patterned in terms of social groups, organisations and societies.

## Sociological Perspective

A perspective can be defined as a way of looking at and seeing something. To have a perspective, therefore, means to look at something in a particular way. For sociologists, are looking at is the social world - in effect, the various ways that human beings behave in a social way. All sociologists necessarily look at the social world from exactly the same perspective, not that sociologists are always in complete about what they are seeing, how behaviour could or should be understood and so forth. The sociological perspective is made-up of a number of quite different sub-perspectives. However, it is possible - and at this stage of your course desirable, to identify a number of common ideas which most, if not all, sociologists believe. We can note these as follows:

— Human beings are social animals. That is, we need to co-operate with others in some way to produce the social world in which we live.

— Human social behaviour is learned, not instinctive. In this respect, the argument is that we have to learn, from the moment we are born, how to be not just a human being but also a recognisable member of the society into which we happen to have been born.

— To understand human social behaviour we have to focus our attention on the groups to which people belong. These groups are many and varied, as we will see in a moment, but the largest group to which people belong is a society.

— Sociology is a perspective that looks at the totality of relationships in an individual's life. In this respect, sociologists do not restrict their studies to a single dimension of an individual's life (economics, politics, history, geography, psychology and so forth). Although each of these is significant and interesting, to varying degrees, it is only by looking at how these relationships affect each other that we can arrive at a complete picture of human social behaviour.

This final idea leads us briefly to consider other, possibly complimentary, social sciences. You should note that sociologists do not reject out of hand the contributions of writers in areas such as economics, politics and psychology. However, the existence of sociology as an academic discipline is based on a recognition that human beings are not one-dimensional beings but rather multidimensional beings.

## Sociology and Commonsense

Commonsense ideas and explanations represent a form of social perspective since they claim to represent the things that "everyone knows" about the social world and / or human behaviour. These ideas, whatever they may be, are not necessarily incorrect, but they do tend to have one characteristic that sets them apart from sociological forms of knowledge, namely that commonsense ideas are simply assumed to be true. Sociological knowledge, however, has greater validity than most forms of commonsense knowledge because it has been tested through some form of observation. In simple terms, sociologists try to base their statements about human behaviour on evidence rather than simple assumption. There are two particular points to note when you consider the following ideas:

— Sociological knowledge is frequently at odds with "what everyone knows", mainly because it is the product of theory development and testing.

— Sociological knowledge is not simply the "statement of the obvious" using lots of long, complicated, words whose main purpose is to obscure the fact that all sociologists are really doing is making simple, self-evident, statements.

We can illustrate some differences between commonsense and sociological perspectives by examining a number of commonsense statements about various forms of human behaviour.

# 2

# Sociology of Cultural Diversities

Sociology is a subject made up of competing theories on society. All the differing theories within sociology are best described as basically involved in the project of describing and explaining 'social order'. In other words sociology has always sought to understand how the components of society, the social relationships and the social institutions, contribute to, or deflect from the continued existence of 'society'. This is not to suggest that sociology is not concerned with social conflict and social change too. However these concerns are essentially one's which derive from, and supplement, the major objective of understanding social order.

Culture theory is that branch of anthropology and other related social science disciplines (i.e., for example, sociology) that seeks to define the heuristic concept of culture in operational and/or scientific terms. In the 19th century culture was used by some to refer to a wide array of human activities, and by others as a synonym for "civilization".

In the 20th century, anthropologists began theorizing about culture as an object of scientific analysis. Some used it to distinguish human adaptive strategies from the largely instinctive adaptive strategies of animals, including the adaptive strategies of other primates and non-human hominids, whereas others used it to refer to symbolic representations and expressions of human experience, with no direct adaptive value. Both groups understood culture as being definitive of human nature.

According to many theories that have gained wide acceptance among anthropologists, culture exhibits the way that humans interpret their biology and their environment. Culture becomes such an integral part of human existence that it is the human environment, and most cultural change can be attributed to human adaptation to historical events. Moreover, given that culture is seen as the primary adaptive mechanism of humans and takes place much faster than human biological evolution, most cultural change can be viewed as culture adapting to itself.

Although most anthropologists try to define culture in such a way that it separates human beings from other animals, many human traits are similar to those of other animals, particularly the traits of other primates. For example, chimpanzees have big brains, but *ceteris paribus* human brains are bigger. Similarly, bonobos exhibit complex sexual behavior, but human beings exhibit much more complex sexual behaviors. As such, anthropologists often debate whether human behavior is different from animal behavior in degree rather than in kind; they must also find ways to distinguish cultural behavior from sociological behavior and psychological behavior.

Cultural rules, therefore, provide a structure for people's behaviour, effectively channelling behaviour in some ways but not others. The stress here, therefore, is on the way our behaviour is constrained by the rules of the society into which we are born. Whenever you enter a building, your behaviour is constrained by its physical structure, layout and purpose. For example, if you want to move from one room to another, then you have to use the doors that have been provided by the designer and builder. Similarly, it would be difficult for you to cook a hot meal in a room designed to be a bathroom, just as you might find it difficult to sleep in a kitchen. These things are not, of course, impossible, but it cannot be denied that physical structures constrain our behaviour.

A culture, with its attendant roles, statuses, values and norms similarly constrains our range of possible behaviours. This is not a physical constraint, as such, but rather a mental one that leads to the individual choosing to limit his or her range of behaviour. We feel inhibited, for example, about doing things that people find culturally distasteful. Social structures, according to this way of seeing things, operate at an institutional level in society. We experience structural pressures whenever we adopt a particular role, since as we have seen, by taking on a role we take on certain norms, give expression to certain values and have a particular status in society. Following are the basis for a consensus theory of social organisation:

— If
  — Society always has a culture
— And
  — Everyone is necessarily socialised into that culture
— Then
  — A general consensus over values and norms must exist
— Because
  — Everyone is socialised into the same set of general ideas.

A major problem this theory is that of how to explain the very clear differences in behaviour that we see all around us everyday. People, for example, do not behave in exactly the same way and there are clear cultural differences present in the same society. The solution to such a problem is usually created by arguing that there are different levels of socialisation in any society.

*Level 1* is that of the society as a whole. This is a level of socialisation that applies to everyone and involves certain basic cultural values and norms. At this level, there is little or no disagreement and involves what are called core social values. These values define such things as what it means to be:

— English rather than French,

— A man rather than a woman,

— A child rather than an adult and so forth.

The ideas involved at this level tend to be fairly general and abstract. For example, they may involve such things as:

— A respect for the democratic process.

— The right to free speech.

— The right to a fair trial or

— The freedom of the individual.

*Level 2* is that of the different groups within a society. This level relates to the fact that membership of different sub-cultural groups itself generates certain norms and values that are important in an individual's life since, in general, these are the values and norms that we learn through our direct experience in the social world These values and norms may be accord with general social values and norms, or they may be in opposition to these values and norms. Clearly, therefore, the situation exists for a certain level of argument and disagreement over values and norms at this sub-cultural level. Consensus theorists tend not to deny this, but argue that this disagreement is itself part of the necessary dynamic process whereby societies adapt and change.

In a peculiar way, therefore, conflict and deviance can be functional for a society because it will eventually produce a new, stronger, consensus over core values. We can see an example of this argument in the work of the Consensus theorist Robert Merton when he analysed the nature of crime and deviance in American society in the 1930's.

Merton explored the idea that, in American society, there existed a disjunction between the socially-produced and encouraged ends or goals for people's behaviour and the means through which they could achieve these desirable ends. Merton was arguing that:

a. People were encouraged, through the socialisation process, to want certain things out of life. In simple terms, they were socialised into the American Dream of health, wealth, personal happiness and so forth.

b. American society was so structured as to ensure that the majority of people could never realistically attain these ends.

The means that American society provided were simply not sufficient to ensure that everyone could obtain the desirable goals they were socialised to want. In this respect, whilst American society placed a high social value on success in all its forms, the means to gaining legitimate success were effectively closed to all but a few. The vast majority of people would never achieve such goals by working. He argued, if people are socialised into both wanting success and needing to be successful by working - yet they are effectively denied that success through such means, strains develop in the normative structure of society.

— On the one hand, you have people actively desiring success.

— On the other, you have a large number of potentially very unhappy people when they discover that the supposed means to such success does not deliver the goods. In such a situation, anomie occurs.

Merton argued that the disjunction between wanting success and the lack of legitimate opportunity for success did not mean people gave-up wanting success. The whole thrust of their socialisation was geared towards the value of success. In a situation whereby people desired success - yet were effectively denied it - he argued they would find other, probably less legitimate, means towards desired ends. Before we look at the way Merton characterised a wide range of possible responses to this anomic situation, we should note that in explaining how people tried to resolve this "ends / means" problem, Merton was aware that different social groups had different expectations about the meaning of success.

For someone who has been unemployed for many months, the simple fact of getting a job may be considered as success - a desired end has been met.

Merton elaborated five basic responses to the anomic situation which he claimed to see in American society. He classified these types of conformity and deviance in terms of acceptance and denial of basic ends and means:

| *Response* | *Means* | *Ends* |
|---|---|---|
| a. Conformity | + | + |
| b. Innovation | - | + |
| c. Ritualism | + | - |
| d. Retreatism | - | - |
| e. Rebellion | Rejects means | Rejects ends |

An example of each category might be as follows:

— The law-abiding citizen. Accepts both socially-produced ends and the sociallylegitimated means to achieve them.

— Could apply to both "entrepreneurs" who develop new means / operate on the margins of criminal / non-criminal means and criminals - people who pursue desired ends by illegitimate means.

— Someone who conforms to socially-approved means, but has lost sight of the ends. This person is likely to be someone who "goes through the motions" - possibly more likely to be elderly?

— Someone who "drops-out" of mainstream society. The drug addict who retreats into a self-contained world, the alcoholic who is unable to hold-down a steady job and so forth.

— Political deviance is a good example of "the rebel" - whether this is expressed in terms of working for a revolutionary party / group or in such ways as political terrorism / freedom-fighting.

Merton's analysis illustrates the relationship between core cultural values and subcultural values. In particular, it shows that people may turn to crime because society denies them the opportunity to achieve a core social value. It also explains a number of different types of potential deviance, based around the particular experience that the individual has of the social world.

The reason for choosing to conform to or deviate from social norms was to be found, according to Merton, in the theory of differential socialisation. Different subcultural groups socialise their members in slightly different ways, depending upon their particular social circumstances. Whilst we do not need to explore this idea in any great depth, a classic distinction - between "working-class" and "middle class" socialisation - might serve to illustrate the point: Merton saw the working classes as being heavily involved in criminal behaviour and this observation was confirmed by Official Statistics about crime. The reason for this, he suggested, was that the socialisation of this group tends to be "less rigid" in relation to their acceptance of and conformity to "conventional" means of gaining desired ends.

This seems to contradict Merton's claim that social order is based on a number of core shared values. However, since the working classes, by definition, are the least successful members of any society, they are the sub-cultural group to whom conventional means to success have least meaning.

The cultural experience of working class adults leads them to socialise their children in ways that will give them the greatest possible advantage in their adult lives . This means adopting illegitimate / deviant means. Over time, these illegitimate means come to be seen as relatively normal; therefore, the working classes can violate "conventional norms / means" more easily and with less feelings of guilt etc.

The socialisation process acts a channel for deviant behaviour whereby the individual is socialised into deviant norms, which increases / decreases the likelihood of different forms of adaption to social strains (anomie).

## Conflict-Based Structuralist Theories

One of the main Conflict perspectives you will meet from time to time during the course is better known as Marxism, after the founder of this particular way of looking at the social world, Karl Marx. There are, however, other forms of Conflict Structuralism at which we will look, the most important of these being Weberian sociology, named after its founder Max Weber. Like its Functionalist counterpart, Conflict theories agree that society and culture influences individual behaviour, almost but not quite to the point of determining it, by the way it structures the way people are able to think and act.

The emphasis on the importance of structure and its influence on the individual does not, however, lead writers in this perspective to stress consensus as the basis of social organisation. In fact, the reverse is true. Conflict theorists stress the extent to which individuals, groups and classes within society are in competition with each other for whatever people in society consider to be important or worthwhile. This does, of course, seem to raise a fundamental problem. On the one hand, Conflict theorists, by definition, argue that groups in society are always fighting each other. On the other, their

Structuralist perspective leads them to suggest that the structure of a society produces social order and, in many respects, consensus.

The defining characteristic of any society, from a Conflict perspective, is inequality. Marxists, argue that economic inequality is at the heart of all societies. In basic terms, some people will have more than their fair share of a society's economic resources and others will consequently have less than their fair share. It is in the interests of those who have wealth to keep and extend what they own, whereas it is in the interests of those who have little or no wealth to try to improve their lot in life.

Consensus theorists do, of recognise social inequality, but they argue that inequality is functional for society (for a variety of reasons - giving people incentives, encouraging people to find new ways of creating wealth, making sure that the bestqualified people perform the most important jobs and so on). Thus, these theorists start from the fact of culture and then use it to explain inequality in society. This leads them to stress things like competition as being a core social value. Conflict theorists, on the other hand, reverse this idea. They start with the idea that every society will be economically unequal. From this fact, those who are most powerful in society try to socialise the least powerful into accepting inequality in any way they can.

Therefore, is two different interpretations of the same thing:

— Consensus theory stresses how common values are the starting point for social organisation.

— Conflict theory stresses how common values are the end result of economic organisation and inequality, once the most powerful in society have been able to convince everyone else that things like economic inequality are socially necessary.

The way this is carried-out is through cultural socialisation. The rich and the powerful occupy the most important and influential positions in society and they use their positions to advance their own interests. This socialisation takes two main forms:

— It is desirable to convince people that their lack of power, influence, status, wealth and so forth is basically their own fault. If you can encourage people to compete against each other, then some will win and others will lose. If losers can be convinced that the competition is free and fair then their inability to achieve the good things in life can be rationalised as being their own individual fault. This is where cultural institutions such as religion, education and the media are important, since their role is basically to encourage people to see the world in this way.

— However, if for whatever reason people fail to be socialised completely into these values, then force is available to make them see the error of their ways.

This is the least desirable socialisation option, mainly because if you force someone to do something against their will you are setting up the conditions for conflict and resistance - something you avoid through the first form of socialisation where people do your bidding because they see it as in their interests to do so.

Conflict theory and culture by outlining an example of the way in which it is possible to show the relationship between cultural socialisation, inequality, values and norms. An example we can use is one drawn from education and focuses on an idealised relationship between teacher and student.

Therefore, although this is a situation that contains the potential for conflict, it is in the interests of both to cooperate in the exchange of commodities. This is not an equal relationship, however, since the person who controls the valued social resource has the advantage in this relationship and they can use this advantage to extract more from the student than they provide in return. In the above example we can see, in very idealised terms, the idea that even where an apparent consensus exists this is built on a potential conflict.

Thus, whoever controls resources considered culturally valuable will always have an economic advantage over those who desire access to these resources. As the example, suggests, however, in order to occupy a dominant social position it is necessary to control a resource that other people want - and this is where we can look at other aspects of culture from a Conflict perspective.

Conflict theorists, unlike their consensus counterparts, tend to argue that all modern societies consist of the appearance of a common culture, shared by everyone in society, which masks the reality of competing cultural forms. Marxist Conflict theorists in particular have argued that every society consists of social classes defined in terms of whether they own or do not own the means of economic production in society in simple terms, society ultimately consists of two great classes:

— The bourgeoisie (or upper and middle classes) who own and control the means of producing economic survival (they own factories, businesses and the like) and

— The proletariat (or working class) who survive by working for the bourgeoisie.

In this sense, each of these two classes have very different interests and experiences in society. The bourgeoisie, for example, are the wealthiest in society whose interests lie in hanging-on to their privileged position. The proletariat, consisting of the least wealthy majority, have according to Marxists the common interest of taking away the wealth of the bourgeoisie. As can be imagined, the relationship between these two great classes is built upon a fundamental conflict of interest. For Marxists, therefore, the bourgeoisie have two main problems in terms of their relations with other social classes:

— How to maintain their privileged position from one generation to the next.

— How to stop other classes taking away their wealth and privilege.

One solution is to develop and enhance cultural artefacts relevant to the bourgeoisie for two main reasons:

— Firstly, to give the members of this class a sense of having things in common (a common culture and hence class identity) and

— Secondly, to try to impose the cultural ideas useful to this class on the rest of society. If this happens it makes it appear that everyone in society has much the same interests, making it less likely that the working class will see themselves as fundamentally different and opposed to the ruling class.

In this respect, many Marxist sociologists have tried to show how cultural artefacts can be used by a dominant economic class to enhance their social status over other classes in society, This, therefore, is where a distinction between high culture and low culture can be an important one.

The status of a ruling class is enhanced through claims that their culture is superior to the culture of the rest of society. By its ability to spread its concept of superior (high) and inferior (low) cultural forms (through ownership and / or control of cultural institutions such as religion, education and the mass media), a ruling class is able to impose cultural ideas on the rest of society that reflect its interests.

High culture, therefore, refers to what are the greatest artistic and literary achievements of a society. Clearly, what counts as "the greatest" is going to ultimately be a matter of values - judgements about what should or should not count as high culture. However, according to Marxists, the people who are in the most influential positions in society are able to impose their definitions of "great" - and these definitions invariably reflect the kinds of activities and ideas that are most relevant and useful to a ruling class. Cultural forms such as opera, classical music, the literary works of Shakespeare and so forth all fall under the heading of high culture.

Low culture, on the other hand, refers to a wide variety of cultural themes that are characterised by their production and consumption by "the masses". At various times, low cultural forms have included the cinema, certain forms of theatre, comics, television. A simple example illustrates the difference between high and low culture:

— A painting of a nude woman hanging on the wall of a gallery is "art" (part of high culture), whereas a picture of a naked woman published in a mass circulation newspaper is certainly not "art" (and may, under certain conditions, be labelled as pornography) but the very opposite of art, namely low culture.

— The justification for the distinction is found not in the cultural form itself but in the theoretical elaboration of that form.

— Thus, when a painting is hung in an art gallery what is being admired is the skill and composition, the cultural references and representations. When a picture appears in a newspaper, these are absent and all that is left is a titillation factor.

Whether or not you are convinced by these arguments is probably a matter of your perspective on culture, since there can ultimately be no cultural absolutes on such matters, just cultural preferences - the argument being that one social class is able to impose its cultural preferences on other classes in society.

## Elite Theory

Marxist Conflict theorists, by concentrating on the way cultural artefacts are used, generally tend not to make judgements about the relative worth of various cultural artefacts - although as we will see in a moment, there are exceptions to this.

Elite theorists, on the other hand, have tended to try to isolate those aspects of a culture that are "the best in thought and deed" and to separate them from the worthless, the mass produced and the artificial. Shils, argues we can characterise this approach by the way it argues that modern societies are characterised by three basic cultural levels:

— Highbrow (the superior and refined, containing the best qualities of a society).

— Middlebrow (the mediocre that aspires to be highbrow but which lacks originality, subtlety or depth) and

— Lowbrow (the brutal and worthless aspects of a culture. Forms which lack any pretence at sophistication, insight or refinement and which supposedly characterise many of the cultural forms of modern, working class, culture).

For elite theorists, modern societies basically consist of a small, cultured, elite and a large, acultured, mass (acultured means, in this context, a culture that is relatively shallow and worthless in terms of the things it values). The problem, as such theorists see it, is how to protect, preserve and accentuate high culture from the negative effects of low culture.

The rise of mass culture is related to the rise of modern societies, where the process of industrialisation brought cheap, mass produced, ideas and items to the mass of society, replacing, in the process, the folk cultures and traditions of pre-industrial societies. The main agency responsible for this diminution and cheapening of popular cultural forms is the mass media and, in particular, cinema and the popular press. The basic idea behind this theory is that the masses, easily lead and manipulated by an unscrupulous media pursuing their own narrow interests and profits, are sold cultural products that appeal simply to the lowest common denominator is society. These products lack depth and subtlety and their consumption by the masses supposedly made them easy to control and manipulate.

***Problems***

Criticisms of this types of elite cultural theory are numerous, but we can note that some of the most frequent are as follows:

— Elite theorists conveniently assume that high culture is inherently superior to what they term low culture, yet it does not seem possible to differentiate this easily between cultural differences without making an arbitrary judgement. I may feel that the works of William Shakespeare represent a higher cultural level than the works of Jeffrey Archer, for example, but it is difficult to see how this belief could be supported objectively.

— The easy distinction between elite and mass / popular culture is oversimplified.

— Many critics of this approach argue that there is little evidence to support the notion that popular culture is, by definition, brutish and impoverished. On the contrary, whilst some cultural forms are undoubtedly manufactured simply for profit and seem to have little intrinsic cultural value or longevity, many originally popular cultural forms have evolved into something of lasting value and worth.

— Finally, elite theorists contrast an idealised pre-industrial past filled with poor-buthappy peasants participating proudly in a dynamic folk culture with a supposedly moribund present where manufactured (both literally and metaphorically) cultural artefacts are passively consumed by an unthinking, forever unsatisfied, mass.

This is an important source of criticism (the idealisation of the past as a contrast to an unhappy present) and we can divert slightly to look briefly at the concept of folk culture.

***Folk Culture***

The distinction between folk culture and mass culture rests on the difference between two basic types of society. The first, in which folk culture is said to dominate, is characteristic of preindustrial societies. That is, societies that existed before the invention of machines and mass power sources (steam, gas, electricity, etc.) and in which the main type of economic production was agriculture. An example of this type of society is Britain before the Industrial Revolution and the development of a Capitalist economic system. The second, in which mass cultural forms are held to dominate, is characteristic of industrial societies such as present-day Britain. This type of society is characterised by factory production based around machines, rather than agriculture.

Elite theorists in particular characterise folk culture as a vibrant lower class culture (music, dance, medicine, oral traditions and so forth) variously expressed through popular gatherings such as festivals, fairs, carnivals and so forth. This culture is passed from one generation to the next in a variety of traditional forms, in particular folk songs, fairy tales and word-of-mouth.

Industrialisation is the villain of the situation, in that it destroyed much of the basis of folk culture by forcing people away from agriculture into towns and factories, breaking-up the traditional communities on which much of this traditional culture was based. The cultural vacuum left by this break-up was filled by popular / mass culture, manufactured and sold to people as a substitute for this traditional past. Unlike traditional folk culture which was seen to be active and participatory, popular culture was seen to be characterised by its passivity. In basic terms, people simply consumed whatever was put in front of them, such was their desire for cultural products. In modern Britain, for example, modern elite theorists criticise the "Heritage Industry" that recreates the things of the past - buildings, communities and the like - and sells the "experience" to its customers who visit, watch the video and buy the T-shirt before moving-on to consume another pre-packaged slice of culture.

Trowler summarises this view thus: "Capitalism quickly polluted folk culture and replaced it with a plastic commodity culture - mass culture. The old traditions were quickly wiped out. The working man and woman have become passive recipients of culture, not active participants in it. Today they sit in the cinema rather than take part in the folk dance. They buy fast food rather than make good food themselves with traditional recipes. Advertising has given them the constant desire for things which they can't have. The world is filed with characters from the television who they don't really know, though they spend hours reading and talking about them as they once might have done about characters in the village. The mass media's role has been to transmit and propagate mass culture".

The above is a politically Conservative view of culture. A more politically-radical interpretation was given by a group of Marxist Conflict theorists, writing from the 1940's, known as the Frankfurt School. These writers offered a different solution to the problem of the development of mass culture. They argued that mass culture was a way of distracting the working classes from the real causes of their problems in Capitalist society. In simple terms, the development of a mass culture that encouraged passive consumption of the pre-packaged products of big business not only destroyed vital, communal, aspects of folk culture, but also provided the working classes with an illusory sense of happiness, togetherness and well-being.

A modern example of this might be the tabloid newspapers' preoccupation with the monarchy. People are encouraged to take an interest in the lives of people with whom they have little or nothing in common, seeing them as soap-opera figures to be watched with passive fascination rather than active criticism. Thus, vital questions about the role and purpose of a monarchy are overlooked in favour of questions about who is sleeping with whom, how much each will get from a divorce, whether Charles will marry the real "love of his life" - the permutations are endless. To aid our involvement, distant people with distant lives are personalised with pet names - Chas 'n' Di, Fat Fergie, the Royal Mistress and so forth. Through these devices, the argument goes, we are encouraged to view these people as somehow "just like everyone else, except they are fabulously wealthy". The behaviour of royalty is further portrayed, soap-opera fashion, as a series of scripted events and set-pieces.

Both the Elite and Frankfurt School viewpoints have things in common, even though they are politically far apart. For example:

— The working classes are seen as passive consumers of pre-packaged cultural forms.

— Working class culture lacks creativity.

— Working class cultural life is brutish and debased.

Although both of these basic theories have modern-day advocates, the main argument levelled against them (apart from charges of political bias) is that neither accurately captures or reflects the true complexity of cultural developments and forms of behaviour. In particular, both see working class culture as dangerous and worthless.

More modern theories and arguments about culture and class, within the general Conflict perspective, have focused much more on the nature and development of different cultural forms. In this respect, these theories tend to be less damning of working class cultural forms and activities.

This perspective is representative of a group of writers who, while emphasising the idea of competition between different groups in society, reject Marxist interpretations of culture. The general term for these non-Marxist Conflict theorists is "pluralist" because they see societies as made-up of a variety (or plurality) of different groups and classes, each with their own different interests and agendas.

Thus, pluralist writers stress the idea that societies are made-up of various groups who develop their own cultural values and norms, some of which they have in common with other cultural groups. This perspective, therefore, focuses on the idea of cultural diversity. The pluralist view of culture, therefore, rejects the idea that a mass culture exists in modern societies. Pluralists reject the idea that cultural forms can be understood in simple "good or bad" terms. For example, the idea that lower class culture in preindustrial society was somehow superior to lower class culture in industrial society is dismissed as both a gross over-simplification and the product of a romanticised view of lower class life.

The main characteristic of pluralist perspectives, therefore, is the focus on the choices people make from a range of possible cultural forms. Clearly such choices will be made against a background of the individual's personal and social circumstances, but they reject the idea that cultural activities are simply passive forms of consumption. Instead, they emphasise the expanding range of cultural developments and forms. They also reject the idea that some cultural forms are inherently superior to others. In short, the cultural choices people make reflect a complex, changing world in which cultural activities develop or die-out on the basis of their relevance to peoples' lives.

**Humanistic Marxism**

This modern version of Marxism sees cultures as involving ways of doing and thinking. In this respect culture is not simply a matter of personal choice and preference (although this is an important aspect of culture). It also reflects a wider sense of (class) struggle in society. This is because cultures are integrating mechanisms in society. What this means is that cultures bind people together by giving them things in common. Religious groups, for example, develop a common sense of culture based around things like a belief in the same god(s), practices and rituals. This common culture gives such groups an identity (they are different to other groups) and a common cause. In addition, these cultures give their individual members a sense of identity.

Humanistic Marxists such as some argued that different social classes develop different cultural backgrounds and identities based on their different experiences in the social world. A rich white male, for example, experiences life in modern Britain very differently from a poor black female. Cultures, as a "design for living", develop to reflect these experiences precisely because they are ways we use to equip ourselves for living and coping in society.

Although this seems to reflect a pluralist view of culture, one of the main differences is that Marxist Conflict theorists see society in terms of large social groups rather than the much smaller groups characteristic of pluralist perspectives. Thus, broadly, each social class develops its own cultural norms that reflect its particular experiences in the world. This perspective stresses two important ideas:

— Class groups develop different cultural outlooks.
— Class groups are in a constant state of conflict with one another.

Unlike in the past when a ruling economic class could establish its leadership in society through force and terror, in modern societies leadership has to be earned. That is, a ruling class cannot take its "right to rule" for granted. Members of this class must, in short, convince both themselves and others in society that they have the "right to rule".

What this involves is a dynamic relationship between different class cultures. Rather than a ruling class simply imposing its culture on the rest of society, the process is more complex. This class, for example, seeks to propagate its values throughout society, since if people can be convinced of certain values this will influence their normative development along particular lines. If people can be convinced that Capitalism is the best possible economic system then they will develop norms that encourage them to try to succeed according to Capitalist values. In this way, Capitalism as an economic system survives.

The concept of hegemony is useful because it provides a sense of cultural diversity and dynamic political struggle. It can be used to explain, for example, how and why cultural forms are adopted and used by people of diverse cultural backgrounds. In this respect, hegemony solves the problem of how to explain:

— The fact that basic cultural forms survive over time.

— The fact that cultural forms evolve, adapt and change over time.

Finally, therefore, the idea of a popular culture is one that, for modern Marxist Conflict theorists, should be used to show the dynamic and creative nature of cultural forms and behaviour. People develop new cultural forms as a means of coping with their position in the social world, challenging the old order and, perhaps, creating forms of "cultural space" that provide a sense of meaning and identity in the modern world. Finally therefore, having dealt at some length with a variety of Conflict perspectives on cultural development, we can now turn to a perspective (Interactionism) that lays much theoretical stress on the idea of human meanings and purpose as people go about the daily task of creating and recreating the social world.

## Interactionist Theories

Interactionist theories are different in scope to the type of Structuralist theories that we have considered. While Interactionists write about much the same type of things as their Consensus and Conflict counterparts, the theoretical emphasis is different. This is something that we now have to elaborate when we look at the various ways that Interactionist sociologists have interpreted the concepts of culture and identity. In general, Interactionist perspectives tend to concentrate upon relatively smallscale levels of social interaction and, for this reason, they are sometimes referred-to as a micro level of sociological analysis.

Interactionist theories of culture identifying a number of the basic characteristics of human cultures. It is a product of social interaction. That is, cultures develop out of the way people act towards one another in a way that involves both purpose and meaning. The question to answer, therefore, is how do we avoid these problems? Many animals, avoid them because their behaviour instinctive. Their behaviour in any situation is governed by genetically predetermined responses to certain forms of stimulation. Many cats, signal to another animal that they do not intend to attack it by raising their tail vertically. This is an instinctive action that does not have to be learnt - the cat instinctively knows that this is the correct signal to give in a non-threatening situation. This is efficient, but limiting. A system of behaviour based on simple signals limits the ability of animals to develop beyond very simple groups, mainly because they lack the ability to communicate and share anything beyond a relatively simple set of meanings.

Humans, on the other hand, can solve these problems by taking advantage of two major biological advantages we have over most animals:

— The ability to communicate through language. This allows us to develop meaning in our behaviour.

— The ability to remember meanings and act purposefully on the basis of this stored cultural knowledge.

These abilities mean we can develop cultural systems that can be learnt through a socialisation process. Thus, our ability to communicate symbolically gives us the ability to develop very rich cultures that may be unlimited in scope. This gives us the ability to control and shape our environment in ways that are unimaginable for animals. Symbols are different to signals since:

— A symbol does not need any direct relationship to the thing it symbolises.

The symbol "elephant" only means "a large animal with four legs, big ears and a long nose" because that is what we have learnt to interpret it as meaning. It could equally mean "a small furry animal with two legs".

— Symbols can be related to one another to create very complex ideas and meanings.

An example of the way we both communicate symbolically and use this ability to create very complex cultural rules and meaning might be: Imagine you were standing at traffic lights waiting to cross the road. If you see a car go through a red light you may interpret that behaviour as "wrong" (because it is dangerous) / "illegal" (because it breaks the law). If, however, the car has a flashing blue light and a wailing siren you may interpret that behaviour as "understandable", because you assume the police officers in the car have a very good reason for acting both dangerously and illegally.

This also illustrates the idea of symbolic meanings, since there is no absolute relationship between a "red light" and the action "stop"; it is only because we have been socialised to make an association between the two things that a red light actually means stop to us. Someone from a society where cars do not exist would not associate red traffic lights with "stop" or "it's dangerous to cross the road when the light is green" because that symbolic association between the two things would not be a part of their "symbolic system of meaning".

The ability to develop shared meanings is the key to understanding human interaction. Our ability to think is both the problem and the solution, since what we effectively do, according to Interactionists, is to create a sense of society and culture in our minds. We behave "as if" these things physically exist. Thus, the world humans inhabit is a social construction. This involves the idea that society is a product of our ability to think and express our thoughts symbolically. The things that we recognise as being "part of our society" or "part of our culture" are simply products of our mind. This is one reason why Interactionists reject the idea that society has an objective existence that is separate from the people who, through their everyday relationships, create a sense of living in a society.

Society is an elaborate fiction we create to help us make sense of our relationships and impose some sort of order on them. We create this fictional universe to make social life possible, since without a sense of shared meanings about what we see and do, interaction would, at best, be very difficult and, at worst, impossible.

Cultures, therefore, represent the general store of shared meanings that people create to give them a feeling of having things in common and as the basis for constructive social interaction. Think of any dealings you have had with people who do not behave in ways that conform to your cultural expectations. People who are drunk, for example, frequently fail to observe expected cultural norms and this makes it very difficult for us to interact with them on anything but a very basic level of understanding.

## Social Construction of Meaning

Humans have the ability to impose a sense of order and predictability on a potentially disordered and unpredictable social world by creating shared meanings about situations. This system of meaning (culture) involves the standard sociological ideas of role play, values and norms, but the question to finally consider is how do we go about the task of creating a culture in the first place?

In simple terms, therefore, we have to consider the process whereby individuals "agree to agree" about what they are doing (the purpose of interaction) and why they are doing it (the meaning of interaction). Interactionists generally start to explain this process by referring to the concept of a definition of the situation. That is, how we define a situation affects how we behave when we are in that situation. To make sense of the confusing world that we experience on a daily basis, Interactionists argue that we use a process of categorization and labelling. That is, as we interact we categorise similar experiences in some way. For example, we create categories of people based around our perception of them as:

— Male or female.
— Young or old.
— Employer / employee.
— Traffic warden / police woman.
— Husband / wife.

Each category of related phenomena is like a little box that we hold inside our mind and, for our convenience, each little box has:

— A name or label that identifies it for us (for example, the label "mother").
— A set of social characteristics inside. That is, a set of related ideas that we associate with the label on the box.

Thus, when someone we meet reveals one of their social labels to us we mentally "open the box" that contains our store of knowledge about "motherhood". This might include objective (factual) information (a mother is someone who has given birth to a child) as well as subjective (based upon opinion or values) information (I love my mother so all children love their mothers; a mother has a duty to look after her children and so forth).

By categorising the social world we give it the appearance of order and regularity, since when we meet people we are able to interact with them on the basis of the "general things that we know about this type of person". When we meet a police officer, for example, we might give them an exaggerated respect because we realise that they have the power to arrest us if we do not give the appearance of recognising their authority.

The socialisation process, therefore, is one that focuses on the teaching and learning of common cultural meanings, since this is the basis for all meaningful social interaction. One of the most important things we learn, in effect, is how to recognise different situations and how we are expected to generally behave in that situation.

Macro and micro sociological perspectives both see cultures as specifying the ground rules for peoples' social behaviour. By the establishment, teaching and learning of these basic rules of behaviour, social interaction is made possible, orderly and reasonably predictable. Macro perspectives focus more on how these rules affect our behaviour by placing restrictions (constraints) on our possible range and choices of behaviour. The focus here is upon large social groups and institutions in society. Micro perspectives focus more on how and why these rules are created. That is, the focus is on small-scale interaction between conscious individuals.

Both perspectives have their advantages and disadvantages in terms of how completely or incompletely they are able to produce theories that explain human behaviour. For the moment, it is probably easier to see these sociological perspectives as complimentary, in the sense that each explains some aspects of our behaviour plausibly. As the course develops the differences between each of the perspectives will become more apparent and so will the basis for seeing these perspectives as having fundamental differences that make them incompatible with each other.

## Cultural Diversity

### *Identity*

All societies develop rules of behaviour that are used to structure the behaviour of their members. This, in turn, leads to the idea that all societies are socially organised. In this respect, it is impossible for a society to exist if it is not organised around a framework of rules. This idea is as true of animal / insect societies as it is of human societies.

— Some animal and insect societies are very complex social structures.

— Human societies also involve complex social structures. A society such as our own, for example, involves the organisation of some 60 million people.

Underlying both these forms of social organisation are rules that provide a structure for organisation and behaviour, although sociologists argue that the basic organising structures / frameworks are radically different in animal and human societies:

— In animal societies, behaviour is structured around the framework of instinct.

— In human societies, behaviour is structured around the framework of culture.

Social organisation, therefore, exists to help a society's members to solve problems, the most basic of these being the problem of existence. We have noted that the basic problems of existence that face all human societies if they are to survive and develop are:

— The economic problem of how to produce the things needed for human survival.

— The political problem of how to ensure that society is orderly and stable. The problem here, therefore, is one of government and control over people's behaviour. In short, the need is the need to enforce rules of acceptable behaviour.

— The family problem of how to ensure that children are born and looked after in a way that allows them to grow into functioning adult members of society.

— The cultural problem of how to make people feel they have things in common with others. How, in short, to make people feel they belong to a common culture / society.

From the above, we can initially note, therefore, that human cultures develop out of the various ways that people choose to solve these basic problems of existence. This idea of choice is significant because it reflects the idea that humans have self consciousness. Most animals do not have self consciousness. Only the higher primates such as baboons and chimpanzees - the closest relations we have in the non-human world - seem to have a similar form of consciousness. In addition, the concept of choice allows us to explain the fact that:

— The same species of insect, for example, always develops the same form of social organisation precisely because they have no choice. Bees of the same species develop the same basic hive organisation in Britain as they do in Germany.

— Human cultures vary widely in their organisation and content because humans are able to exercise choice in their range of behaviour.

Having noted the idea of a problem of existence that provides the basic human need for social organisation, we can now turn to look at the various similarities and differences in human cultures under the general heading of cultural diversity. In basic terms, our interest here is in trying to understand the rules, routines and responsibilities that structure peoples' lives within the same society and between different societies. In this respect, therefore, there are two main aspects of cultural diversity that we need to analyse:

— Basic cultural similarities and differences that exist between different societies. This is called an inter-cultural form of analysis.

— Basic cultural similarities and differences that exist within the same society. This is called an intra-cultural form of analysis.

In addition, to help us do this we can structure our analysis around a number of basic ideas:

— Structural and Cultural Universals - an examination of the organisational features that seem to exist in all societies.

— The concepts of ethnocentrism and cultural relativity.

— Sub-Cultural Forms - an outline of the different sub-cultural groups that exist within any society

## Structural and Cultural Universals

A structural universal refers to issues that must be addressed if a society is to survive and evolve. We have referred to these earlier as the basic problems of human existence. In effect, we are talking here about the kinds of social tasks that people must accomplish for their survival as a society.

Structural universals are not particularly difficult to find, given that all human societies have, at one time or another, to solve certain problems if their are to survive. In general therefore, we can note the following examples of structural universals.

— *Communication:* People have to develop ways of communicating their ideas to each other. This usually takes the form of language, although it may also involve the use of writing. Writing is not a universal feature of societies, however. Many societies, especially in the past, had no way of communicating their beliefs through writing and these are called pre-literate societies.

— *A Family system:* This relates to the structural problems of regulating relationships between members of a society, the socialisation of children and the like.

— *Religion:* All known societies have, at some point, developed religions. A reason for this may be that the belief in a god or gods is a very effective means of bringing people together. Not only do religions give people a sense of having things in common, but the fact that they involve the belief in a supra-human force or forces means that they represent very effective sources of social control.

— *Social control systems:* These vary from informal controls (values, norms, etc.) through to the highly-developed control systems we find in modern societies.

— *A division of labour / role allocation system:* Even in very small societies there exists a variety of tasks to be performed if people are to survive. Societies have, therefore, to devise ways of sharing-out these tasks amongst their members.

— *Social stratification*: This refers to the way different roles are ranked against each other in terms of social importance. During this course we will be looking at a variety of ways people are stratified in different societies on the basis of such things as:

— Social class - stratification based on work role.

— Gender and age - biological systems of stratification.

— Ethnicity - stratification based around the cultural background of different groups.

A cultural universal refers to possible similarities in the particular way a society chooses to solve structural problems of existence. For example:

The problem we have, when looking at the idea of cultural universals is that of deciding how specific something has to be in order to count as a universal feature of human social organisation. In effect, how widely or narrowly we draw the definition of universal affects the conclusion we reach about cultural patterns.

In some ways, this question appears rather academic since it refers to a very fine distinction. However, there are major two reasons for seeing it as important:

— Firstly, in terms of sociological theory it is important because if we are to understand and explain the nature and process of human social development it is necessary to ensure that all theories of cultural development refer to the same thing.

— Of more immediate practical significance is the idea that if it is possible to identify universal cultural features, this can lead to the idea that one form of cultural organisation is natural, and by implication right and better, than another form of organisation. Thus, non-universal features can come to be seen as unnatural or deviant.

This introduces the concept of ideology, which can initially be defined as:

> "A systematic set of beliefs which serve the interests of some social group in society. Ideologies are associated with power and the ability to present ideas as right and natural for everyone in society. Perhaps the best way of describing ideology is as ideas

> that are out forward for a purpose - to fulfil the aims of a social group in society and which may or may not be true."

In this respect we have to be careful about how we try to understand the idea of cultural universals because of the way knowledge can be used to promote the political and ideological aims of various social groups. This is not to say that, as sociologists, we should suppress what we believe to be true for political convenience. Rather, we have to be careful about the information we present as true. This idea will be developed when we look at the ideas of ethnocentric and culturally relative approaches to the study of cultural development. Having noted this, the next question to address, therefore, is whether or not it is possible to identify customs and practices that are truly universal cultural features of human society.

## Ethnocentrism and Cultural Relativity

The level of cultural diversity that seems to exist amongst human societies means that it is important to avoid the trap of ethnocentricity when trying to understand the nature and scope of human cultures. Ethnocentrism can be broadly defined as an attitude whereby you judge other societies by the standards that apply in your society. Classifying people who live in technologically-undeveloped societies as "primitive". Additionally, ethnocentrism can also refer to the way the lifestyles, experiences, values and norms of one group in a society are assumed to be common to everyone in society. The assumption that everyone lives in a loving, two-parent family, is an example of ethnocentrism on a group level, as is the idea that because some women in our society are economically successful this applies to the experience of all women in society.

Ethnocentric attitudes of both kinds are not uncommon but, sociologically, we need to move away from thinking that there are universal cultural standards that somehow point to fundamental truths about "human nature". Sociology is not about making moral judgements, disguised as objective truth, about the worth or otherwise of people's lifestyles. Rather, it is about the attempt to understand and analyse the reasons for the development of cultural diversity.

Cultural relativity is an attempt to understand the cultural development of societies and social groups own their own terms; that is, without trying to impose absolute ideas of moral value and trying to measure different cultural variations in terms of some form of absolute cultural standard.

In this sense, under specific circumstances, any form of human behaviour can appear to be good or bad. A good example here is our attitude to the killing of another human being. In peace time this may be considered to be murder or manslaughter (deviant), whereas in war time this may be considered a duty. As this example suggests, what is significant is not the act itself. However, the concept of cultural relativity does present problems, since if we apply it politically, not just sociologically, we have to accept any form of behaviour as acceptable as long as it conforms to the cultural expectations of the society in which it takes place.

Cultural variations that develop between social groups in the same society. Since one of the developing themes of this both this section and the course as a whole is that of various ways social groups can be classified on the basis of common, defining, cultural characteristics, this final section will be divided into analysing the nature of sub-cultural groups based around the concepts of:

— Social class (class sub-cultures).

— Age (in particular, youth sub-cultures).

— Cultural background (ethnic sub-cultures).

***Sub-Cultures***

People develop cultures to provide a structured framework of rules for their behaviour. In turn, people's behaviour is influenced by their cultural background (socialisation) and setting. People do not just form cultures, however. They also form much smaller groups within society which we term sub-cultures. An initial definition of a sub-culture is provided by Farley when he notes that, "A subculture is defined as a set of cultural characteristics shared among a group within a society that are distinct in some ways from the larger culture within which the group exists, but also have features in common with the larger culture. Usually, a group that forms a subculture has some sense of identity, some recognition that people in the group share something among themselves that others in the larger society do not. A subculture can develop any time a group of people share some situation or experience that is different from that of others in their society."

As this definition suggests, a sub-cultural group can develop around any number of social activities (family, work, education, religion, geographic region and so forth). This makes the study of sub-cultures potentially difficult since we would have to produce theories of sub-culture that accounted for the behaviour of groups such as stamp collectors, football supporters, athletes, Government ministers and so forth. To make our task more manageable, therefore, we are going to restrict our observations to a number of major forms of sub-cultural groupings in our society. This will allow us to focus on some of the main theoretical accounts of the existence and development of various types of sub-cultural groups.

When we use the term sub-culture sociologically, we are referring to a group of people whose behaviour has features that set it apart from the wider (or dominant) culture of the society in which it develops. Such groups are considered to be subcultures, rather than cultures in their own right, because they retain links to and features of, the wider culture. One of the most frequent uses of the term sub-culture is used in relation to young people. In Britain we recognise the youth category teenager as a distinctive sub-cultural group. Although teenagers may develop interests and behaviour that are unique to this group and which set them apart as a sub-cultural grouping, they nevertheless remain within the general cultural framework of society. Teenagers live in families, they go to schools, they work, hold religious beliefs and so forth.

Finally, we need to recognise that the relationship between the dominant culture and sub-cultural groups is not static. Social behaviour is always dynamic; people's behaviour constantly changes to take account of new situations and relationships. Additionally, cultures and sub-cultures, although different, are not self-contained units in society; on the contrary, there is a continuous flow of influences from culture to sub-culture and vice versa.

In the following, to help us understand the nature and differences between subcultural types we are going to classify sub-cultural groups in terms of two main types. These types should be considered as theoretical ideals, in the sense that sub-cultures do not necessarily belong to one type. As with most typologies their main use is as a means of helping us get to grips with social phenomena that are frequently difficult to comprehend. You should bear this idea in mind at all times. In addition, as we outline each sub cultural type it will be useful to provide examples of groups that conform to these types. To help us, therefore, we can relate each type to some of the other major cultural influences on people's behaviour, such as:

— Social class.

— Gender.

— Age.

— Religion and

— Ethnic background.

***Sub-Cultural Types***

The first sub-cultural type we can note is that of a reactive or oppositional subculture. A reactive sub-culture is one in which the members of a particular sub-cultural group develop norms and values that are both a response to and opposition against the prevailing norms and values that exist in a wider, dominant, culture. In this respect, this form of sub-culture is sometimes called oppositional rather than reactive.

The central idea in the above is that a sub-cultural group forms as a reaction to what someone else is trying to do to them. By reacting to this pressure, the emergent sub-cultural group effectively tries to oppose the pressures being placed on them. In the form of sub-cultural grouping the members of the group adopt a set of norms and values that are effectively self-contained and specific to the group. Where these values, in particular, differ from those of the wider culture in which the sub-culture exists, they may not necessarily be in opposition to such values. Such sub-cultural values represent is an independent product of - and solution to - the problems faced by people in their everyday lives.

The basic idea here is that a sub-cultural group develops around the interests and experiences of the people who come together to form such a group. In this respect, such groups are independent of other groups in the sense that they do not arise as a reaction to what some other group is doing. This does not mean that independent sub-cultures have no contact with other cultural or sub-cultural groups. For our purposes, however, the idea of independence relates to the reasons for the formation of such sub-cultural groups.

Having outlined these two basic types of sub-culture, the following section looks briefly at some examples of different types of sub-cultural groups and tries to suggest reasons for their development. As you may imagine, the vast number of cultural and sub-cultural groups in our society makes it difficult to do anything more than scratch the surface of sub-cultures; therefore, the discussion here will simply focus on some general examples.

***Independent Sub-Cultures***

An alternative form of explanation for the development of youth sub-cultures is provided by this interpretation. This involves the argument that we should see youth sub-cultures as developing independently of other groups. That is, out of the experiences and cultural needs of the people who form such groups. In this sense, the development of youth sub-cultural values and norms represent is an independent product of - and solution to - the specific problems faced by people in their everyday lives.

Some argue that it is significant that youth sub-cultures are a modern phenomenon. They represent an attempt by young people to manage the transition from childhood to adulthood in modern societies. Thus, childhood involves one set of norms and adulthood involves a different set of norms. Modern societies lack the kinds of rites of passage and rituals common in pre-modern societies for marking the passage from childhood to adulthood. Therefore, teenagers have to develop their own ways of managing this transition - hence the development of sub-cultural groups. In this respect, youth sub-cultures are functional for society and the individuals involved because they provide group settings in which young people can gradually learn the norms of adulthood.

This idea explains why such sub-cultures are mainly developed by young people. They are a passing phase not because people get fed-up with them but because these groups are no-longer functional. As a teenager moves into adulthood, they have completed the social transition from child to adult and simply do not need this type of sub-cultural organisation any longer. This also explains why youth sub-cultures appear and disappear with great rapidity. In simple terms, people grow out of them once such groups are no-longer relevant to the individuals involved.

***Youth Sub-Cultures: An Alternative View***

Although we've looked at a number of different perspectives

on youth sub-cultures, some argues that youth sub-cultures should not be considered as sub-cultures at all. This view is worth noting because it provides an alternative sociological view to generally accepted ideas about sub-cultures. It also provides an example of the way theories can be criticised not only by conducting studies that "prove them to be wrong" but also by questioning the basic assumptions on which the theory is built. If he is right then it means that these writers have been trying to explain something that does not need explanation.

Youth sub-cultures are not coherent social groupings that arise as a reaction to social forces. Rather, the mass media manufacture them by focusing attention upon possibly-unconnected forms of behaviour and giving them the appearance of coherence and structure. The media, in effect, provide a framework of "explanations that make sense" for something that may just be a relatively simple collection of individuals. In this respect, media labelling results in the creation of youth sub-cultures by giving a meaning to the behaviour of people. The media, therefore, provide a "meaning structure" for behaviour that, prior to the labelling process, may well have not had any coherent meaning to the people involved.

By applying a meaningful label to behaviour, the media create something out of nothing. That is, they provide both society and the people involved with a framework in which to locate their behaviour. A classic recent example of this is acid house - groups of people who had nothing in common except a desire to party are manufactured by the media into some form of social collective with common interests, aims and beliefs.

The role of the mass media is that of a socialising agency. They react to some form of youth behaviour and write about that behaviour as if the behaviour was part of a wider, sub-cultural, phenomenon. By publicising the behaviour:

— The people involved start to see themselves as part of a wider social movement. They see themselves as having

> something in common and a "youth sub- culture" begins to take shape. The attention of wider society is focused not on a "few, relatively isolated, youths", but on a full-blown youth movement - a potentially troubling scenario, since it implies that the participants share certain values, beliefs, attitudes and so forth. Such groups are far more likely to be considered a threat about which "something must be done".

In this scenario, the media takes a role as mediator between wider society and the youths involved. Not only does the media "explain" behaviour for its audience, it also provides feedback about how members of the youth culture are expected to behave.

***Ethnic Sub-cultures***

With ethnic groups the situation is slightly different because we are initially talking about people who have arrived in a new country. For this reason we will look at the idea of independent sub-cultural development first because this has a bearing on the development of reactive sub-cultures.

a. *Independent sub-cultures.* The issue of immigration is significant here because of the idea that immigrants bring with them a set of cultural traditions, values and norms from their home society. In this sense, therefore, any immigrant group will generally automatically form a subcultural group in the host society. Independent sub-cultural groups are many and varied. Jews, for example, form a distinctive sub-cultural grouping in Britain, whereas Italian and Irish immigrants initially formed a distinct subcultural identity in America.

b. *Reactive sub-cultures:* These forms of sub-culture are also fairly commonplace amongst ethnic minority groups, mainly because of the presence of things like racial discrimination. Thus, the idea here is that groups who feel themselves to be unjustly persecuted develop subcultural responses to the situation.

# 3

# Intercultural Communication

## Human Communication

Communication is everywhere. Even when they are alone, people are bombarded with communication. Human communication-that is, the ability to symbolize and use language-separates humans from animals. Communication with others is the essence of what it means to be human. Communication is the vehicle by which people initiate, maintain, and terminate their relationships with others.

### *Nature*

Because of its ubiquitous nature, communication is very difficult to define. Although there is no universally agreed upon definition of communication, there are certain properties of communication upon which most communication scholars agree describe its nature.

1. *Process*. A process is anything that is ongoing, ever-changing, and continuous.
2. *Dynamic*. The terms "process" and "dynamic" are closely related. Part of what makes communication a process is its dynamic nature. Something that is dynamic is considered active and/or forceful.

3. *Interactive-Transactive.* Communication is interactive and transactive because it occurs between people. Communication requires the active participation of two people simultaneously sending and receiving messages.

4. *Symbolic.* A symbol is an arbitrarily selected and learned stimulus that represents something else. Symbols can be verbal or nonverbal. Symbols are the vehicle by which the thoughts and ideas of one person can be communicated to another person.

5. *Intentional.* Perhaps one of the most debated issues regarding the communication process centers around intentionality. Intentional communication exists whenever two or more people consciously engage in interaction with some purpose. Unintentional communication may exist, however.

6. *Contextual.* Communication is dependent on the context in which it occurs. A context is the cultural, physical, relational, and perceptual environment in which communication occurs.

7. *Ubiquitous.* That communication is ubiquitous simply means that communication is everywhere, done by everyone, all of the time. Humans are constantly bombarded with verbal and nonverbal messages. Wherever one goes there is some communication happening.

8. *Cultural.* Culture shapes communication and communication is culture bound. People from different cultures communicate differently. The verbal and nonverbal symbols we use to communicate with our friends and families are strongly influenced by our culture.

Communication then, is the dynamic process of encoding and decoding verbal and nonverbal messages within a defined cultural, physiological, socio-relational, and perceptual environment. Although many of our messages are sent intentionally, many others, perhaps our nonverbal messages, can unintentionally influence others.

## Nature of Culture

Like communication, culture is ubiquitous and has a profound effect on humans. Culture is simultaneously invisible yet pervasive. As we go about our daily lives, we are not overtly conscious of our culture's influence. Yet most of our thoughts, emotions, and behaviors are culturally driven. Culture has a direct influence on the physical, relational and perceptual environment. Culture is defined as an accumulated pattern of values, beliefs, and behaviors, shared by an identifiable group of people with a common history and verbal and nonverbal symbol system.

1. *Accumulated Pattern of Values, Beliefs and Behaviors.* Cultures can be defined by their value and belief systems and by the actions of their members. People who exist in the same culture generally share similar values and beliefs. The values of a particular culture lead to a set of expectations and rules prescribing how people should behave in that culture.

2. *An Identifiable Group of People with a Common History.* Because the members of a particular culture share similar values, beliefs and behaviors, they are identifiable as a distinct group. In addition to their shared values, beliefs and behaviors, the members of a particular culture share a common history.

3. *Verbal and Nonverbal Symbol System.* The verbal and nonverbal symbols with which the members of a culture communicate are culture bound. Although two cultures may share the same verbal code they may have dramatically different verbal styles. Nonverbal codes systems vary significantly across cultures also.

Within most cultures there are groups of people, or microcultures, that coexist within the mainstream society. Microcultures exist within the broader rules and guidelines of the dominant cultural milieu but are distinct in some way, perhaps racially, linguistically, or via their sexual orientation, age, or even occupation.

### *A Model of Intercultural Communication*

Intercultural communication occurs whenever a minimum of two persons from different cultures or microcultures come together and exchange verbal and nonverbal symbols. Intercultural communication occurs within a variety of contexts, including a cultural, microcultural, environmental, perceptual, and socio-relational context. The intercultural communication is defined by the interdependence of these various contexts.

1. The largest, outer circle of the model represents the cultural context. This is the largest circle because the dominant culture permeates every aspect of the communicative exchange, even the physical geography.

2. The next largest circle in the model is the microcultural context. These groups are in some way different than the larger cultural milieu. Sometimes the difference is ethnicity, race, or language.

3. The next largest circle in the model is the environmental context. This circle represents the physical geographical location of the interaction. While culture prescribes the overall rules for communication, the physical location indicates when and where the specific rules apply.

4. The two circles in the model within the socio-relational context represent the perceptual contexts of the individuals interacting. The perceptual context refers to the individual characteristics of the interactants, including their cognitions, attitudes, dispositions, and motivations.

5. The circle encompassing the perceptual contexts in the model is the socio-relational context. This refers to the relationship between the interactants. Whenever two people come together and interact they establish a relationship. In the model, the socio-relational context is graphically represented by two circles labeled nonverbal and verbal messages.

6. The nonverbal message circle is larger than the verbal message circle because the majority of our communicative behavior is nonverbal. Whether we are using words or not, we are communicating nonverbally through eye contact, bodily stance, and space.

7. The verbal message circle is a series of dashes in the shape of a circle to represent the digital quality of verbal communication. By digital, we mean that, unlike our nonverbal communication, our verbal communication is made up of words that have recognizable and discrete beginning and ending points.

## Intercultural Communication and Uncertainty

When we interact with someone from a different culture we are faced with a lot of uncertainty. Uncertainty about the other person may make us feel nervous and anxious. To some extent, to effectively interact with someone from a different culture we must be able to predict how our interaction partner is likely to behave and, based on those predictions, select our appropriate verbal and nonverbal messages.

Some types of communication situations may be more or less anxiety producing than others. Initial interaction with someone or interacting with someone from a different culture may produce heightened anxiety. If we are too anxious about interacting with strangers, we tend to avoid them. This type of communication anxiety can be labeled intercultural communication apprehension; that is, the fear or anxiety associated with either real or anticipated interaction with people from different groups, especially different cultural or ethnic groups.

### *Intercultural Communication Apprehension*

Successfully interacting with someone from a different culture requires a degree of communication competence. Most models of communication competence include a cognitive, affective, and behavioral component.

1. The cognitive component refers to how much one knows about communication.
2. The affective component includes one's motivation to approach or avoid communication.

## Barriers to Intercultural Communication

Ethnography is the direct observation, reporting, and evaluation of the customary behavior of a culture. Ideally, ethnography requires an extended period of residence and study in a community. The ethnographer knows the language of the group, participates in some of the group's activities, and uses a variety of observational and recording techniques. In a sense, the accounts of 15th-century explorers of the unfamiliar cultural practices they encountered were primitive ethnographies. Modern ethnography tries to avoid questionnaires and formal interviews in artificial settings; observation in natural settings is preferred. The objective is an analysis of cultural patterns to develop a grammar or theory of the rules for appropriate cultural behaviors.

An ethnographic approach to understanding the dialogue between the magistrate and the defendant would use the perspective of the parties themselves to analyze the problems that each faces in the attempt to communicate. A cultural approach attempts to develop an ideal personification of the culture, and then that ideal is used to explain the actions of individuals in the culture. For example, using the cultural approach, it would be important to know that the Aboriginal people began arriving on the Australian continent from Southeast Asia 40,000 years before North and South America were inhabited and that it wasn't until 1788 that 11 ships arrived carrying a cargo of human prisoners to begin a new British colony by taking control of the land. Liberman describes the unique form of public discourse that evolved among the isolated Aboriginal people of central Australia: Consensus must be preserved through such strategies as unassertiveness, avoidance of direct argumentation, deferral of topics that would produce disharmony, and serial summaries so that the people think together and "speak with one voice." If any dissension is sensed, there are no attempts to force a decision, and the discussion is abandoned. Western European discourse style is direct, confrontational, and individualistic. Thus, it can be said that the Aboriginal defendant in the example finds it difficult to communicate a defense by opposing what has been said and rather frequently concurs with any statement made to him.

The ethnographic and cultural approaches are complementary and together can help our understanding of breakdowns in intercultural communication. Every culture and subgroup provides its members with rules specifying appropriate and inappropriate behavior. Were you to approach intercultural communication from the perspective of attempting to learn the norms of all cultures and subgroups, it certainly would be an impossible task. There is no way that you could learn all the rules governing appropriate and inappropriate behavior for every culture and subgroup with which you came into contact. You'd always be doing something wrong; you'd always be offending someone. Your communication would likely suffer, as your violation of norms would be a form of noise limiting the effectiveness of your communication.

In fact, you wouldn't even know if you were expected to conform to the other's norms or if you were expected to behave according to your own culture's norms while respecting the other culture's norms. A better approach is to examine on a general level the barriers to intercultural communication. LaRay M. Barna has developed a list of six such barriers:

— anxiety,

— assuming similarity instead of difference,

— ethnocentrism,

— stereotypes and prejudice,

— nonverbal misinterpretations, and

— language.

These barriers will be used when discussing problems that can arise in intercultural encounters.

*Anxiety*

The first barrier is high anxiety. When you are anxious because of not knowing what you are expected to do, it is only natural to focus on that feeling and not be totally present in the communication transaction. For example, you may have experienced anxiety on your very first day on a new college campus or in a new job. You may be so conscious of being new-and out of place-and focus so much of your attention on that feeling that you make common mistakes and appear awkward to others. A 1993 survey reported 168 Japanese employees of Japanese companies working in the United States and 135 of their U.S. coworkers. Only 8% of the U.S. coworkers felt impatient with the Japanese coworkers' English. While 19% of the Japanese employees felt their spoken English was poor or very poor and 20% reported feeling nervous when speaking English with U.S. coworkers, 30% of the Japanese employees felt the U.S. coworkers were impatient with their accent, and almost 60% believed that language was the problem in communicating with the U.S. coworkers. For some, anxiety over speaking English properly contributed to avoiding interactions with the U.S. coworkers and limiting interactions both on and off the job to other Japanese only.

*Assuming Similarity Instead of Difference*

The second barrier is assuming similarity instead of difference. In 1997, a Danish woman left her 14-month-old baby girl in a stroller outside a Manhattan restaurant while she was inside. Other diners at the restaurant became concerned and called New York City Police. The woman was charged with endangering a child and was jailed for two nights. Her child was placed in foster care. The woman and the Danish consulate explained that leaving children unattended outside cafés is common in Denmark. Pictures were wired to the police showing numerous strollers parked outside cafés while parents were eating inside. The Danish woman had assumed that Copenhagen is similar to New York, that what is commonly done in Copenhagen is also commonly done in New York.

When you assume similarity between cultures you can be caught unaware of important differences. When you have no information about a new culture, it might make sense to assume there are no differences, to behave as you would in your home culture. But each culture is different and unique to some degree. Boucher, for example, has shown how cultures differ as to whom it is appropriate to display emotions. If you assume that display of emotions is similar to your culture, you might see people in some circumstances as lacking emotion and others in other circumstances as displaying emotions inappropriately. The inverse can be a barrier as well. Assuming difference instead of similarity can lead to your not recognizing important things that cultures share in common.

*Ethnocentrism*

The third barrier to effective intercultural communication is ethnocentrism, or negatively judging aspects of another culture by the standards of one's own culture. To be ethnocentric is to believe in the superiority of one's own culture. Everything in a culture is consistent to that culture and makes sense if you understood that culture. For example, assume that global warming is a fact and, as a result, assume that summers in the United States average 43°C (109°F). It would be logical to make adjustments: Rather than air condition buildings all day, you might close schools and businesses in the afternoons to conserve energy. Such adjustments would make sense.

A less extreme form of ethnocentrism can be labeled cultural nearsightedness, or taking one's own culture for granted and neglecting other cultures. For example, people in the United States often use the word Americans to refer to U.S. citizens, but actually that word is the correct designation of all people in North and South America. Its careless use is a form of ethnocentrism. Cultural nearsightedness often results in making assumptions that simple things are the same everywhere. Designing forms for something as simple as a person's name is not that simple if you recognize how widely practices vary. For example, in Mexico people may have two surnames, with the first from the father's first surname and the second from the mother's surname.

Often, only the first surname is used and the second abbreviated. When a woman marries, she usually retains both of her surnames and adds her husband's first surname. Or consider China with 1.3 billion people and only about 3,100 surnames, with 90% of the population sharing 100 of them. Based on its 1982 census, China has 87 million people sharing the name Li-the most common surname in the world. The name Smith is shared by 2.4 million people in the United States.

Another example is Eurocentric ethnocentrism. This would include, for example, recognizing only Western holidays in schools or basing curriculum only on Western history, music, and art. The terms "the West" and "the East" themselves have been labeled Eurocentric ethnocentrism. Asia is east of Europe, but to call Asia "the East" makes its identity dependent on Europe. In 1913, members of the Pueblo tribe challenged the degree of control that Congress exercised over tribal affairs. In its decision on United States v. Sandoval, the Supreme Court ruled, "Always living in separate and isolated communities, adhering to primitive modes of life, largely influenced by superstition and fetishism, and chiefly governed according to crude customs inherited from their ancestors, [the Pueblos] are essentially a simple, uninformed and inferior people. . . . As a superior and civilized nation, [the U.S. government has both] the power and the duty of exercising a fostering care and protection over all dependent Indian communities within its borders." Extreme ethnocentrism leads to a rejection of the richness and knowledge of other cultures. It impedes communication and blocks the exchange of ideas and skills among peoples. Because it excludes other points of view, an ethnocentric orientation is restrictive and limiting.

Everything that occurs within a school, and especially in the classroom, involves communication, the act of sharing information. Sometimes communication involves the use of oral or written verbal symbols. On other occasions, communication involves various types of nonverbal symbols, including body language.

Communication is the medium for instruction, assessment, interpersonal relationships, group interactions, parent and community relations and counseling. Most behavior problems in schools, and their resolutions, involve some type of communication. In sum, communication permeates education.

Communication is culture bound. The way an individual communicates emanates from his or her culture. Of course, a person may know more than one culture or may be competent in a combination of cultures. Nonetheless, one basic truth prevails: communication is a product of culture.

Students with different cultural norms are at risk if teachers have little knowledge, sensitivity or appreciation of the diversity in communication styles. Such teachers may perceive differences as problems and respond to students' diversify with negative attitudes, low expectations and culturally inappropriate teaching and assessment procedures. Culturally and communicatively diverse students, in turn, may respond with low self concepts and low academic achievement to a school climate they perceive as hostile. The result is reflected in these students' excessive placements in special education, reduced placements in talented and gifted programs and high suspension rates.

The United States is currently experiencing radical demographic shifts which are changing the colors and the cultures of its citizenry. According to recent statistics, one American in four currently defines himself or herself as non white. By the year 2010, because of higher birth rates and immigration trends, non whites are expected to constitute more than one third of the American people, and upwards of 50 percent of its school aged population. By the year 2050, the average U.S. resident will trace his or her descent to Africa, Asia, the Hispanic world, thc Pacific Islands, the Middle East almost anywhere but white Europe.

### *Cross Cultural Communication Issues in Schools*

The failure of many schools to take cross cultural communication issues into account can contribute to school related problems experienced by specific groups of children. The current crisis of African American males in many of the nation's schools demonstrates this point. According to recent statistics, the percentage of African American males who graduate from high school has decreased since the mid 1970's. A similar trend exists for the percentage who go on to college. In 1989, 34 percent of young African American males attended less than four years of high school and only 11 percent attended four years of college or more. In 1990, one out of four

(23%) African American males ages 20 29 were in the criminal system, while only 6% of white males and 10% of Hispanic males were in the system.

Within many schools, it is a well documented fact that African American males are disproportionately placed in special education and speech language pathology programs, and are more likely to be recipients of disciplinary actions. Recent research has shown that language and communication norms among African American males, particularly those of lower socioeconomic status, are related, at least in part, to these problems. For example, lower SES African American males are likely to see the speaking of ethnically based English vernaculars, and the use of urban argots, to be markers of masculinity and defiance of white standards.

While adherence to ethnic vernaculars allows validation to be achieved within the African American male peerage, their employment within the school setting virtually guarantees academic problems and, sometimes, social problems. When students' communication norms conflict with the school's communication norms, erosion of academic performance and acceptable classroom behavior frequently follows. Thus, while the use of Black vernacular speech by African American males may be perceived as "fresh" by peers, it is viewed by teachers, all too often *and incorrectly*, as indicators of a slow learning, violent, undisciplined, and obnoxious individual.

In order to address these issues, schools must build into their curricula (particularly in the language arts area) the notion that there is a time and place for all language. In this way, respect can be given to students' culturally based vernaculars when used in informal, nonacademic activities, while teaching them the necessity and validity of the school's language in formal academic settings. Indeed, the creative teacher uses the vernacular linguisitic system for contrastive analysis during the process of teaching standard English. This approach encourages the African American male to adapt a bidialectal approach to language use.

In addition, the school must provide examples of strong male images who are able to alternately speak the school's language or the vernacular language, as necessary. Jesse Jackson, Spike Lee and Arsenio Hall represent good examples of highly successful and popular African American males who can serve as positive role models for young students, and who demonstrate competence in the standard language required in formal situations as well as the community language when required.

### *Culture, Communication and Language*

Now that your "cultural eye" has been sharpened, let us look at how culture influences students' language skills and their learning of standard English, the language of education.

The concept of communicative competence, based on one's knowledge of the rules of language structure and language use within a given culture, will be useful. A major responsibility of teachers at all grade levels is to teach the language and communication skills needed for academic success, and for career and social mobility.

#### *Sociolinguistics*

Sociolinguists examine social and cultural influences on language behavior. Among the most important concepts to emerge are those relating to dialects and language standards.

Sociolinguists have documented the presence of dialects in every language. These dialects, all of which are legitimate, are associated with educational, economic, social and historical conditions. To linguists, the word "dialect" refers to a way of speaking a language, and not to an incorrect way of speaking a language. While all dialects of a given language are linguistically legitimate, some achieve social prestige. In literate, economically developed societies, the dialect spoken by those with the most formal education, the highest socioeconomic status and the greatest degree of political power tends to acquire the greatest social prestige. Typically, it becomes the standard for the culture, for writing and for education.

Standard dialects also provide a medium through which persons from different linguistic backgrounds can communicate with one another. Social and regional variations may exist within standard dialects as long as they conform to specified linguistic rules, largely grammatical in nature. Standard English, therefore, should not be considered "Northern English" or "White English," since it is spoken, in one form or another, in all parts of the United States and by some members of all racial and cultural groups.

At the other end of the social spectrum, so called nonstandard dialects are generally spoken by the "have nots:" the powerless, the less educated, the less economically well off and the less socially prominent. While legitimate linguistically, these dialects tend to be unacceptable to the "haves" of society.

In the United States, the schools' failure to teach standard English is reflected in the poor performance of nonstandard English speakers on achievement, aptitude and diagnostic tests. Perhaps the most alarming evidence of this failure is the low performance of nonstandard English speakers on tests used to place students in remedial or gifted programs. Virtually all of these tests presume competence in standard English.

Many African American children, usually from working class homes or communities, speak a nonstandard variety of English. This variety, often referred to as Black English Vernacular, is thought by many sociolinguists to reflect African influences on American English, and is reinforced by social isolation, segregation and group identity.

### *Cultural Differences in Discourse*

In addition to differences in pronunciation, vocabulary and grammatical structures among cultural groups, variations also exist in the rules for general discourse in oral communication, covering such specific acts as narratives and conversation. In communicating with one another, teachers and students naturally will follow the assumptions and rules governing discourse within their respective cultures. Discourse rules govern such aspects of communication as:

— Opening or closing conversations;

— Taking turns during conversations;

— Interrupting;

— Using silence as a communicative device;

— Knowing appropriate topics of conversation;

— Interjecting humor at appropriate times;

— Using nonverbal behavior;

— Expressing laughter as a communicative device;

— Knowing the appropriate amount of speech to be used by participants; and

— Sequencing of elements during discourse.

In this section, we will present examples of cultural and communicative tendencies observable among African American and white students from several cultural groups in the United States. Tendencies are not universal. In order to avoid generalizations and stereotypes about cultural groups, variations within cultures must always be considered. Highly educated people of a given cultural group are less likely to reveal indigenous language and communication patterns than less educated persons. Moreover, many people communicate in ways influenced by other cultures.

Unfamiliarity with cultural communication differences can lead to misinterpretation, misunderstanding and even unintentional insult. For example, the African American student who shows little reserve in stating his or her feelings may be misperceived as hostile, or perhaps as dangerous. The student, meanwhile, may see himself or herself as an honest person willing to share feelings as a necessary first step in resolving problems.

Similarly, the African American student who looks away from speakers during conversation may be erroneously perceived as showing disrespect or not paying attention. The African American student who freely states his or her position to the teacher may be perceived as challenging the teacher's authority when the student may be demonstrating honesty and pride in the value of his or her opinion.

Teachers, like all human beings, have their own expectations about communicative behavior. The teacher should 1) recognize any incongruencies that may exist between his or her expectations and those of the child; 2) make certain that behavioral norms in the classroom are sufficiently broad to embrace all cultural groups; and 3) teach the rules of standard American culture and the reasons for them.

A variety of cross cultural communication problems can arise in school, and it is important that teachers not automatically blame the student or the student's family or culture. Problems often result from misunderstandings or value conflicts between teachers and students who are obeying different culturally based communication rules.

Today an Internet search on the topic of intercultural communication or cross-cultural communication yields over 100 000 results. In recent years practitioners in a wide variety of fields—scientific cooperation, academic research, business, management, education, health, culture, politics, diplomacy, development, and others—have realised just how important intercultural communication is for their everyday work. Fast travel, international media, and the Internet have made it easy for us to communicate with people all over the world.

The process of economic globalisation means that we cannot function in isolation but must interact with the rest of the world for survival. The global nature of many widely diverse modern problems and issues such as the environment, governance of the Internet, poverty and international terrorism call for cooperation between nations. Intercultural communication is no longer an option, but a necessity.

Because important decisions in business, politics, education, health, and culture these days usually effect citizens of more than one nation, the question of whether communication between people of different nations is effective and whether all parties emerge with the same understanding is of crucial importance. Individuals who deal with people from other cultures want to learn how to improve their performance through improving their communication skills.

The world today is characterized by an ever growing number of contacts resulting in communication between people with different linguistic and cultural backgrounds. This communication takes place because of contacts within the areas of business, military cooperation, science, education, massmedia, entertainment, tourism but also because of immigration brought about by labor shortage or political conflicts. In all these contacts, there is communication which needs to be as constructive as possible, without misunderstandings and breakdowns. It is our belief that research on the nature of linguistic and cultural similarities and differences here can play a positive and constructive role.

Lack of knowledge of another culture can lead, at the best, to embarrassing or amusing mistakes in communication. At the worst, such mistakes may confuse or even offend the people we wish to communicate with, making the conclusion of business deals or international agreements difficult or impossible.

At the dawn of the twenty-first century, Marshall McLuhan's vision of a global village is no longer considered an abstract idea but a virtual certainty. Technological and socio-political changes have made the world a smaller planet to inhabit. The technological feasibility of the mass media to bring events from across the globe into our homes, businesses, and schools dramatically reduces the distance between peoples of different cultures and societies. Telecommunication systems link the world via satellites and fiber optics. Supersonic jets carry people from one country to another faster than the speed of sound.

Politically, the end of the cold war has brought decades of partisan tensions to an end. Countries that were once bitter enemies are now joining forces. Mass migrations force interaction between people of different races, nationalities, and ethnicities. Noted historian and Pulitzer Prize winner Arthur Schlesinger warns us that history tells an ugly story of what happens when people of diverse cultural, ethnic, religious, or linguistic backgrounds converge in one place. The hostility of one group of people against another, different group of people, is among the most instinctive of human drives. Schlesinger contends that unless a common goal binds diverse people together, tribal hostilities will drive them apart. By replacing the conflict of political ideologies that dominated in the twentieth century, ethnic and racial strife will usher in the new millennium as the explosive issue. Only through intercultural communication can such conflict be managed and reduced. Only by competently and peacefully interacting with others who are different than ourselves can our global village survive.

# 4

# Understanding Human Social Behaviour

Human behaviour is different to non-human behaviour because it is guided by reference to values. In turn, the development of values that have meaning to people is dependent upon two ideas:

— Consciousness, which involves things like the ability to think and an awareness of the world around us, and

— Self-consciousness, which involves an awareness of ourselves as unique individuals.

These ideas are crucial for the understanding of the basis of human social behaviour since it is only because we possess conscious and self-conscious abilities that we develop values that, in turn, provide us with a sense of culture. Clear evidence of this is provided by:

— The cultural differences that exist between different societies.

— The sub-cultural differences that exist between groups in any society.

In a simple sense, therefore, we are all products of our social environment. However, this simple statement hides a multitude of controversies and interpretations over the precise relationship between us as individuals and the social groups to which we belong. This perhaps illustrates the tension between thinking, conscious, individuals and the society in which we live.

— At one extreme, we have Structuralist sociologists who argue that we are the product of society. Society shapes people in its own image.

— At the other extreme are Interactionist sociologists who emphasise the creative aspects of human individuality. People shape society in their image.

The majority of sociologists probably fall somewhere in the middle of these two extremes. On the one hand we recognise that people do have individual levels of consciousness, creativity and understanding, whilst on the other it is evident that for all our supposed individuality we demonstrate very clear and broadly predictable patterns of behaviour that can only have been imposed on us in some way through our contacts with the social world.

### Development of Self

Although it is clear that human beings have the capacity for self-consciousness and self-awareness, the earlier work we've done on culture and socialisation demonstrates that we do not develop this ability automatically. Rather, sociologists argue that it has to be learnt, just like any other social skill.

In basic terms, therefore, through social interaction we are able to build on the biological capacity to "see ourselves as others see us".

— If we do not interact socially, we do not develop this capacity in any way that is recognisably human. Thus, people need society in order to develop as individuals and social interaction allows us to develop the capacities given to us by our human biology. This is called a symbiotic relationship, which means that the one depends on the other.

Through our ability to think we are able to create the context in which our individual capacities can be developed, but by creating this context we automatically place limits upon our ability to act freely. This is because cultures involve shared meanings that govern social interaction.

It is here that we can start to develop the concept of identity, which relates to ideas about who and what we and others believe us to be. A cultural identity, therefore, involves a set of characteristics that define us as individuals, groups, societies and so forth. These characteristics can be almost anything, but it is evident that things such as gender, class, ethnic background, region and age are some of the most important sources of identity in any society.

Thus, in order to develop a sense of identity, it is necessary to have self-awareness. However, we develop this sense of self through the socialisation process when we learn how to interact socially on the basis of various cultural identities. The one, in short, is dependent upon the other.

— We can perhaps understand this a little more easily if we think more specifically about how we learn self-awareness.

## Social Construction of Self (personality) and Identity

We can start to examine these ideas in a general way by looking in more detail at various theories of Self development, beginning with a general overview of the type of Interactionist theory suggested by Mead. For Interactionist sociologists, the development of our individual Self / personality is rooted in the twin processes of:

— Negotiation and

— Interpretation.

In basic terms, the relationships that we form and enter provide us with a relatively flexible structure of rules which we have initially negotiated with others. Clearly, this idea of negotiation has to be interpreted widely, since in many situations the relationships we enter into are already surrounded by rules of behaviour, the basic boundaries of which are difficult if not impossible to change. For example, when you first began school at the age of 4 or 5, you where given no choice about whether or not you wanted to attend.

Similarly, the basic role relationship between you and your teachers was not negotiable, since the roles of teacher and pupil in this situation are already very clearly defined in terms of their basic content. However, even in this situation, relationships are negotiable and negotiated. With some teachers you establish a friendly, easy-going, relationship, yet with others you establish a cool and distant relationship. How you choose to play the role of pupil is also a matter for negotiation, since you may try to push the boundaries of the relationship to see how far it will go.

Other social situations are, however, more clearly negotiated in the sense of being created by the relationship between the participants. Think, for example, about the range of relationships you form in your school / College on a daily basis which have to be recognised and maintained through some form of negotiation. For example, as you walk around, you may encounter the following relationships:

— *Strangers:* These are people that you recognise as human beings and will respond to if required (for example, if they ask you for directions), but in the ordinary course of events you do not acknowledge their existence.

— *Acquaintances:* These might, for example, be people from your class. Some you may have spoken to in class, others might just be vaguely recognisable faces or names. However, it may or may not be appropriate to recognise them as you walk around (depending on a number of factors), but if you do recognise your relationship its content might involve things like:

- making brief eye contact and smiling as you pass.
- saying "hello".
- stopping for a few seconds to hold a fairly meaningless conversation about the weather.

— *Friends:* These are people that we know well and we have to recognise this fact when we meet them. We are expected to stop and talk to them when we meet and a range of topics will be included in the conversation. Unlike acquaintances, for example, we will know a reasonable level of detail and depth about their personal background and we are willing to reveal appropriately more about ourselves to them.

— *Close friends:* This involves people with whom we are emotionally close, although we are probably not sexually involved with them. They include people of the same and / or opposite sex and are, for most of us, few in number. When we meet in passing we are more likely to stop to talk to them and the conversation will cover a range of topics. More emphasis is likely to be placed upon the personal feelings of the people involved than is the case with friends or acquaintances.

— *Intimate friends:* People in this category are likely to be those with whom we share a loving / sexual relationship. Unlike with most other relationships, this is more likely to involve public (and private) touching behaviour (holding hands, kissing, etc.).

These are a small sample of the relationships we are likely to recognise and remember during the day. These relate to our peers and there is, of course, an even greater range of non-peer social relationships in our lives.

All of the above are clearly negotiated relationships. We can demonstrate this by thinking about how these relationships can change over time. However, these different relationships also demonstrate the second aspect noted above, namely the significance of interpretation.

If you think about the above relationships, our ability to differentiate between strangers, acquaintances, friends and so forth is based upon the way we are able to interpret the meaning of such relationships. Thus, we need to develop ways of identifying the different relationships we have and, most importantly, the content and meaning of such relationships to both ourselves and the other people involved.

If we now try to apply some of these basic ideas to the way in which our personality develops through social interaction, we can use an example to illustrate the basic nature of this developmental process:

— Imagine two people meeting in the street. They recognise the fact that they are friends and stop to talk to each other accordingly. In this situation a number of things are apparent:

   a. They have decided they have something in common.

   b. This assumption involves imposing on each other certain expectations. They will stop walking; they will greet each other in an appropriate manner; they will talk to each other and so forth.

   c. By doing this, each effectively tries to control the behaviour of the other, even though in this situation they may not consciously believe they are doing this, mainly because it seems somehow natural that this is how friends behave.

In this situation, therefore, as in numerous other small-scale social encounters, social interaction involves:

— Trying to understand something about the people we meet.

— Using the behaviour of others to tell us something about ourselves.

On the other hand, what might we think about ourselves if we recognise someone as a friend and prepare for the inevitable friendly encounter and they simply ignore us or give us a withering, scornful, look as they pass quickly by on the other side of the street?

In the above example, we can note a fundamental idea about the development of our identity, namely that we use the way other people interpret our behaviour as evidence of who and what we are. Charles Cooley referred to this idea as the "looking-glass self". That is, the theory that we use the behaviour of others towards us as a kind of mirror in which is reflected an image of the person we are.

This suggests that "who we are" or "who we believe ourselves to be" is a reflection of what others think about us. Up to a point this is true. We look to the behaviour of other people around us to confirm the impression that we have about ourselves.

However, this is not the whole story since we are not simply "prisoners" of other people's behaviour (that is, we do not simply take the reactions of other people towards us as the single, defining, aspect of "who we believe ourselves to be". This is not the whole story of our personality development for a number of reasons:

— We do not simply believe everything that people tell us about ourselves.

— Other people rarely tell us directly what they think about us. We have to interpret what the behaviour of other people towards us means and this creative aspect of interpretation means that we frequently interpret the behaviour of others in ways that confirm the image we have of our selves.

— Some people are more significant to us than others and their views carry more weight with us. These significant others are more influential in shaping our personality than people whose behaviour and opinions we care little about.

— As thinking individuals, we try to manipulate the impression that other people have of us. We are not "passive victims" of other people's behaviour and this idea of impression management is one we can now develop.

## Presentation of Self

Erving Goffman uses a theatrical metaphor to illustrate his ideas about personality, self-development and social identity. In basic terms, the social world is represented as a play in which the various members of society adopt certain roles and speak certain lines. Unlike a play, however, the lines that we speak are created by us, not for us. Social life, therefore, is a series of dramatised encounters which vary in importance and significance. These encounters, just like in a play, have scenery that defines the situation for the actors and props.

Whenever we have a social encounter (such as sitting in a classroom, getting married or whatever) Goffman argues that a complex process of social interaction is always created, even around the simplest of activities. We usually only recognise this complexity when we are faced with situations where we are unsure of our ability to play a role), uncertain about how we are expected to behave or have never encountered the situation before.

— Trying to manage your impression of them.

— Reacting to your attempts to manage their impression of you.

To aid your performance, you use various props. These props are used symbolically. That is, we use them to project an image of ourselves from the perception of others about the meaning of the symbol. For example, wearing an expensive piece of jewellery may give others the impression that you are rich. At the end of the party, your performance in that particular situation is concluded, but you have collected and created a set of social characteristics that serve to identify you to the people with whom you have interacted. These impressions are remembered and used to identify you when or if you meet them again. There are a couple of key ideas in the above that we need to clarify and elaborate.

Firstly, we have noted the importance of role play and a role, for Interactionist sociologists, represents a kind of mental map that we use to guide us through the social world. In this respect, adopting a role does not simply involve learning a set of rigid guidelines concerning appropriate and inappropriate behaviour; rather, a role involves learning a set of flexible behavioural principles (or rules of a situation) that are used to govern various forms of social interaction.

Secondly, as we interact socially and develop a sense of self, we also begin to establish an identity - an understanding of who and what we are. There are a number of dimensions to social identity but what we will eventually need to think about is how the type of sociological theories we have just outlined concerning self development can be related to both identity and concepts such as class, gender, age, ethnicity and region.

## Labelling Theory

Labelling theory seeks to illustrate and explain the relationship between individual actors and the wider society in which they live. In particular, it tries to show how the audience for our behaviour is influential in the creation of personal identities and to understand this theory we first have to understand the significance of social labels. As human beings we live in a symbolic world. Basically, this means that the meaning of everything we encounter has to be interpreted. Nothing is self-evident and the meaning of something is highly dependent upon the context in which it exists. For example, even the relatively straightforward act of me shaking my fist at you can have a range of different meanings, depending upon the context in which it takes place.

One of the main ways in which we interpret the meaning of an action is through what is called "taking the role of the other". That is, we use our ability to metaphorically put ourselves in the shoes of the person with whom we are interacting in order to understand the meaning of their actions.

For humans, the most symbolic system we develop is language. Words are created to symbolise certain things or ideas. Thus, the word "elephant" is symbolic of "a large grey creature with big ears and a long nose called a trunk".

It is symbolic precisely because there is no real or logical connection between the word and the thing it describes. Language, therefore, is a system of labels or names that we apply to things. A label identifies and represents a class of objects and categorises them as being similar.

The sociological importance of labelling is not just that it enables us to communicate using a patterned system of shared meanings. In social terms, therefore, labelling is extremely significant since the labels we attract, either through choice or because they are forced upon us, are going to be significant in terms of:

— Our self-image and behaviour.

— The perception that others have of us and their interpretation of our behaviour based around those perceptions.

Having outlined the basic ideas involved in labelling theory, we will develop and apply these ideas in the next section that looks specifically at the concept of identity. Next, however, we need to look briefly at alternative conceptions of self development to those discussed above. In this respect, we need to look at Structuralist perspectives and in particular those ideas put forward by Functionalist and Marxist Conflict sociologists.

## Structuralist Perspectives on Self-Development

In Structural sociology, the focus is placed more firmly on the way society, in all its forms, shapes the behaviour of individuals. Although Structuralists differ in the emphasis they place on structural forces and the ability of individuals to shape their own lives, there is a general agreement that what really matters in terms of individual and group self-awareness and development is the way that these structural forces effectively seem to make people behave in certain more or less predictable ways.

In addition, structuralists tend to place a great deal of emphasis on the socialisation process as the means through which societies shape the beliefs, perceptions and behaviour of their members. In many respects, therefore, socialisation is viewed as a powerful guiding force in terms of the way people are:

— Made into self-aware beings.

— Categorised into particular forms of cultural identity.

*Functionalist perspectives.*

As we have seen earlier writers within this perspective stress the importance of socialisation and the way people learn the already-existing norms of expected behaviour. Functionalist writers argue that it is only by learning cultural rules that social interaction becomes possible.

Cultural rules, therefore, provide a structure for people's behaviour, effectively channelling behaviour in some ways but not others. The stress is on the way our behaviour is constrained by the rules of the society into which we are born. Social structures, according to this way of seeing things, operate at an institutional level in society. We experience structural pressures whenever we adopt a particular role, since as we have seen, by taking on a role we take on certain norms, give expression to certain values and have a particular status in society.

In order to exist, societies create numerous roles that have to be successfully filled and performed. In education, for example, roles such as student, lecturer, administrator and so forth have to be filled and performed if this institution is to fulfil its allotted purpose in society. If we see societies as structures of social relationships, it follows that people are socialised into already-existing and defined roles.

We can see this most clearly in small scale-societies where the number of roles people are required to perform is very limited. In such societies people's behaviour tends to be very conservative and limited in scope. In Modern societies, such as Britain in the 20th century, the situation is more complex since there are a huge range of possible roles and a wide range of socialising agencies. However, the basic principles remain the same.

From this perspective, human consciousness clearly exists, but it is not given the same level of significance that Interactionists give it. Clearly, humans have to be conscious of the world and they have to be able to recognise cultural needs and develop cultural rules to organise solutions to these needs - but the fact that people are forced to react in this way relegates human consciousness to a secondary position in the great intellectual scheme of things.

If you have understood the principles behind this idea of structuralism, it becomes a relatively simple matter to develop these ideas sociologically (rather than linguistically) and apply them to the ideas of both Structural Functionalism and, in a moment, Marxist Conflict Structuralism. If we substitute a social need such as the "problem of survival" for the "problem of communication" and, as a solution to this problem the idea of "social institutions" instead of "language" it should be possible to grasp the basic ideas involved concerning the development of individual self awareness. In basic terms, every human being is the product of the culture in which they live and have been socialised to accept. Our sense of self, identity and behaviour is, therefore, created and sustained by the culture with which we identify.

### *Marxist Perspectives*

Although, as with all sociological perspectives, there are a variety of competing interpretations in Marxist perspectives, Marxist Conflict theory differs from its Functionalist counterpart in important ways.

While Functionalism stresses the idea that society is a functioning entity that involves consensus over basic values, Marxists argue that although consensus necessarily exists, it is a form of consensus that is manufactured to reflect the interests of powerful groups or classes. That is, whereas Functionalists argue that consensus over values is the bedrock of any social system, Marxists argue that consensus is a phoney construction. It creates a sense of unity of purpose that obscures the fact that the rich and powerful benefit far more than the poor and powerless by maintaining the fiction of a basic value agreement.

Marxists, therefore, argue that social life involves inherent conflicts of interest, the most important of which is economic conflict; that is, the conflicts that arise from the fact that in capitalist societies, for example, some groups have greater access to economic rewards than others.

In basic terms, social classes are defined primarily in economic terms, usually by reference to what is called the means of economic production (that is, the way a society is organised to produce the things needed for its survival). Some people are in a position to own the means of production, while others have little opportunity for ownership. This situation, Marxists claim, produces a classbased system of social stratification. A simple expression of this might be:

a. *Upper or Ruling class* - people who own businesses.

b. *Middle class* - professional workers who help to run businesses on a day to day basis.

c. *Working or Lower class* - people who have no economic ownership and are not involved in the control of businesses.

Social class is considered to be the most important source of self image and social identity although, as we have suggested, many Marxists argue that people may not always be consciously aware of this.

## Identity

In this section we will be exploring in the various ways that conceptions about individual and group identities are socially constructed. That is, created against a social background that tries to make social interaction meaningful, understandable and ordered by categorising people in various ways. As we have seen, sociologists are interested in identifying and explaining the nature of identity as a social phenomenon. That is, we are interested in the relationship between social categories such as age and gender and how these affect people's perception of both themselves and their relationship to others. In this respect we are particularly interested in the various ways that different cultures develop and use biological categories and physical categories as props around which individual and group identities are built. In the main, therefore, we will be looking at five basic sources of identity, namely:

— Gender.

— Social class.

— Age.

— Region and

— Ethnicity.

These are not the only sources of identity, nor do they necessarily appear in all known societies, but they are a significant selection of the main sources of identity in modern societies such as our own. In addition, one of the reasons for looking at identity is to explore the idea of its social construction and we can do this most clearly by using examples that will be relatively familiar from your own experiences.

On the contrary, sociologists believe that identity is a dynamic feature of social life. That is, it is something that is constantly evolving and changing. For some people, identity can change rapidly and dramatically, of course, but for most of us our identities evolve slowly and imperceptibly. This is perhaps one reason as to why we tend to think of our personality as being relatively fixed and unchanging, but we only have to compare our behaviour and attitudes over time to appreciate just how much we do change.

### *Explaining Identity*

If you keep in mind the categories identified above, the first thing you should note is that they are all examples of labels. That is, they are names that our society gives to a variety of different social categories. As we will see in a moment, one of the most significant things about each of these labels is that they are associated with a set of social characteristics that tell us something about the meaning of each category.

The kinds of social categories noted above exist because they represent attempts to understand and explain the differences that exist between people.

To summarise these ideas, therefore, we can note that:

— Observed differences between people need to be explained.

— These differences are named (labelled) and categorised. Thus, people who share certain similarities (such as being biologically female) are placed in a particular social category.

— Each category of person is given or develops certain general characteristics that broadly define the category.

— These characteristics become general expectations about how to be a person of that type.

— On the basis of these different expectations people hold about different categories of person, the people placed in these categories have different experiences in society. A man, for example, has different experiences to a woman; a child has different experiences to an adult and so forth.

The easiest way to visualise the idea of different social categories is to think in terms of social roles. Each role that we play has:

— *Observed differences:* The role of student is different to the role of student.

— *A name / label that categorises the people playing a particular role:* A role involves people sharing a common belief about how to play the role and so forth.

— *General characteristics:* These relate to norms of behaviour when playing a particular role. There are for, example, certain norms relating to how it is appropriate to play the role of female, male, child and so forth.

— *Expectations:* When others relate to you in terms of a particular role, they have expectations about how you should behave (values and norms). Similarly, when you play a role you internalise various norms (the expectations others have of you) in order to try to play your role in an appropriate manner.

— *Experiences:* As you play various roles you find that people relate to you in different ways, based on the expectations they have about the role you are playing. These expectations are like a hidden force acting upon you and they affect your behaviour in the sense that:

  — People are trying to make you conform to certain ideas they have about appropriate role behaviour.

  — People will try to punish you if you deviate from the expectations they hold.

Thus, the characteristics people in different societies assign to the type of categories we have noted are important because they represent general rules of expected behaviour. That is, the various ways people are expected to behave in terms of the social roles they have achieved, such as teacher, student, etc. or been given (ascribed), such as male, female, Northerner, etc.

## Gender

Gender is defined in terms of the particular cultural characteristics that people give to different biological sexes. In our society, for example, we recognise only two sexes (male and female) defined by the physical differences between the two. Although some societies recognise a third sex (hermaphrodites - people born with various combinations of male and female sexual organs) which is a combination of male and female, for our purpose here it is enough that we simply recognise biological differences as the basis of sex labelling.

At the moment of birth, therefore, perhaps the first conscious label applied to human infants is that of sex, followed closely and intimately by that of gender. These labels are significant because they will be used to tell people such things as:

— How to raise a child appropriately in terms of its gender.

— The types of behaviour that a culture expects from different genders.

— The types of roles different genders will be expected to fulfil.

In this respect, gender is a very significant source of identity in our society, mainly because of the social characteristics we give to children of different genders. If we have different perceptions of people based around, in part, their gender, then this will clearly:

— Affect the various ways that we behave towards them.

— Affect the way they see themselves through our behaviour.

In basic terms, what we are referring to here are the rules that apparently govern the roles that we play in life. Thus, to be male or female in our society means conforming to various cultural rules and expectations around what it means to be male or female. The assumption here, for the moment, is that a society develops certain norms about masculinity and femininity that people then try to socialise into us. The first thing we need to do, therefore, is to identify the rules of gender in our society. When we have done this we can then think about how and why these rules develop, are maintained and can be changed.

*Gender Identities*

These are not separate features of social life but rather they are wholly interdependent. In this respect we can look generally at various types of gender expectations (or gender appropriate norms) in a variety of ways. Aspects of male roles, reflecting the kinds of assumptions we make about how men should behave, include:

— Leadership,

— Taking control of situations,

— Making decisions and being

— Active, worldly, unemotional and aggressive.

— In addition, men are not supposed to be particularly emotional. Men are allowed, by and large, to be blunt, loud, sloppy in their behaviour and dress. In their sexual relationships, men are expected to openly take the initiative and they are allowed much greater scope in their sexuality.

Aspects of female roles on the other hand, again reflecting the kinds of assumptions we make about how men should behave, include:

— Physical dependency (especially during pregnancy),

— Emotional behaviour,

— Lack of control,

— Passive, motherly and family-orientated.

— In addition, women are encouraged to take more care with their appearance how they dress, use of make-up and so forth. Femininity involves caring for others, especially children, and this is related to one of the primary roles associated with women in most Western societies, namely motherhood.

There are, of course, many other aspects of gender identity that we could note, but the important thing for our current purpose is the idea that gender identity involves the belief that you have things in common with others - in this case, your biology and particular ways of seeing and behaving in the social world. Conversely, in the case of gender identity we are perhaps more usually aware of having a particular identity when we look at opposite identities. That is, when we mix with people of the opposite sex, although clearly we do behave in ways, with our own gender, that reinforce gender norms, experiences and beliefs.

## Age

As we have seen, the concept of age is rooted in biological development. In this respect we clearly all pass through various phases of physical development, although once again this fact is probably less important to sociologists than the various norms of behaviour that are associated with age / physical development.

As with the concept of gender, age group has clear cultural connotations with regard to identity. That is, people are socialised into normative associations between age and behaviour. In our society, for example, we can identity four very broad cultural groupings based around age, namely:

— Childhood,

— Youth,

— Adulthood and

— Old Age.

Each of these groups reflect certain cultural assumptions about how it is appropriate / inappropriate for people of a certain age to behave. In many ways these assumptions about behaviour are related to things like lifestyle and people are generally encouraged to identify themselves with different kinds of behaviour based around their biological age. For example:

*Children:* During this phase, a child is encouraged to see themselves as largely dependent on adults. Much of their behaviour is closely controlled and little independent behaviour is seen as possible or desirable. Youth: This is a period between childhood and adulthood where the young person is being prepared for full acceptance into adulthood. Young people are increasingly given independence from adults during this period, although much of their behaviour is still fairly tightly controlled .

Some cultures, have clear rites of passage relating to the formal passing from childhood into adulthood. In Britain, we tend to mark the passage from childhood to adulthood at age 18 by symbolically giving the new adult "the key to the door".

*Adults:* Full adulthood brings with it full legal rights and independence as an individual in our society. It also brings with it a range of responsibilities, depending on the choices that people make. In many ways this is probably the least distinctive and most general of the age groupings in our society and it is usual to sub-divide this group into a variety of age-based categories. For example, one relatively modern category is "thirtysomethings" to denote relatively young, socially-successful, individuals.

*Old Age:* In our society, one of the most important rites of passage is that undergone between adulthood and old age. The most frequent rite is official retirement from work which has the effect of literally and symbolically marking-off the elderly as different from the rest of society.

Each of the above cultural groups confer a sense of identity on people; that is, a sense of belonging to a specific grouping with its own values, norms and forms of behaviour.

This leads us to a second interpretation of the relationship between age and identity in terms of the concept of sub-culture. Youth and the elderly are much more likely to think of themselves in sub-cultural terms - as an identifiable social grouping where people have important things in common that they do not share with other groups. · Youth sub-cultures, for example, frequently and periodically arise in Western society. These tend to be based around fairly unique lifestyles involving symbolic forms of dissent (music, dress, attitudes, behaviour and so forth). Most people will be familiar with such sub-cultural styles as skinheads, punks, ravers and so forth. The wide variety of different youth sub-cultures and styles is considered in more detail in other parts of the course.

## Region

Region is a further example of the way we use our perception of physical objects as a means of constructing a sense of identity. Initially we can focus on two main aspects of region:

— The concepts of Nation and nationality and

— The idea of regional variations within different Nations.

The concept of a Nation relates, geographically, to the idea of dividing the world into various States. For our purposes, a

Stâte is simply an area of land that is administered by some form of national government. Nation states are usually clearly defined in terms of geographic boundaries.

Sociologically, however, Nation-states are also what Anderson has termed an "imagined community". That is, the people who are born and live within certain geographic boundaries have a sense of belonging to or being a part of a particular Nation. That is, people imagine themselves to have a specific nationality.

As you may also be aware, sociologists are generally wary of discussing concepts of nationality and race as if they are the same thing, since both are seen to be social constructs. That is, they are debatable ideas around which certain social characteristics are developed.

When we start to think sociologically about this type of current controversy, we find that it highlights some of the difficulties we face when thinking about concepts like nationality.

The idea of nationality as an imagined community and this is significant because it illustrates the way that various national characteristics - and by extension, national identity - are developed around the idea of physical region. It is, for example, reasonably clear that when people talk about "being English" or "being French" they are saying that each nationality can be uniquely defined in terms of various social characteristics.

In significant respects, therefore, national identity is something that is created in relation to perceived differences with other nationalities. We also need to note a further dimension of nationality since it also involves idea of claim to loyalty. Turning briefly to the second aspect of region noted above, it is clear that within a particular nationality people can develop a more specific and personal sense of regional identity. That is, the idea that being born and raised within a particular geographic area within a Nation-state also has some significance for our sense of identity. This is because regional cultural variations create social characteristics that can be used to impose or develop a sense of local identity.

## Ethnicity

There tends, in everyday language, to be some confusion over the use of the terms ethnicity and "race" and we need, initially, to resolve any possible sociological confusion. The term "race" refers to the idea that human beings can be classified in different ways on the basis of various supposed racial types - European, Nordic, Aborigine, African or whatever. At various times this idea has been popular in both the biological sciences and everyday language, but there seems to be little or no genetic evidence to support the idea that there is sufficient genetic variation between human beings to support the idea that there are definite racial types. A major problem with this type of usage is not simply the question of whether or not distinctive racial types actually exist, but rather that the concept of race is frequently used to justify the alleged superiority / inferiority of one "race" over another.

Sociologists recognise that the term "race" is frequently used in everyday language even though its academic use is increasingly rare. Thus, whenever the term "race" is used it should always be qualified by the use of "quotation marks" to denote that although we recognise its everyday use, we do not necessarily agree with its everyday meaning.

Of more use to us is the concept of ethnicity, which basically means a recognition that different people develop different forms of culture. Thus, whereas "race" has frequently been used to denote supposed biological / genetic differences between human beings, ethnicity is now more often used to denote cultural differences between different peoples.

One advantage of the concept of ethnicity - aside from the fact that we can talk about cultural differences free from the stigma of doctrines relating to "racial superiority" - is that it forces us to focus on the different ways of life that human beings develop. In addition, we can also focus on the concept of ethnicity in terms of cultural identities. Although this is not the place to develop theories about the nature of ethnic group interaction, it is clear that people draw a sense of identity from the fact of belonging to this or that ethnic group and culture. This sense of belonging is particularly evident when we look at relationships between ethnic minorities and the wider cultures within which they reside. In very general terms, ethnic group identity can be based around a number of different areas, singularly or, more usually, in combination.

## Social Class

Social class is an important concept in Sociology and it usually refers to the various ways that people can be classified on the basis of their occupation. Thus, within Sociology, class has tended to be used as an economic or occupational classification system.

The concept of class is frequently a difficult one to come to terms with, mainly because:

- It can be defined in many different ways.
- There are frequent disagreements as to the significance of social class.

Some sociologists, for example, use the concept as a convenient way of classifying different occupational groups in society. In this respect social class is seen to be a statistical category that does not have much significance outside the fact that it allows us to conveniently group people of similar occupations. This usage is probably closest to the Functionalist perspective in Sociology. Other sociologists, however, view social class as far more than a convenient classification of related occupations. Marxist sociologists, for example, see social class as a much more active concept. That is, social class is seen to influence people's experiences in the social world and, most importantly, how they see the nature of their world.

For the moment, we will assume that a simple definition of social class involves identifying three major social classes:

— The upper class - consisting of people who own and control businesses.

— The middle class - consisting of people who, although they do not own businesses, are charged with the day-to-day running of these enterprises.

The working class - consisting of people who lack both ownership and control and simply work for a wage. Although this is a very simplistic view of social class, it will suffice for our purposes for the moment, since it conveys the main idea of people experiencing the world differently based upon their working situation.

In terms of culture and identity, the basic idea here is that different classes develop different ways of life based around their different experiences. Values and norms frequently develop in different ways for different social classes, such that the culture of an upper class male or female will appear very different to that of a working class male or female.

One way that social class can be used to provide people with a sense of identity is through their work / occupation. In this sense, where people work together, doing the same kinds of job they develop something in common with each other - in effect, they identify themselves through what they do.

Another way that social class relates to identity - although perhaps one that may be rapidly declining in significance in modern societies - is through the idea of community. That is, the idea that people of a similar social class tend to live and work in the same area and develop common bonds through sharing similar experiences in the social world. For example, traditional mining villages consisted of people who shared roughly the same type of employment and experiences - and this fact gave them a sense of common identity.

Finally, perhaps, the third area relating to class and identity is class consciousness. That is, an awareness of belonging to a particular social class with its own way of life, traditions and interests. Many people, for example, are keenly aware that they are working class or upper class and this awareness helps to create a sense of social identity; that is, the idea that you can broadly define both yourself and others in class terms. This idea has further significance if we see social classes as having different interests in society. If this is the case we can talk about things like class solidarity· These and other ideas about social class will be developed further as we go through the course.

In this section of the course we have looked - briefly and in general terms - at a variety of different sources of identity. In particular, we have looked at the various ways that conceptions about individual and group identities are socially constructed. That is, created against a social background that tries to make social interaction meaningful, understandable and ordered by categorising people in various ways.

We have focused on a number of major sources of social identity, mainly to give you an idea about how these social categories can be and are used for the purpose of creating and maintaining individual and group identities. In all of these cases, the basic concern has been to show some of the ways that membership of social groups helps to create a sense of belonging in human beings. This sense of belonging - of having certain things in common with people - is important to us, as social animals, mainly because we can use it as a source of telling us who and what we are. The sociological concept most often used in the context of identity is that of social integration. Thus, as social beings we need to feel that we belong to various groups.

This need to "feel we belong" is significant because we draw from these groups a sense of identity. That is, by becoming integrated into a social group we feel we belong to it and, by extension, we are able to define ourselves in terms of the groups to which we belong. Group membership gives us not just a sense of identity, but also a sense of purpose to life.

## Sexual Behaviour

Sexual behavior is not only of basic biological importance, but of central social importance. Not only does it perpetuate the human species, but it is the central behavior around which families are formed and defined, a vital aspect of the psychological wellbeing of individuals, and a component of a variety of social problems. Among current concerns tied in part to sexual behavior are the familial problems of marital harmony and divorce; criminal problems of rape, incest, child molestation, and prostitution; reproductive problems of infertility, sterility, unwanted and mistimed pregnancies, and abortion; and health problems related to sexually transmitted diseases (STDs).

About 17% of adults 18-59 have had an STD and the lifetime infection rate is likely to be over 20%. Moreover, with the advent of AIDS the medical problem of STDs has taken on increasing urgency. Deaths from AIDS rose at a rapid pace in the 1980s and early 1990s. By 1992 AIDS had become the number one cause of death among men 25-44. Only recent improvements in medical treatments have curbed the rising levels of HIV to AIDS conversions and lowered the death rate from AIDS. Most HIV infections have resulted from sexual behavior and heterosexual intercourse is increasingly becoming a mode of transmission. Because of both the importance of sexual behavior in general and the health crisis of AIDS in particular, we need to arm ourselves with a thorough, scientifically reliable understanding of sexual behavior and especially to study high-risk behavior.

### *Premarital and Adolescent Sexual Activity*

Premarital sexual intercourse become increasingly common

over the last century. This increase was not merely the result of the so-called sexual revolution of the 1960s. The change was underway for decades prior to the 1960s and has continued since then. Rates among men were moderately high even from the beginning and climbed steadily. Women had low rates of premarital intercourse to begin with, but their rates grew more rapidly than those of men and the gap between men and women has narrowed over time. By the 1980s women had almost as much sexual experience as men prior to marriage. This increase in premarital sexual experience is confirmed by community studies and longitudinal panels.

Then in the early 1990s the century-long increase in the level of premarital and adolescent sexual activity reached a peak and then declined for the first time in decades. The decrease appears to be greater for males than females, but both genders show a levelling-off and then some reversal.With the increase in levels of premarital sexual intercourse came a fall in the age of first intercourse. In 1970 5% of women age 15 and 32% age 17 were sexually experienced, by 1988 this had grown to 26% at age 15 and 51% at age 17. This trend may also have levelled-off and reversed since then, but the evidence is inconclusive.

When the increase in levels of premarital sexual intercourse is coupled with the rising age at first marriage, this means that men and women are spending longer and longer periods of their sexual life outside of marriage. Between 1960 and 1997 the median age at first marriage rose from 22.8 to 26.8 for men and from 20.3 to 25.0 for women. For women the median age of first premarital intercourse in 1960 was about 19.0, meaning on average only a short period of premarital sexual activity. In 1990 the median age at first sex was 16.9 for women, meaning an average exposure of 8.1 years. For men the period of premarital sexual activity now averages 10.7 years.

With people spending longer periods engaged in premarital sexual activity the number of lifetime sexual partners has also grown for both men and women. Between the pre-1910 birth cohort and the 1940-49 birth cohort the portion of men with two or more premarital sexual partners rose from 49% to 73%, while for women the gain was from 3% to 26%. This trend continued until recent years. For example, among sexually experienced women ages 15-19 living in metropolitan areas 38% had had 2 or more sexual partners in 1971 while by 1988 this had increased to 61%. More recently there is evidence of a reversal of this trend. On the Youth Risk Behavior Surveys (YRBS) the % of male high school students with 4+ sexual partners declined from 1989 to 1997, but the trend among females is unclear.

### *Cohabitation*

The rise in premarital and adolescent sexual activity, coupled with delays in marriage, has led to more people living together. Since 1970 the rate of living together outside of marriage has increased more than 6 fold, from 1.1% to 7.0% of couples. Similarly, the portion of single mothers who were cohabitating grew from 2% in 1970 to 12% in 1995. While the proportion of couples and adults cohabitating at any one point in time remains small, a large and growing percent live together at some point. Currently over a third of adults in their mid-twenties to midthirties cohabited before their first marriage and half of this age group has cohabited at some point in their lives.

Cohabitation after and between marriages is even more common. According to the General Social Survey (GSS) among those 25-44 who are in a second marriage, 61% cohabited with their new spouse before marriage. Cohabitation differs little by gender or race. It is higher among younger adults, the divorced and never married, those in urban areas, and among those who attend church less frequently. Current, but not prior cohabitation with ones spouse, is higher among the less educated and those with lower incomes. Cohabitation is usually a short-term arrangement, typically resulting in either marriage or a break-up after about a year.

Cohabitation has often been characterized as a trial marriage and about 40% lead to marriage within two years and about 60% eventually culminate in marriage between the cohabiting partners. However, marriages formed after cohabitation are rated as less stable and result in more divorces than marriages not preceded by living together." Those who are cohabiting have fewer sexual partners than those who are unmarried and not cohabitating. However, people who are cohabitating have more sexual partners than married couples. For example on the 1993-94 GSS the married averaged 0.97 partners last year, the never married who were cohabiting had 1.38 partners, and the non-cohabitating, never married had 1.63 partners. That fact coupled with the transitory state of most cohabitations makes living together riskier than marriage when it comes to STDs.

***Non-marital Births***

With the link between sexual activity and marriage breaking down, the connection between marriage and procreation has also lessened. In the 1960s when premarital sexual intercourse resulted in conception, the women's pregnancy usually in turn led to a marriage before the child was born. Since then, the propensity of unmarried parents to marry before the birth of their child has steadily fallen. By the 1990s less than 25% of women who conceived children before marriage got married before their child's birth.

As a result of the higher level of premarital sexual activity and the decline in marriages after a conception but prior to birth, there has been a large increase in out-of-marriage births. In 1960 only 5% of all births were to unmarried women. This climbed to 14% by 1975 and 33% by 1994. Then, after over 30 years of increase, the rate leveled-off in 1994-96 at 32-33%.

The trend in the United States has been parallel to changes in culturally similar, advanced industrial nations and not unique to the US. While the percent of births to unmarried mothers climbed from 5% in 1960 to 32% in 1995 in the US, it rose from 5% to 34% in Great Britain, from 4% to 26% in Canada, and from 6% to 37% in France. The rate of increase has been much greater for Whites than for Blacks. For Whites the percent of unmarried births has expanded ten-fold from 2.3% of all births in 1960 to 23.7% in 1996, while the Black level grew by just over three-fold from 21.6% in 1960 to 70.4% in 1994. While the Black to White ratio has fallen from a little over 9:1 in 1960 to under to 3:1 in 1990s, the gap between Blacks and Whites rose from 19 percentage points in 1960 to 44-46 percentage points in from 1980 to 1996.

This means that almost a majority of White or Black mothers would have to change their marital status to equal that of the other race. The cumulative difference between Whites and Blacks is further shown by the fact that by ages 30-34 only 23% of never-married, White women have given birth, while 69% of never-married, Black women have had a child. While both Whites and Blacks have a greater proportion of births occurring outside of marriage, they have achieved the gains through decidedly different paths.

For Whites the unmarried birth rate rose throughout the period. It increased more than 4 times from 9 in 1960 to 38 in 1994-95. For Blacks their rate was quite variable over time. It fell from 98 in 1960 to 79 in 1985 before climbing again to 91-93 in 1989-90 - still below their birth rate in the 1960s. In the early-1990s the Black unmarried birth rate then again declined, falling to 76 in 1996.

In addition, there is also a high level of unintended births. Of women 15-44 in 1995 who have had a child, 28% reported that they had an unintended birth and this reached 36% for women 40-44. On those with an unintended birth, 80% reported the birth as mistimed and 20% as unwanted. In brief, over the last century premarital sexual activity become more widespread, sexual initiation started at younger ages, the period of premarital sexual activity lengthened, and the number of premarital sexual partners increased. This expansion in premarital sexual activity in turn led to major increases in cohabitation and unmarried child bearing.

But during the 1990s a small, but historic, reversal of some of these trends occurred. The level of premarital and adolescent sexual activity levelled-off and in some aspects retreated and the proportion of births outside of marriage reached a plateau. These changes are partial rather than across the board and even those behaviors that have levelled-off or reversed are at near record high rates. But even limited changes to a massive, century-long trend are highly notable and potentially important from a public health perspective.

## Adult and General Sexual Behaviour

Compared to the amount of information available on premarital and adolescent sexual behavior, until recently there has been little scientifically reliable data on the sexual behavior of adults or of the population in general. Moreover, the dearth of representative and credible studies has created a vacuum that has been filled by unrepresentative and incredible misinformation from popular magazines, sex gurus, and others.

## Extra-marital Relations

There are probably more scientifically worthless "facts" on extra-marital relations than on any other facet of human behavior. Popular magazines, advice columnists, popsexologists have all conducted or reported on "studies" of extra-marital relations. These studies typically find extremely high level of extra-marital activity. Hite for example reported that 70% of women married five or more years "are having sex outside of their marriage." They also often claim that extra-marital relations have become much more common over time. Claims that 50% of married women now have sex outside of marriage, double the level of a generation ago.

But representative, scientific surveys indicate that extramarital relations are less prevalent than pop and pseudo-scientific accounts contend. The best estimates are that about 3-4% of currently married people have a sexual partner besides their spouse in a given year and about 15-17% of ever-married people have had a sexual partner other than their spouse while married.

There is little direct and reliable trend information on extra-marital relations before 1988. Since then, levels have not changed. Prior to then there is indirect evidence that extramarital relations may have increased across recent generations. The figure of ever having extra-marital relations rises from 13% among those 18-29 to 21% among those 40-49. It then falls to 8% among those 70 and older. Since these are lifetime rates, one would normally expect them either to increase across age groups or to increase until a plateau is reached. The drop among those 50 and older suggests that members of birth cohorts before about 1940 were less likely to engage in extra-marital relations than are spouses from more recent generations .

Some recently married people have difficulty adjusting from a premarital pattern of multiple sexual partners to a monogamous partnership and in general recent marriages are more likely to end in divorce than long-term marriages. The rates of extra-marital relations are about twice as high among husbands as among wives. Extra-marital relations are also more common among Blacks, those with lower incomes, those who attend church less frequently, those who have been separated or divorced, and those who are unhappy with their marriage. It also may be more frequent among residents of large cities, but the overall relationship with community type is statistically significant only for the last 12 months. Finally, extramarital relations in the last year are more likely to occur among the less educated, but the lifetime pattern with education is mixed and unclear.

## Gender of Sexual Partners

Few discusses have been so contentious as the controversy over the sexual orientation of Americans. The gay and lesbian communities have long adopted 10% as the portion of the population that is homosexual.However, a series of recent national studies indicate that only about 2-3% of sexually active men and 1-2% of sexually active women are currently engaging in same gender sex. These national American estimates are consistent with figures from local communities in the United States, indirect measurements, and statistics from Great Britain, France, Norway, and Denmark.

Rates of same gender contact increase as the reference period is extended. Recent figures indicate that 3.0% of sexually active males have had a male sexual partner in the last 12 months, 3.9% during the last five years, and 5.9% since age 18. As the time frame is lengthened, the % of men with only male partners declines. Over the last 12 months 2.4% are gay and 0.6% are bisexual, over the last five years it is 2.5% gay and 1.4% bisexual, and since age 18 less than 1% are gay and 4%+ bisexual. Most of those who report both male and female sexual partners since age 18 report only opposite gender partners during the last year. Lesbians follow these same patterns.

There is little reliable evidence on whether sexual orientation has changed before the late 1980s.In terms of attitudes levels of approval of homosexuality slightly declined from 1973 to 1991, but then rose notably in 1992-98. Since then, no change seems to be occurring in the sexual orientation of the public. Studies of male and female homosexuality both in the United States and Europe regularly find a higher proportion of males are gay than the share of females who are lesbian. Sexual orientation does not vary much across socio-demographic groups.

The most distinctive pattern for both gays and lesbians is that they are less likely to have married. About 60% of those with a same gender partner during the last 12 months have never been married compared to the 16% of female heterosexuals and 21% of male heterosexuals who have never been married. Second, gays, but not lesbians, are distinctive in congregating in the largest central cities. About 8.5% of men in large central cities have had a same sex partner in the last year as have 9.6% over the last 5 years and 14.7% since age 18. Rates are lowest outside of metropolitan areas. Lesbians, like gays, are under-represented in non-metropolitan areas.

Third, more gays are found in the lower income categories and among Blacks. Race is unrelated to being lesbian and low income is only marginally related to being lesbian. This may partly reflect both homosexual activity in prisons and male, homosexual prostitution. Education does not consistently differentiate among homosexuals. Fourth, lesbians, but not gays, are more common among younger age groups. This could indicate an increase in homosexual activity among women across cohorts. Finally, lesbians, but not gays, attend church less than heterosexuals. About 3.4% of women who rarely attend church have had a female sexual partner in the last year compared to only 1.3% of those who attend regularly.

## Frequency of Sexual Intercourse

There is some evidence that the frequency of intercourse rose from the 1960s to the 1970s and may have declined in the 1980s. Among teenage males 17-19 living in metropolitan areas the rate fell from 59.8 times per year in 1979 to 39.0 in 1988, but then among all males ages 17.5-19, it rose from 30 to 49 times per year between 1988 and 1991. Among unmarried women ages 20-29 the rate showed a more modest decline from 59.8 in 1983 to 56.0 in 1988-93. However, no meaningful change has been occurring among all adults since 1988. On average adults engage in sex about 61 times per year, a little over once a week.

The overall adult average is relatively uninformative however since the frequency of sexual intercourse varies notably across socio-demographic groups. The factor making the biggest difference is age. Among those 18-29 frequency averages about 84 times per year. This then falls off steadily to 64 times per year for those in their 40s to 9.8 times per year for those 70 and older. Among the married the decline is even more striking, dropping from 112 times per annum for those under 30 to 16 times per annum for those 70 and older. This age related pattern is nearly identical to one shown in the 1988 National Survey of Families and Households and is consistent with a large number of other studies. This decline with age also occurs within marriages. First, the so-called honeymoon effect leads to the highest rates of intercourse among the recently married and those recently married tend to be younger. Second, biological aging reduces hormonal output and poor health in general and impotency in particular increases with age. As a result, even among couples who rate their marriages as very happy and among those who say they are still "in love" frequency of intercourse declines with age.

Marital status also influences sexual activity. Frequency is greatest among the currently married. The never married and divorced have lower rates, probably because of less continuous and convenient availability of a partner. The widowed have by far the lowest rates, a function of their age as well as their marital status. The edge of the married over the non-married becomes even more apparent when age is taken into consideration. Activity is 25-300% greater among the married compared to the non-married at various ages. Among the married intercourse is more frequent among those who have happier marriages.

Husbands and wives closely agree on the frequency of intercourse in the aggregate and in most paired comparisons of partners. However, unmarried men and women differ considerably with men reporting more activity than women do. This is true even if the surplus of widowed females is accounted for. A multivariate analysis indicates that more sexual intercourse is separately and independently related to a) being younger, b) having been married less than 3 years, and b) rating ones marriage as happier. It is unrelated to gender with controls for these other factors.

There are little differences by race, community type, education, or income and these are mostly related to age and/ or marital status.

### *Sexual Inactivity*

Sexual inactivity takes on three distinct forms: 1) the period prior to first sexual intercourse, 2) periods of extended inactivity after first intercourse and prior to last intercourse, and 3) the possible period after last intercourse. The first has been dealt with above in the discussion of premarital sexual relations. The latter two are discussed here. They can not be readily separated from one another with the available data. Sexual inactivity appears to have modestly declined since the early 1980s. Both among women of childbearing age and among all adults the proportion not engaging in sex over extended periods has decreased in the 1990s.

Among adults there is a u-shaped curve with sexual inactivity most frequent among the youngest and oldest adults. Sexual inactivity among the elderly is fairly common and is a function of general aging, poor health, and unavailability of a partner. As we saw in the section on frequency of sexual intercourse, sexual activity decreases markedly with age even when a partner remains available. This is a function of both a reduction in the rate of sexual intercourse among those remaining sexually active and also an increase in the proportion sexually inactive. Among those over 70 61% are not currently sexually active. Among this age group sexual abstinence reaches 33% among the married and among the nonmarried it hits 92%.

Sexual inactivity is much less common among younger adults. Among the currently married only 1.5-3% of those 18-

49 are sexually inactive. Almost all of this group either have poorer than average health and/or rate their marriage as unhappy. While 7% of married couples of all ages are sexually inactive over the last year, fully 16% of married couples have not engaged in sexual intercourse in the last four weeks. Sexual abstinence is much higher among the non-married ranging between 16% and 27% for those under 50. Most other socio-demographic differences are small and merely reflect underlying differences in age and/or marital status, but sexual inactivity is lower in households with higher incomes. While there has been long-term and massive increases in all aspects of premarital and adolescent sexual activity, there is little evidence that similar changes in regards to adult or overall sexual behavior have occurred. Moreover, adult sexual behavior appears to be more restrained and traditional than it has commonly been portrayed.

### *Impact of AIDS on Sexual Behavior*

AIDS is a deadly and infectious disease that has mainly been transmitted through tainted blood products, sexual intercourse, and the sharing of needles by users of illegal injection drugs. With the safeguarding of the blood supply current transmission occurs largely through sexual intercourse or the sharing of needles with a HIV positive individual. The only means of restricting the spread of the disease is to have people adopt safer sexual and injecting drug use behaviors.

On the one hand, the long latency period of AIDS greatly complicates matters since infected people often are not aware that they are HIV positive and therefore pass the infection on to others. On the other hand, since the mid-1980s over 90% of the public have known that HIV is spread by sexual intercourse and knowledge about AIDS in general has grown over time. Given the existence of widespread, if imperfect, knowledge about the role of sexual intercourse in spreading AIDS, the question arises whether behavior has been modified in light of the known risk.

***Changes in Sexual Behavior***

A number of studies have asked people whether they have changed their sexual behavior because of AIDS or have taken steps to avoid AIDS. Early surveys in 1986-87 showed that only about 7-11% of adults reported any change. At that time these levels were commonly seen as indicating that people were either not informed about the risk of AIDS or were not reacting responsibly to the risk of AIDS. But the recent studies on sexual orientation, extra-marital relations, and sexual abstinence indicate that the number of people at risk was smaller than initially feared.

And if relatively fewer people were engaged in risky sexual behavior, it would be understandable that few reported altering their behavior. This was directly supported by a 1987 Gallup question in which 68% reported they had not changed their behavior because they were not at risk. Likewise, the low-level of behavioral change among the married (3-12%) compared to the non-married (17.5-51%) reflects the lower level of risky behavior engaged in by married people.

Similarly, more change is reported by higher risk groups such as younger adults and Blacks. Of people reporting a change in sexual behavior because of concern about AIDS, about 45-50% mention reducing their number of sexual partners - including having only one partner and getting married, 20-35% cite the use of condoms, 17-30% indicate they have sex less frequently or abstain completely, 10-30% say they are restricting their partners to people they know well, and less than 10% report they have stopped having sex with bisexual men or injection drug users.

Among all adults a number of sexual changes are reported as having been made to avoid AIDS. Monogamy and/or limiting the number of sexual partners is mentioned by about 20%, 10-12% report using condoms, and 5-7% practice abstinence. Reports of behavioral change have risen somewhat over time, apparently indicating that risky sexual behaviors are increasingly being modified and that more people are taking precautions to avoid AIDS. However, since these questions have not apparently been asked after 1993, it is unknown if this trend continues.

Moreover, because of the nature of retrospective questions on behavioral change both the increased trend and the reports themselves are less than ideal.To reliably track changes due to AIDS, time series monitoring of the relevant risk behaviors are needed. We therefore consider what changes have occurred in sexual behaviors that relate to risk of HIV infection -gay sexual activity, number of partners, familiarity between partners, and condom use. Homosexual Behavior By the time AIDS was identified, its mode of transmission via sexual intercourse documented, and tests for HIV infection developed, the disease was already widespread among the gay population, especially in San Francisco and New York City.

Combined efforts by gay community organizations and public health officials led to the rapid dissemination of knowledge about AIDS and the adoption of safer sex practices by gays. The result was "a dramatic decline in risk practices for HIV transmission...gay men have reduced the number of sex partners, have fewer anonymous sexual encounters, have switched from shorter to longer term relationships, and engaged in less anal intercourse or consistently used condoms." Of late however, there has been little further increase in safe sex practices among homosexuals and even some back sliding among some who have tired of the diligence and restrictions required by safer sexual practices, among some minority groups, and among younger gays who did not experience the initial onslaught of the epidemic.

As a result, same gender sexual intercourse among men remains most frequent mode for the transmission of AIDS. Number of Partners While the overall number of sexual partners among all adults has not diminished in recent years, some change has been occurring among teenagers and young adults. Among young males the number of partners was probably rising for most of the century until the early 1990s. However, the evidence is somewhat mixed for the 1980s.

The mean number of lifetime partners among sexually active males 17-19 in metropolitan areas fell from 7.3 to 6.0 between 1979 and 1988, while among sexually active males ages 17.5-19 the mean number of sexual partners in the last 12 months rose from 2.0 in 1988 to 2.8 in 1991.

During the 1990s there appears to have been a decline in number of partners. The % of male high school students with a lifetime total of 4 or more partners declined from 31% in 1989 to 16% in 1997. For young females there is less clear evidence that the long-term increase in number of partners reversed in 1990s. The YRBS data indicate year-to-year fluctuation rather than any definite trend. However, the GSS shows that from 1988-1990 to 1991-1996 the mean number of sexual partners during the last 12 months for the 18-24 age group significantly decreased from 2.4 to 1.7.

Even if the reductions in number of partners among teenagers is real, many adolescents are still at risk of AIDS and other STDs because of having multiple partners. Whether the possible decline in number of partners accumulated by teenagers and young adults will translate into a lower number of lifetime sexual partners is unknown. If it does, it will reverse an expansion that began several generations ago. We can see evidence of that rise in the figures on number of sexual partners since age 18.

The increase in the number of sexual partners from ages 18-29 to 40-59 mostly represents the accumulation of partners over ones lifetime. The sharp drop in cumulative partners for those 60 and older occurs because this age group represents a generation that came to age before the peak in premarital sexual activity described above. That is, this generation had fewer premarital partners, married relatively early, and, as a result, has accumulated a lower number of sexual partners than subsequent generations. Among adults, having multiple sexual partners during the last year and during the last five years is most strongly associated with being young, unmarried, and male. It is also higher among Blacks, residents of large central cities, those with low incomes and less education, and infrequent church attenders.

The adult lifetime figures show a similar pattern except that there is no relationship between income or race and number of sexual partners and the less educated have fewer partners than the better educated. The reversal of the education relations results from less educated, earlier cohorts having fewer partners than more recent and better educated cohorts have had. Multiple partners are thus found in two main social niches, among young, unmarried adults and adolescents who have not yet "settled down" and among disadvantaged segments of society in general and among inner-city minorities in particular who also tend to lead less stable and conventionally-ordered lives.

***Relationship to Sexual Partners***

Risk increases not only with one's number of sexual partners, but also with the casualness and transitoriness of relationships. When it comes to STDs one "sleeps not only with a partner, but with all of that partner's partners." Closer relationships are associated with mutual monogamy, while casual relationships come without any likelihood of exclusivity.

The trends in relationships are mixed and depend on the measure and data set being examined. First, since 1988, the GSS item on relationships to sex partners during the last year shows little change in relationships between sexual partners either among all adults or among unmarried people under 40.

Most people are engaged in close and presumably mutually monogamous relationships as spouses or cohabiting partners, but each year 3-4% of sexual partners are pick-ups, one-night stands, prostitutes, or other casual couplings. In addition, another 4-5% of partners are better known, but are not considered close friends or regular partners. Second, there was a small, but statistically significant, drop in whether one was in a continuing relationship with ones most recent sexual partner from 92% in 1996 to 90% in 1998.

Finally, across birth cohorts of women relationship with their first sexual partner have become more casual over time. Of those born in 1951-55, 32% were engaged or married to their first sexual partner, 51% were going steady, 16% were less closely involved, and 1% were in other relationship. For those born in 1976-1980, 4% were engaged or married, 73% were going steady, and 23% were less connected. More casual relationships are most prevalent among the young, unmarried, and males. They are also more common among Blacks, residents of large central cities, and those with lower incomes.

Similarly having ones last sexual encounter with someone that one did not have an "ongoing relationship" with is more common among men, Blacks, the young, never married, city residents, the less educated, and infrequent church attenders. Household income is not related to non-relational sexual encounters. "One-night stands" are equally common for Black and White males, but less frequent for Black females than for White females. In general, we see that those socio-demographic groups with a high number of partners also tend to have less familiar partners.

***Prostitution***

At a time when prostitution could be a major avenue for the spread of AIDS into uninfected areas and groups, we know little about its magnitude or how the situation has been changing. As the National Academy of Sciences' Committee on AIDS Research observed, "(I)nformation about women who work as prostitutes is scant, and knowledge of their clients is sketchier still ." Because prostitution is an illegal and socially stigmatized occupation, the amount of reliable information on it is limited. The only time series data come from the arrest records compiled by the FBI. They show that the arrest rate climbed from around 30 per 100,000 total population in the early 1970s to a high of 59 in 1982 and 1983. The rate then fell back to the lower 40s by 1988 and has remained at that level since then. Whether this represents shifts in the prevalence of prostitution or variations in law enforcement efforts is unknown. While the illegality of prostitution is probably the main barrier to accurate counts, estimates are also complicated by the prevalence of many part timers, the continual occupational turnover, and the apparent geographic mobility of prostitutes.

There are some more recent and limited studies that have tried to overcome these serious problems and either to estimate the number of prostitutes or of certain types of prostitutes in given localities or to measure the proportion of women who have engaged in sex for pay. In addition, there are recent estimates of what proportion of men have engaged in paid sex. Although all three of the community, aggregate-estimate studies were carefully done and show a high degree of consistency, all estimates of the number of prostitutes are fraught with uncertainties since they deal with what one study aptly calls a "covert" population.

Surveys of general populations of women are equally limited. The studies cover sub-groups in local areas, have very small to medium sample sizes, use different measures, and show different levels of involvement in paid sex.

In additional, two recent samples provide the first national estimates of the proportion of women involved in paid sex. A 1991 survey of 1,669 women ages 20-37 found that 2.0.% had ever had "oral, anal, or vaginal sex in exchange for money or drugs" and the 1991-98 GSS of 5,700 women 18+ indicated that 1.6% of women had "had sex with a person you paid or who paid you for sex" since age 18. Given the differences in ages and measurements, the Dallas survey and the two national samples are in close agreement. They suggest a much higher rate of female participation than the aggregate counts, but the two sets of estimates are not directly comparable.

In brief, the available studies are extremely limited in number and most are unrepresentative of the United States as a whole. In particular, extrapolations from these few local studies to national estimates could well be wrong, especially if prostitution is heavily concentrated in urban centers. This possibility is supported by the fact that on the 1988-1998 GSSs 0.3% of men living in rural areas reported having sex with a prostitute during the last year, while 2.0% of those living in the 12 largest central cities reported having sex with a prostitute during the last 12 months. In.addition, the lifetime figures show a similar pattern.

Reports by men on paying for sex indicate that 0.6% of men had a prostitute for a sex partner during the last year, 5.9% within the last five years, and 16.3% at some point during the past . Unfortunately, these figures are not consistent. The five-year figures are more than twice what would be expected based on the annual figures. In addition, comparing the annual rates to estimates of FTE prostitutes comes to only 9.9 clients per prostitute.Thus, if the estimates of number of prostitutes are correct, this would suggest that men are underreporting their number of paid sex partners. Alternatively, the number of FTE prostitutes may be overestimated.

Based on the analysis of reported contact with prostitutes during the last year and during one's lifetime, sexual activity with prostitutes does not consistently vary by education or age. As one would expect, lifetime contact generally increases with age, but current use is unrelated to age. Lifetime contact is unrelated to education and current use has an irregular relationship. Contact is higher among those living in metropolitan areas, Blacks, those with lower incomes, veterans, those who attend church less frequently, and those having gone through a divorce (it appears to be especially high among separated men). Among married men paying for sex during the last 12 months is strongly related to low marital happiness.

***Use of Condoms***

Undoubtedly because of the advent of AIDS and the dissemination of safer sex messages, condom use doubled from the late 1970s/early 1980s to the late 1980s. From the mid-1960s to the mid-1970s just over a fifth of women used a condom at the time of their first intercourse. By the mid-1980s this had almost doubled to 42%. Similarly, in 1979 21% of teenage males reported using a condom at the time of their most recent intercourse and in 1988 the level increased to 57.5%.

Condom use has continued to increase since then. For example, the YRBS shows that condom use steadily increased for both males and females in the 1990s and condom use at last intercourse among never married males 15-19 grew by 10 percentage points from 1988 to 1995. However, while condom use has grown appreciably, it is still far below the general and consistent use called for by safer sex practices. Among sexually experienced college students in 1995 only 38% reported always using a condom. Likewise, a 1991 national survey of men 20-39 found that only 26.5% of sexually active men had used a condom during the last four weeks and even among unmarried men with no regular sexual partner only 46% had used a condom during the prior month.

Similarly, among unmarried women 15-44 in 1990 with 2+ partners in the last 3 months only 16% always used condoms and 39% never did. Also, among both men and women 18-24 in 1996 whose most recent sexual partner was not someone they were in an ongoing relationship with only 56% had used a condom.

Condom use is higher among socio-demographic groups that have multiple, sexual partners and less committed and on-going relationships with sexual partners. Condoms are used more frequently by Blacks, the young and never married, residents of large cities, those with lower incomes, and those who attend church less regularly. Use generally increases with education, but drops off among those with graduate degrees.

Men tend to report greater condom use than do women, but both men and women agree on the trends and general patterns reported here. Among adults 21% of men and 18% of women reported using a condom the most recent time they had sex.

Condom use declines among youths and young adults as they age. This is believed to be largely because sexual relationships become more established and enduring. However, this connection has not been well-established in the studies to date. Condom use also varies by status of sexual partner. A 1991 study of Hispanic adults and of non-Hispanic White adults living near Hispanics in the Northeast and Southwest indicated that even among those with two or more sexual partners only about 50% always used a condom with their secondary sexual partner(s). In addition, condom use is often notably lower among primary partners than among secondary partners. This increases the chance of spreading AIDS and STDs to one's primary sexual partner.

# 5

# Cultural Sociology and Pluralistic Society

From a sociological standpoint, pluralistic approach promises to be more useful in addressing an important contemporary problem, namely how particular groups with different traditions contribute and respond to globalization. If meaningful responses to globalization are likely to take different forms instead of crystallizing into one set of shared sacred symbols, as one influential perspective on the subject suggests, then pluralism would seem to fit the demands of the global age. A fairly conventional "substantive" definition of religion offers one powerful entry point into the predicaments of the global age.

The point of advocating pluralism is to be cognitively inclusive. In effect, we propose to sidestep familiar controversies about defining religion because interested not in finding the correct way to think about religion but in pursuing the most useful tools for global cultural analysis. At this still-embryonic stage of global analysis, it would be premature to rely exclusively on one definition.

Minimally, then, advocating pluralism in definitions implies the pragmatic judgment that, at this point, the competitive pursuit of distinct agendas will help to maximize our collective cognitive gains. Singling out one particular definition as exclusively valid or useful would once again prematurely limit our vision of problems worth pursuing.

*Staal and Saler are right:* Religion is no universal category, it has no universal core. Defining religion, in any conventional sense, would therefore seem to be fruitless. Better to focus on universal categories that can by studied "by themselves" than to persist in misapplying a modern prejudice. Others might reply that there is, after all, a type of human enterprise that uniquely features the "inclusion of culturally postulated superhuman agents". Saler advocates a third approach: to avoid drawing sharp lines that distort, a cross-culturally useful concept of religion should be based on resemblances in a family of related phenomena, which can vary in their degree of "religiousness" along several dimensions.

The skeptical rejection of religion as universal leads us to view it as part of a larger whole, proponents of substantive definitions lead us to pursue systematically the implications of one powerful definition, and the family resemblance approach leads us to think of religion in terms of variable dimensions.

Some philosophical reasons support this pragmatic effort to sidestep struggles over definitions. Strictly speaking, definitions don't matter: theories do. In the classic Popperian model, theories address problems. Definitions are mere instruments in the development of theories. Judging a definition by itsef, without considering the theory of which it is a part, makes little sense.

The validity of theories does not turn on any feature of their definitions in any case. Of course, some definitions serve the purpose of their theories better than others, for example by being clear and by directing the attention of scholars to critical issues to be resolved. But this is simply means that definitions can be more or less useful, not that we should spend a great deal of energy on getting them "right." At the same time, definitions do matter, for reasons that do not contradict the point we just made but in fact support for pragmatic argument. Definitions can embody prototheories. That is, setting the boundaries of a phenomenon or defining its "essential" features often serves to make some claims about an area of human experience. For example, so-called functional definitions of religion, which define it as sacred beliefs and practices that unify a collectivity, contain claims about the content and role of group culture.

Definitions also may produce interesting questions. For example, so-called substantive definitions of religion, which define it as beliefs and practices confirming the existence of a transcendent reality, lead scholars to question whether all societies contain such religion and, if so, whether this matters equally to all. If definitions operate within theories and may actually contain prototheories, then scholars with different theoretical agendas can legitimately use different definitions. Dissensus on definitions, familiar to students of religion, reflects contrasting scholarly interests, assumptions, and theories. Even one scholar's interests can vary from one context to another. For example, in own work a somewhat unfriendly critic might detect three definitions of religion-substantive, functional, and constructivist.

Globalization, mainly followed the practice of others, notably Roland Robertson, to examine religion as the term and issues associated with it are construed by people and groups themselves. But if, to generalize, different agendas legitimately use different definitions, and if there is no single vantage point from which to favor one agenda over all others, then the reasonable position to adopt is pluralism. Exclusive adherence to one definition would prematurely limit our vision.

This is not to say that all definitions "go" equally well. On the whole, substantive definitions are better than functional ones. To be sure, in view of the points just made, no one can be an unreconstructed substantivist. We also do not mean to imply that the functionalsubstantive opposition is the only important one. Nevertheless, the point holds because functional definitions tend to incorporate false prototheories and gloss over significant questions whereas substantive definitions reflect plausible prototheories that also raise interesting questions.

The implicit functional claims that all collectivities produce "the sacred" and that the sacred is critical to social unity are false. Functional definitions also tend to frame religious change as transformation in always-present, always-important symbols and practices: the more things change, the more they stay the same; and this is also false. Scholars favoring substantive definitions plausibly assert that what is unique to religion as a human enterprise is the "inclusion of culturally postulated superhuman agents," a point already cited. They further claim that this distinctive content has distinctive consequences for how people act and think, though transcendence has no necessary function.

As noted, they imply that this enterprise may not be present in all groups or societies and they raise the question whether the role of religion in this sense may change. In the global age this agenda remains important. One argument against substantive definitions is that they rely on core features of the Christian religious tradition and thus ignore or distort important features of other traditions. This lies behind Staal and Saler's critique of the category of "religion" as such. But substantive definitions are not exclusively Christian. Weber was right to treat Christianity as one member of a set of similar phenomena, i.e. salvation religions centered on some view of superhuman reality. Even if a definition were Christian-inspired, it could still be fruitful, since the Christian way of "doing" religion has spread and the de-Christianization of many western countries raises important questions about religious change generally.

A definition need not be "universal" to be globally relevant.Whatever the benefits of a sound substantive definition, in modern world society there is no one legitimate and binding view of religion. In most places, for most social intents and purposes, religion has become mere culture, to be used and interpreted as individuals and groups see fit. Like definitions of secular phenomena, definitions of religion are practically contested. It is not even clear that defining religion should focus on drawing a boundary between sacred and secular, if we may mix Durkheimian and Weberian terms. Searching for the "correct" definition reflects a desire for boundaries and certitude that modern cultures subvert. If modern cultures, especially modern world culture, have no single sacred core, no one guiding view of the supernatural, no one family of approved religiosities, then pluralism may be one way to do justice to the complexity of actually existing societies. Starting with a substantive definition enables us to get the distinctive features of our current condition clearly in view.

Of course, a pluralistic approach to defining religion should recognize the plurality of cultural contexts in which religiosities appear. If it is true that collective practices organized around a shared conception of the supernatural were most common in one, long period that is coming to an end and that in modern societies many groups and individuals need not follow the precepts and practices of the world religions as they make sense of their lives in ways that resemble, but also deviate from, the historically familiar religious forms-if that is true, then squeezing the investigation of new cultures, of world culture in particular, into the straitjacket of conventional definitions of religion is not necessary. Cultural problems need not be "religious" to be worthy of serious study. The sociology of "religion" need not, indeed cannot, encompass all of human culture.

## Religion in Globalization

How is religion involved in globalization? From South Asia to North Africa to the United States, fundamentalists opposed to the "new world order" attempt to change their societies, drawing global attention. Relying on new communication technology, American Christians export the Gospel, with considerable success in Latin America and Africa. Reviving its universal ambitions, the Catholic Church pursues a new global strategy, diversifying in the process. At the same time, the homelands of Western Christianity experience "gatherings in diaspora", creating new local cultures while forging transnational bonds. On behalf of Tibetan Buddhists, the Dalai Lama urges the world to appreciate human commonalities and to cultivate a universal responsibility for the planet.

Some religious movements experience significant international growth. These examples would provoke little dispute: they refer to global activities by representatives of established "world religions." The fact that they seem uncontroversial suggests that in some sense "religion" has become a global, if not a universal, category: "we" know what "we" mean when "we" talk about religion. But these examples certainly do not exhaust the possible range of involvements one can reasonably consider "religious." Cases in point are environmentalists defending the earth as a sacred place, the struggle by the Church of Scientology to be considered a "proper" religion beyond the U.S., or the increased global importance of preserving "indigenous" cultures.

As these examples only begin to indicate, there is no one connection between religion and globalization. Religion is, and has been, involved in globalization in various ways. This is true analytically because, as several definitions enable us to recognize, one can distinguish different modes of involvement: "religion" can be source, component, or affected party.

Religion has been a source of globalization by creating transnational or inter-state relations, by stimulating and endorsing the expansion of such relations, and by articulating a distinctive awareness of the world as a whole. Religion has been a component of globalization insofar as religions themselves have spread globally, built global institutions, and aspired to being global actors. Religion has been affected by globalization since worldwide social and cultural changes have changed the conditions for its flourishing, relativized the identities of religious groups, and involved religion in addressing the problems of the world as such. Thus, we can view religion as moving force, key dimension, and prime interpreter in globalization.

More importantly for argument, the connection between religion and globalization is variable in a more basic, logical sense: how one thinks of religion in relation to globalization, and what one looks for as relevant evidence, depends on one's view of globalization. If globalization stands for the worldwide extension of a capitalist world economy supported by a multiple-state system, then religion's primary mode of involvement will be ideological legitimation or delegitimation. If globalization describes one world society of differentiated social systems, then religion is involved as attempting to form a functionally distinct system that addresses residual problems.

If globalization captures humanity achieving a new awareness of global coherence among relativized units, then religion's role lies in its contribution to that consciousness and problematic coherence. Of course, none of these definitional frames prevents anyone from taking an interest in the findings of fellow scholars, but each reflects a theory or perspective that has a distinct and selective "logic."

Once again different agendas, relying on different definitions, have different implications. Thus, for example, a world-systemic approach to global analysis that is essentially agnostic when it comes to defining religion, is unlikely, on materialist grounds, to search for "religion" as a source of globalization. A Luhmannian view of religion as a distinct global social system depends in part, to use its jargon, on the way such a system is structured by communication processes world society; what counts as "real" religion is not simply up to the defining observer.

One implication of the "creolized hybrid" view of global change is that while "religion" will not be submerged in more powerful "secular" flows, it is likely to become attached to other symbols and ideas in a particular "form of life". Insofar as religion was/is involved, so we can phrase the reasoning in each case, it took/takes this form. That does not mean religion must be unimportant. For example, if globalization raises a question of ultimate meaning, as we may infer from Robertson, then historic providers of answers to such questions are likely to play strong roles. Yet even Robertson's focus is on culture as the site of contention, without presuming that religion is the soul of culture. That few scholars take a strong formal-theoretical stance on religion's involvement in globalization is not surprising.

Globalization refers to an historical phenomenon. We can study some of its features through analytical abstraction, of course, but questions about the phenomenon and its bearing on religion are bound to be historical.

The extent to which religion has served as source of globalization is also mainly an historical question. Those who have addressed it actually tend to rely on a fairly conventional substantive definition of religion, which, conveniently, fits the Christian case particularly well. In the European Middle Ages, some would argue, Christendom constituted a world civilization. The organizational resources of the Church and its missionary ambition contributed to European expansion. The Reformation schism further divided Europe politically and contributed to competition that became a key feature of the capitalist world system.

The civilization that spread from Europe also had distinctively Christian characteristics, not least its rationalizing and individualistic thrust. In a more basic way, Europeans' ultimately religious orientation to world mastery provided a powerful stimulus for their actual technical and social domination. The contrasting argument suggests that religion followed the juggernaut of politicaleconomic expansion. Churches provided the civilizational veneer for a capitalist project, missionaries pacified natives, and so on.

Religion, in short, became the useful superstructure of the world-system. From one point of view, then, world society is partly of Christian design; from another, the world would have looked the same without Christianity or any other form of religion.

The influence of the traditions of Western Christianity, much about the emerging global system would have been different, including the way the core pursued riches and dominion, the form of the state, the relationship between individual and society or between self and other. Due to the form and content of the Western Christian churches, the world system also became a world civilization of a particular kind.

Does this traditional debate have any contemporary relevance? Weber's comment on the fate of the Protestant ethic applies here: a set of motivating forces may recede once the new habits and institutions acquire a momentum of their own. From a substantive standpoint, there is nothing intrinsically religious about any global practices or institutions. Insofar as religion is a global "player" at all, it must compete with other sources of meaning and legitimacy in shaping global society. No current global institutions depend on religious legitimation. This is not to say that religion has no role left in creating global relations or awareness beyond "its" specialized purview. Insofar as globalization involves a new awareness of global unity, the "total" perspective of many religious traditions remains a key component.

Views of the good world society, articulated by religious leaders, are themselves factors in the direction it takes. Religions build transnational practices and institutions; they may incubate others. Religion may thus serve as model and stimulus for building components of world society. Religion, then, can still be an important source of globalization, its relative significance varying over time. Measured against the scale and scope of global media, business, states, science, NGO's, professional networks, and so on, that significance now is relatively low, and the makeup of global society militates against any totalizing religion gaining great influence in nonreligious spheres. But like secularization theory of old, globalization theory rules out reversals at its peril.

As we indicated, many of the globally recognized religions are involved in transnational activity-some dramatically so. Under John-Paul II, the Catholic Church has renewed worldwide missionary vigor. Evangelicals have expanded successfully in Africa and Latin America. Islamists aim to change the world, by uniting the ummah and defeating its opponents. Of course, the "world" religions already ranged across large spaces. Since the sixteenth century, however, the Christian expansionary thrust has been much more deliberate than before. Since the nineteenth century, relations between religious groups and bodies have increased as well. In the last century or so, several new religions, from the Baha'is to the Unification Church, have sprung up with explicit ambitions to unite religions, if not the world at large. Several arguments make sense of such developments and identify them as a coherent bundle of events.

Religion has distinct advantages in creating civil society. As Rudolph has suggested, in many parts of the globe it has transnational experience. Its transcendent dimension provides a measure of autonomy, strengthened by Western-influenced ideas of separating state and church. Religion has resources and reasons to create transnational links independent of state structures. As civil society grows in the interstices of a fragile state system, religion is bound to be a globalizing force. As state capacities diminish and competition for allegiance increases, religion can flourish. It builds world society.

Religion can play a special role at the intersection of social and cultural flows. Globalization, Nederveen Pieterse and Hannerz suggest, mixes organizational forms and cultural repertoires, both globally and locally. At the intersection of many cultural flows and institutional pressures, each society, group or individual must define a new global identity. In a hybridized world, such identities are creolized. As source of meaning and identitymodels, religion is bound to play a key role in the mix. Some globally-oriented new religious movements are cases in point. They will synthesize global and local elements, appeal to different audiences, reinterpret heritages while using modern communication tools, and portray themselves as resolving worldwide problems. Religion thus displays key features of globalization.

A contrasting line of argument restricts the possible independent role of religion. Faced with established instrumental systems, religious institutions are forced to form a distinct structure focused on "residual" problems. This does not prevent religion from forming a global system of its own, insofar as religions conform to one model of religion. Indeed, around their own binary coding religions are likely to form a system that resembles those formed in secular spheres, for example by establishing national linkages and developing organizational capacities. Religion, on this view, becomes a global system.

There is indeed evidence that some traditions and organizations are more globally recognized as properly "religious" and that borrowing across boundaries is common. But this does not yet add up to the convergence needed to fix religion as a "system" in its own right. There are still many ways to distinguish between the religious and the nonreligious or between the mundane and the transcendent.

There are still many ways to be religious. No global authority supports one mode to the exclusion of others. Rather than as system, we could describe global religion as a "sphere," a set of activities structured around similar problems and symbols, but internally diverse and competitive. That sphere has maintained some independence form others, and thus has room for further experimentation, a hybrid among hybrids. It may not crystallize as a fullfledged system.

A final reading of current developments would portray religion as potential carrier of world-cultural principles. Though not an institutional element of the world polity, religion nevertheless will experience pressure to organize itself as a rational institution like others and support a universalistic, individualistic global script. If religion is to be a global institution, and institutionalists would see no a priori reason why it cannot be, then it will be subject to the same world polity constraints as any other world-level institution.

Religion, as NGO writ large, will have to enact, or present itself as enacting, certain global principles. The extent of the convergence expected by this institutionalist argument remains to be investigated. Certainly it is possible that different traditions will reorganize as humanistic, voluntaristic, and progressive. Some observers might view convergence along these lines less charitably as the Americanization of world religion. However, there is ample reason to believe that precisely religions can resist such normative pressures and, more generally, can resist the consensual view of world-cultural principles as sacred in themselves.

Religion as diffuse civil society already clearly exists; through religion, people worldwide already recreate identities. On the other hand, religion as global system and carrier of world culture is at best in statu nascendi. Religion as a component of globalization thus appears vital but, in some respects, constrained.

The likely vitality ultimately depends on the direction of overall globalization. That its thrust is economic liberalization, political democratization, social integration, and cultural pluralization. Increasing market competition, decreasing state control, increasing transnational resources, and an open world culture once again present opportunities to religion(s). In pursuing them, however, religion will be subject to the ground rules of all transnational institutions. Whether this will make religion a system like any other, a normal carrier of world-cultural principles remains to be seen. For reasons of doctrine and organization, religion(s) may resist pressure to specialize according to one binary code or pressure to gain legitimacy through isomorphism. Thus far, at least, there does not seem to be the convergence across the religious spectrum required by either differentiation or world polity theory.

### *Interpreter of Globalization*

Globalization affects everyone and everything in many different ways. No group, society, or tradition "responds" to a necessarily complex experience in any unequivocal way. To treat religion as "interpreter" of globalization, then, is to single out one set of responses by one type of affected party. The premise is that globalization presents one universal problem, namely the problem of globality. How can "we" make global life meaningful and coherent? What does the desirable global society look like? How should its constituent parts relate to one another? What Robertson has said about societies applies to traditions and their representative institutions as well: they must identify themselves, position themselves in relation to the globe-as-such. In the process, so observers occupying different vantage points expect, they will formulate "explicitly globally-oriented theologies". To a large extent, we suggest, such religious responses to the problem of globality take the form of new rejections of the world.

The world-as-is must be transcended in the interest of a higher principle. In this way, most globally active religion(s), which encompasses more than the established world religions, interprets globalization critically. To many Christians, that critical mode may be nothing new; as a near-global phenomenon, it is. From a world-system point of view, religion as antisystemic movement challenges the autonomy of the economic sphere, undermines universal rationality, and opposes liberal individualism.

Religion as relativized, synoptic spirituality may issue "holistic and global perspectives transcending the privatized self and the individual state". Religion as a domain of culture particularly exposed to the relativization of actors and identities, in Robertson's sense, will most intensely work through the tension between universal and particular, national and transnational, individual and humanity. Each way of framing religion's responses. But how significant are they? Do religious rejections of the world matter? They do, but according to the accounts examined here they are diverse and secondary.

There is no one type of religious rejection and such rejection is often embedded in secular critique. Elaborating on Robertson's typology of images of world order, there are four ideal-typical ways to formulate images of world order, each with its own distinctive premises and critical thrust. Many groups and movements, intellectuals and activists are involved in advocating each one. Any recognizably "religious" voice is only one among many. It is strongest in what we call "Jihad," following Barber's usage. Conceiving of the world as a congeries of distinct, embattled traditions, Jihad defends against the undermining of one such tradition in the interest of achieving its rightful supremacy.

The commands of ultimate truth must pervade the world as such and all its institutions. The thrust of Jihad, in short, is fundamentalist. Anti-McWorld refers to groups and activists interested in preserving the autonomy and distinctive identity of nation-states as vehicles for achieving democracy and social justice. Conceiving of the world as a system of unequal and competing states subject to economic forces beyond their control, anti- McWorldists aim to foster community through self-governance in a world of equal partners. Some Catholic criticism of capitalist materialism and exploitation may fit into this type.

The new world order refers to a position perhaps least critical of actually occurring globalization. Using George Bush's infamous phrase, it refers to the liberal critique of arbitrary constraints on economic and cultural activity. New world order proponents wish to let freedom reign, within and outside societies. They see the central thrust of globalization as liberating. American evangelical Protestants and their converts elsewhere have at least an affinity with this approach to globality, even if they do not endorse all its implications.Finally, one-worldists put the globe first.

Conceiving of the world as one society to which all humanity belongs in principle, they reject destructive competition or imperial control. Instead, they pursue unification under common principles leading to responsible planetary governance. This position receives support from the global religious left, such as the World Council of Churches in some of its pronouncements or the Dalai Lama in expressing the common concerns of humankind.

Though religious responses are "secondary" in the sense that, with the possible exception of Jihad, they neither originate nor dominate any of these general responses to globality, religious discourse on each is bound to be salient. Globalization, in any version, raises a process noted by Beckford to the global level. Religious themes and symbolism, renovated by bricolage and energized by movements, can be coopted by activists addressing problems under any ideological umbrella. Globalization intensifies the "'freeing up' of relations between religion and other parts of society". Its relative autonomy makes renewed influence possible.

Of course that influence can turn from mere response, satisfying adherents but irrelevant to the larger world, into source, serving as prelude to the reconstitution of world society itself. How and why that can happen remains an item on our collective research agenda. Much depends on the global force of interpretations of the global condition in general.

Clearly, they are more than passive reflections. Multiple responses contribute to cultural pluralization. Responses as critique help to maintain the relative autonomy of spheres. Responses as ways of working out the relativization of global units serve to guide global action. Responses have a logic of their own and thus, depending on social support they receive, constrain possible courses of legitimate action. Of course, responses as global discourse are significant in their own right. Yet, we suggest, there is no one way in which responses shape globalization, no one type of structure-culture dialectic. The role of culture-as-agency will vary by context and over time.

Specifically, pluralism fits the demands of global cultural analysis. At a time when different lines of research examine a variety of responses to globalization, a needlessly exclusive definition would hamper progress. In practice, we have seen, these different approaches lead to different questions about and interpretations of the role of "religion" in globalization.

The more detailed sketch of that role, drawing on the actually existing pluralism in global analysis, leads to conclusions compatible with different agendas: A liberalized world offers a chance of renewed vitality even for groups and traditions opposed to that liberalization. Religion, however defined, may no longer serve as a prime source of globalization, it still builds global structures and displays the dynamics of globalization.

Over time, religion may become more integral to the world polity as a fully constituted global system. There is no one religious response to globalization, but religion does contribute significantly to the critical discourse of globality. That discourse, sociologists of religion naturally expect, is bound to make a difference to the future of the world itself.

## Cultural Sociology of Communication

Communication for social change is part of an evolution of communications methodology that can help accelerate global development. The process began in the first quarter of the 20th century with the use of publicity tools to bring attention to social problems such as hunger and disease. It grew to a reliance on public relations as a means of identifying stakeholders and creating programs to fit the audience's interests.

More recently, social marketing took center stage where sophisticated marketing and cause related advertising tools were applied to influence individual and societal behaviors - such as convincing couples in poor nations to use contraceptives. This was followed by development communications and strategic communications, the latter which rightfully considers communication to be a process rather than as a series of products.

The two authors argue that communication for social change is a distinct way of doing communications - and one of the few approaches that can be sustained. Such sustainability is largely due to the fact that ownership of both the message and the medium - the content and the process - resides with the individuals or communities affected. We believe that this approach can help make greater contributions to the pace of development. From this basic assumption we move to questioning "how" and "if" and "where" we might find interesting work and committed individuals to test the effectiveness of this approach.

In order to do this work, the Rockefeller Foundation has brought together a group of social activists, academics, filmmakers and journalists, funders, electronic communications experts, service providers and professional communicators.

***The Premise***

*This initiative is based on a simple premise:* that recent developments-in communications technologies, in political and media systems, and in emerging development problems- suggest a greatly enhanced, radically different role for communication in development programming. Communication programming has, very simplistically, tended to fulfill three roles in development thinking and practice:

— its role has been to inform and persuade people to adopt certain behaviors and practices that are beneficial to them: for example, to inform people how to protect themselves from HIV and to persuade them to use a condom; to persuade them of the importance of vaccinating their child and to inform them when and where they can do so; to persuade them that simple sugar and salt solutions can cure diarrhea and to inform them how to make them up; to persuade them to have fewer children and to inform them how to do so.

— it has been used to enhance the image and profile of the work of organizations involved in development with a view to boosting the credibility of their work, raising more funding and generally improving public perceptions.

— It has been used on a more targeted level within communities to enable community consultation over specific initiatives.

The communication for social change initiative believes that all these roles are important and communication work in general remains underfunded and undervalued. We argue that these traditional approaches to communication are generally insufficient in addressing the reality of the development problems that exist, and they do not always reflect the complex changes in the communications environments taking place in many developing country societies.

Communication can play a much greater role in enabling people to take control over their own lives, in enabling people and societies to set their own agendas in relation to political, economic and social development; and in enabling, in particular, the voices of the economically and politically marginalized to be amplified and channeled to mainstream public and political debate.

The interaction between communication and the social well-being of people in developing countries will be radically redefined over the next few years. Global economic liberalization of communications, the deployment of the Internet, mobile telephony and other new technologies and the changing political environment in most developing countries are all coinciding to make the cusp of the new millennium a defining moment which will determine how successfully all countries, especially developing nations, adapt to and exploit these changes. Information in society does not simply enable people to know what they should do or think. Information is power-it enables people to make sense of their lives and it enables them to shape their aspirations. Ultimately it can enable them to take control of their lives. In many areas of the world, people have precious little access to information outside their community that enables them to make such "sense."

In other societies, despite a multitude of information outlets, people who are historically marginalized and excluded remain "voiceless" and "invisible" because those who control information channels refuse to share access equitably. Communication for social change principles focus on using direct, many-to-many communications which spring from the affected communities.

The problems are those which have plagued communication practice for decades: how to assess impact beyond counting products produced or net impressions received; how to program communication for social change work on the micro community level and on the macro multinational level, often simultaneously; and how to transfer knowledge and skills to those most in need of "training" who often live and work in hard-to-reach areas. We also struggle with ways to capture the best learning - those cases that illustrate the power of communication for social change yet are not overly simplistic.

*Language is also a challenge:* the notion of how to explain this work in terms that can be readily accessible and used by grassroots activists as easily as by professional communicators. Others, such as sitebased knowledge transfer, are in the early exploratory stages and will require more study, testing and applications, especially in developing nations with scarce human and financial resources. Yet nothing in our questions should suggest lack of conviction nor should they prevent us from energetically embracing the potential of communication for social change to fulfill critical gaps in the development process.

The traditional understanding of the role of communication in development is one that seeks mainly to change individual behaviors. This behavior change communication can be broadly defined as a process of understanding people's situations and influences, developing messages that respond to the concerns within those situations, and using communication processes and media to persuade people to increase their knowledge and change the behaviors and practices that place them at risk.

### *A Changed Communications Environment*

The starting point for this inquiry is the growing evidence that, as a generality, the "communications environment" in which most people on the planet live has changed radically over the last decade. It has changed both in relation to the information people have access to, and the opportunities people have to communicate their own perspectives on issues that concern them. This new communications environment is shaped by three main interlocking trends:

i) Media liberalization and deregulation

ii) New information and communication technologies

iii) The changing global political and economic context

In general, and with important exceptions, these trends are tending to decentralize communications in developing countries, with a trend towards a more fragmented, more horizontal, people-to-people model of communication, and away from a highly centralized, vertical model. In industrialized countries, media liberalization suggests more choice for consumers, which should, theoretically, mean increased access. Yet the way it plays out in countries like the United States is in encouraging the growth of huge media monopolies that result in far less community input to programming. With deregulation, public service programming has become just a fading memory, and station ownership has leaped beyond the realm of possibility for most community-based organizations or individuals of color.

This new communications environment has, we argue, important implications for development programming, an importance that is compounded by the emergence of new development problems-such as HIV/AIDS—that demand new approaches to communication. Our inquiry suggests that there are many opportunities to be seized, as well as real challenges to be faced in understanding and acting upon these changes.

## Media Liberalization and Deregulation

Most people on this planet receive most of their information on issues beyond their immediate communities from the print and broadcast media. Fifteen years ago, much of humanity had one main source for this information-their governments. The means were stolid, formulaic broadcast and print media that had been established with the express purpose of telling people what they should know and think. Two general trends have changed this. First, following the end of the Cold War, a combination of internal pressure from their citizens and external pressure-often in the form of conditions set by donors-have led governments to relax censorship and freedom of speech laws. Second, this pressure for political liberalization has been combined with economic liberalization and deregulation of national media industries.

The result in many of those countries with tightly controlled media has been a blossoming of dynamic, generally populist and highly commercial newspapers, television and radio media in most developing countries, and flourishing of new community media in some. Meanwhile, old monopoly state-run media, particularly broadcasters, have tended to languish, losing their audiences to more dynamic competition. They also face declining government support and funding.

The implications of these changes for those involved in communication are challenging. Monopoly broadcasters have presented a convenient way of communicating simple messages to huge audiences through one medium. In much more fragmented media environments, this opportunity no longer exists and reaching the same audience requires putting messages out through many different media, and adapting it to many different audiences.

Perhaps more importantly, the creation of these more complex and dynamic communications environments raises the deeper question of just what information do people have access to, and does it empower poor people and give them a greater voice-or does it move them further to the economic and social margins?

At their worse, new communications environments have done the latter. They have shifted from providing stodgy and dogmatic government propaganda to providing a uniform diet of often Western popular music. In some countries, state-controlled news has been replaced by no news, or information that is sensational, inaccurate or irrelevant to the daily lives of much of its audience, or news that is derived entirely from international sources. Often operating in anarchic regulatory environments, commercial and private stations have little obligation to provide anything other than entertainment. At its very worst, media have encouraged intolerance, sectionalism and tribalism, the most extreme example being the "hate" radio of RTML in Rwanda which played a key role in the massacres in that country.

At their best, however, commercial, community and, in some cases, newly invigorated state-run news and media organizations have managed to attract large audiences with compelling, popular and informative programming. In Kampala, Uganda, the FM station Capital Radio attracts some of its highest audiences for its Capital Doctor program, which provides advice and information on issues of sex, HIV/AIDS and other health issues. In South Africa, a form of "edutainment" -"Soul City," set in a Johannesburg township-has become one of the most popular soap operas in the country, yet has succeeded in educating people about diarrhea, HIV/AIDS and other issues.

Again in South Africa, deregulation has spurred the creation of more than 80 community radio stations broadcasting in 15 languages. Community stations have made serious inroads into the broadcast markets, often stealing audiences from the well-established public broadcasting stations. Community broadcasting provides communities with information that is relevant to their lives, as well as a voice through which people can make demands. In Cape Town, the tiny community radio station, Radio Zibonele, drew on their audience's anger to play a key role in mediating and resolving the township's gang warfare surrounding the taxi business. In fact, the success of community radio proves, in some small way, the ready market for communication for social change principles to be applied in diverse circumstances throughout the world. In addition to sub-Saharan African nations, community radio has succeeded where little else can from northwest Canada to southeast Asia.

The print media too is changing under similar pressure, with more entertaining, more populist and often more trenchant coverage of news issues. These changes have demonstrated how in the print media in particular, poor reporting undermines many other forms of social and political discourse; high quality reporting can play a major role in promoting and stimulating constructive public debate. Well-informed, investigative reporting in particular can provide a key element of public accountability, both for national governments, for international institutions, and for NGOs and other civil society organizations.

Finally, the last decade has seen an explosion in satellite broadcasting. Take the South Asia region, home to one-fifth of the world's population which is today within the footprint of at least 50 broadcast satellites. In India, Pakistan and Bangladesh alone there are more than 70 million households with television sets, adding up to a total viewership of 300 million. By 2007, there will be 550 million television viewers in these countries. Half of them will be hooked up to cable - able to watch the 350 channels that will be available to them by then.

These changes do not apply to all people in all countries, but in one form or another they do affect the vast majority of people in the great majority of countries. They present many problems; reaching lots of people with prepared messages is becoming more difficult and more expensive. They also present substantial opportunities: to work with communities to enable them to amplify their voices, to enable access to the information that can empower them, to help shape communication environments that can work for people, not against them.

### *New Information and communication technologies*

The current revolution in information technologies represents probably the most profound set of technological developments human society has experienced since the industrial revolution. The innovations of the Internet-and particularly e-mail-have transformed communications capacities in countries with often dilapidated telecommunications infrastructures; and have opened up access to much more information about global issues. The falling costs and increased access to telephony mean that an increasing number of people have the capacity to communicate rapidly beyond their immediate communities, thus opening up new economic opportunities and opportunities for social and political discourse. For many participants in this communication for social change initiative these technologies represent a huge opportunity:

— Centralized control of information by governments or commercial interests becomes much more difficult.

Increasingly, political systems can neither control the information their citizens receive nor monitor or constrain how they communicate with each other. Technology is-for good and ill-increasing access to the kind of information that is uncensored and unfiltered. Technology is growing most rapidly in those areas where its demand is most clearly defined by the users.

— The capacity of people to access information is substantially increased.

— The capacity of people to organize, advocate and lobby beyond physical boundaries is greatly enhanced.

— The capacity for people and organizations in developing countries to communicate information-their aspirations, demands, experiences, analysis-becomes cheaper, more powerful and far more pervasive.

Nevertheless, we also recognize the limitations of these technologies. In particular, the "information gap" between rich and poor is stark. One of the least expensive of the information and communications technologies (ICTs) -- the telephone-illustrates just how far apart the rich and poor worlds are in access to such technologies. One quarter of the countries in the world still have fewer than one telephone line per 100 people.

The majority of the population in developing countries -- 60% of the total-live in rural areas. Yet in these countries, more than 80% of main telephone lines are in urban areas. 1The distribution of new ICTs is no more equal. Eighty four per cent of mobile cellular subscribers, 91% of all fax machines and 97% of Internet host computers are in developed countries.

Telecommunications is nevertheless becoming cheaper, more reliable and more accessible and will continue to do so. Despite the constraints, it seems likely that we are seeing the emergence internationally of organizational structures that are increasingly based on networks, rather than hierarchies. It is this revolution which represents most powerfully the increase in horizontal, people-to-people communication, and which provides profound new opportunities for more inclusive public and policy discuss.

## Changing Political and Economic Environment

The collapse of the Soviet Union and the end of the Cold War have had far reaching effects. However, two key issues should be mentioned. The first is the growing, though uneven, democratization and political liberalization that has swept much of the developing world over the last decade. Many of the highly centralized oneparty states or dictatorships have given way to multi-party democracies, or at least to more open political systems.

This political liberalization has been matched by a still more pervasive economic liberalization and we have seen the rapid emergence of a new global economy. As Manuel Castells argues, "for the first time in human history the entire planet is capitalist, since even the few remaining command economies are surviving or developing through their linkages to global, capitalist markets." As all governments are finding, including China's, maintaining strict and centralized control of information in a market economy is both difficult and often inefficient.

The fragmentation and decentralization of information outlined above is potentially countered by the greater concentration of ownership in communications and media industries ushered in by globalization. According to UNESCO's World Communication Report 1997, "international conglomerates are emerging with the purpose of controlling not only the transmission system but also the programs they convey." An increasing spate of mergers and acquisitions over recent years has seen the emergence of a handful of "world companies" who now dominate global media markets. Time Warner Inc., News International, Sony, Finivest and Bertelsman each have annual sales well in excess of $10 billion, an increasing percentage of which is generated outside the United States. This concentration is compounded by convergence of media and telecommunications industries leading to still greater concentration of ownership.

Such concentration may not matter and may be offset by the more horizontal and decentralized models of communications outlined above. But both these trends-towards a decentralization of information production away from government, and a concentration of ownership of the means of communication in the hands of transnationals-should matter to anyone involved in communication. These trends are bound up intimately with questions of who controls the information that people receive.

***Communication and emerging development problems***

These changes to communication environments come at the same time as important changes in how we think about development. Some of the most important emerging development challenges of the last decade have raised new questions. Issues such as HIV/AIDS, reproductive health and reproductive rights, and others such as tobacco use have highlighted more intensely than ever how disease and poor health are linked not only to poverty and poor nutrition, but also to prejudice, to social, political and economic inequality, and to social dislocation. They have focused an especially strong spotlight on social and political environments where issues of sex and sexuality are habitually hidden or are difficult to debate in public.

Such complexities are forcing societies globally to change-to question long cherished, deeply rooted social, political, and religious mores and practices. A whole range of issues-from HIV to reproductive rights, from domestic violence to female genital mutilation-have crystallized the need for much wider social and political change. Such change is informed by what happens both within countries and by international debates, but if it is to be sustainable, change has to emerge from within societies. The means of how societies change, and who drives such change is contentious and difficult.

Part of such change will come from education about issues such as condom use-but much of the more deep seated changes that need to take place in societies, such as the improvement in the status of women, need to emerge from advocacy and vigorous public debate within and between societies. Such debates depend fundamentally on communication: on communication within societies, within families, within communities, through political discourse; and on communication between societies, at the levels of the individual, of the community and of the global society.

The capacity of people to communicate is intimately bound up with their capacity to effect change. In short, a new model of communication could be emerging from a mixture of political, technological, economic and social change. It is decentralized, pluralistic and democratic; it seeks to empower rather than persuade people; it fosters debate among and between citizens, among and between communities, and between people and government.

This model envisages increasingly horizontal communication allowing people to communicate with each other easily and inexpensively. It also involves the steady disintegration of traditional monolithic vertical lines of communication, where governments owned radio and television stations in order to control flows of information.

***Creating Environmental change***

Communication for social change programming suggests a major shift in development. Above all it is about enabling publics and communities to articulate their own agendas for development at the community, the provincial, the national and the international level. Programming in this area is about making connections-at these different levels and between them. It involves making connections between global trade policies and local communities, and it involves making connections between many different kinds of activities-between the issues themselves and the means that exist for debating and discussing them. community radio, women's radio listeners groups, an informed and responsive national media, quality media programming, telecommunications.

It involves framing and phrasing debates in language and forms that are inclusive. It involves a responsibility of academics in particular, but those concerned with development in general, to communicate research and information not only to their peers, but to the wider public within developing countries. It involves "returning" research and analysis to where it originates. Perhaps, above all, it suggests that the key role for donor and development institutions is to create an environment for change. It suggests a role that sees these organizations continuing to inform and create development strategies, but also in creating the conditions where developing country societies can assess, challenge and adapt such strategies and begin to create strategies for themselves.

It provides new opportunities to open up development decisions and programming to public discuss and dialogue, and to enable publics-and not just experts-to be more proactive in shaping discuss on development issues.

### *Where is Good Work Happening?*

One question that we're asked frequently is "what does communication for social change look like? Who is practicing it, or where is the greatest potential?" In looking for examples of good work, it's important to keep in mind the key principles of communication for social change: it empowers individuals and communities, it engages people in making decisions that enhance their lives, it is many-to-many, it relies on democratic ideals, it allows previously unheard voices to be heard, and both the process of communications and the content of the messages are controlled by the receiving communities. This can be heady stuff -at times bordering on the ideal rather than the practical. Yet even so, we've found examples of innovative social communications work in several locales.

As we work in the United States, Africa and Asia, for example, it appears that the most likely practitioners of communication for social change are small struggling organizations with few resources. Communication for social change in some respects becomes a means of survival. Without the benefit of large communications staffs or budgets, and facing media that are hesitant to cover social issues in substantive ways, some small NGOs and community-based organizations have figured out how to use the people most affected by their work to make the communications process work.

In Africa and Latin America, the community radio movement stands out. By definition, community radio stations cannot succeed without local control, citizen participation, local issuesbased programming and open access. Yet radio remains essentially a top-down methodology; that is, someone decides what will be broadcast, it airs, and is received passively by listeners. The better community radio stations, such as Cape Flats' Bush Radio, Radio Zibonele in the Khayelitsha community of Cape Town, South Africa, and Alexandra Township's community station focus on audience participation.

New programming stems from the suggestions listeners make when phoning into the stations, or when they are working there as volunteer staff. Critical issues facing the communities are discussed - and problem solving happens in real time - on the air. Outreach is daily and continuous - the community radio stations are vital parts of the neighborhoods where they operate. They don't just "cover" issues - they lead the residents in collective decision making.

## Capturing Impact

Recognition of the role of communication in achieving social change is not necessarily new nor surprising, but it receives comparatively little funding. While the case for this kind of programming-for the reasons already given-is building, there remain significant obstacles to it attracting major support. Indeed, many of the communications initiatives that are currently funded-particularly around behavior change-attract support less because they are perceived as addressing the main problem, but more because they can be claimed as having changed something. In the field of HIV/AIDS, for example, much of the funding for communications initiatives has gone into attempts to change individual behaviors.

Such problems are fundamental. Communication for social change programming can constitute only part of the real solution; it can help enable people to shape their own agenda, articulate their own priorities and aspirations of how to address the epidemic, and ensure that donors are following and responding to public and policy debates within developing countries as well as shaping such discuss. Evaluation of impact in this area remains difficult but not, we conclude, impossible. It does, however, mean that we must develop new methodologies.

### *Measurements and Evaluation**

Donors have a right and an obligation to demand evidence that their funds have been spent wisely, that they have achieved what they were meant to, or that there are good reasons for any changes or lack of achievement. However, there are other reasons why impact needs to be measured.

1. *Accountability* - understanding the impact of communication interventions is an essential component of being accountable. The primary accountability is to the people engaged in the communication intervention. Being involved with them in aspects of their lives requires that accountability. They are also the people, proportionate to their means, who will invest the most resources.

2. *Progress* - understanding what is happening and whether it is what people want to happen.

3. *Improvement* - information from any measurement and evaluation is crucial to both large strategic decisions and to fine tuning communication interventions in order that better value is gained from the investments that are made.

4. *Motivation* - a sense of achievement is crucial to motivation. Good motivation is an essential element of any endeavor, including communication for social change programs. The people involved draw energy and drive from knowing that progress is being made. Not knowing can lead to the opposite.

5. *Credibility* - Good data on the impact of communication for social change interventions can only enhance the credibility of this field and the investments - from local to international - that are made.

The long-term goal of all development action is to see positive change in the issues of concern. We all want less poverty, increased employment, better gender equality, to eradicate HIV/AIDS, more girls in school, higher educational achievement, lower child and maternal mortality rates, better nutrition, fewer accidents and no violence. That is the crucial measure of success. Such changes can take five years or a decade, but generally much longer.

People involved in communication for social change initiatives need more immediate data that indicates whether what they are doing is making a contribution to the overall change process. It is not possible to run a program for 15 years before assessing impact and then finding that the wrong things were done. More immediate information on the contribution of communication to change is required. Although communication for social change activities tend to have less specific and immediate objectives and targets, they nevertheless need to develop a similar set of indicators both to measure and indicate progress and to drive the nature of the programming.

## Intercultural Education

In most European countries the term multiculturalism is only used to explain the existence of 'The Other', the 'stranger' who does not belong. In this sense it can be argued that "Multiculturalism has been racialised". On reflection, it indeed turns out that issues of discrimination and diversity in Britain were used by activists and others because of racism against those who were seen to be visibly different, to privilege discrimination against themselves. The ways in which policies arising from such a political stance were devised tended to suggest that there was a singularity towards exclusion and discrimination.

The essentialist rhetoric of these policies has led to some communities being designated as "the other" and created binary oppositions. This has negated possibilities of an inclusive polity based on intercultural policies. The situation today is that despite two decades of such focus, black students are still not performing well, the situation for poorer white boys is no better in educational terms in England. Hence, while racism still remains a problem so are issues of exclusion, based on other indices of diversity that exist in our society. In fact, one can argue that failure to deal with inequalities because of racial discrimination now raise issues of religious identity, discrimination and fundamentalism.

The British state colluded with the racialisation of multiculturalism, because it was seen as a way of ensuring that social diversity was in fact seen to be merely a result of post-World War II migration, particularly from people who were coming from the old empire and now the new Commonwealth. Statements, like the ones made by the ideas 1965 which said in the 'School Curriculum' document that "our society has become multicultural", can only be explained as a way of camouflaging the more complex issues. The situation now is different because after the devolution of power to Scotland and Wales through democratic means, we can no longer throw a cloak of monocultural and monolingual illusion over the British State.

The future for intercultural studies in Britain is therefore much brighter than it was before. This is because of the peaceful and democratic transition at least in Wales and Scotland and the way in which there are lessons to be learned from the conflictual situation in Northern Ireland which needs to be built into intercultural teaching. To support teachers' work it is important to develop a framework of analysis based on historical and contemporary aspects of diversity and the relevance to developing an inclusive curriculum which integrates intercultural citizenship education. Issues of identity whether in singular or its multiple forms are also relevant to intercultural education. Within complex socially diverse societies where technological changes may be leading to high levels of unemployment, greater stress needs to be placed on democratic institutions.

The need to deepen democracy entails a critical appraisal of issues of societal concern and the development of collaborative community participation as well as curricular and pedagogic changes. Also, it is not only what children are taught and what they learn hut also their actual experiences at school which contribute to their understanding of their rights and responsibilities as future citizens. So, a democratic school ethos is important and this needs to be experienced in the context of the wider community.

The role of youth work, further and other formal and non-formal life-long learning are all important. There is an African adage that says, "it takes a whole village to educate a child". There is obviously a lot to this adage bur nowadays it is possible that the whole village might require re-educating itself. This therefore not only entails a rigorous education for teachers bur also continuing education for them. The terms 'social diversity' and 'multiculturalism' also raise issues about which there is currently not very much agreement. The comparative educationalist Nicholas Hans referred to factors such as languages, religion, social class and territory, which form the basis of nations. If one examines British society using this taxonomy then the society can be seen as being historically diverse.

In linguistic terms the use of Gaelic and Celtic languages and different forms of regional English make our society historically multilingual. Likewise in religious terms, the pre-Christian religions, the various denominations of Christianity, Islam and Judaism make Britain a multi-faith society. The historical distinctions between social classes and rural and urban differences are also indicators of differential access to public and social institutions and, of course, education is critical in this context. The British polity has been constitutive of the Welsh, Scottish, English and Irish nations and in addition, the presence of the non-territorially based and largely socially invisible Traveller / Gypsy communities. All these therefore form the historical basis of the multicultural past of the British nation.

A similar taxonomic analysis of the Swedish society in historical terms would demonstrate the historical multiculturality of the Swedish society especially because of the historical presence of Sami people and the Finnish community. Secondly, Sweden has also been an emigration country. Educators need to use that experience, its. history and rationale to build a more sympathetic understanding of current immigration.

Hence, a complex understanding of the historical and contemporary aspects of societal diversity within such a framework which allows educators and young people to develop a more textured and layered understanding of their polity, and would ensure that issues of diversity are not marginalised and laid at the doors of the immigrants and strangers.

Devolution within Britain presents an opportunity to develop coherent historical and contemporary understanding of societal diversity within a framework which ought to provide young people with a view of the complexity of the nations of belongingness, of different groups.

Comparative work needs to be developed to inform intercultural educational practices with a country like Sweden which would help in the development of policies and practices, which is more integrated into mainstream public and social policy institutions and framework. Marginalised and peripheral policies can have negative impact and be counter-productive.

The challenge for intercultural education is the moulding of the one out of the many and to construct appropriate education responses to difference and diversity within complex societies especially in the light of the new and emerging constitutional and institutional arrangements. For both Britain and Sweden the continuing integration of the European Union and its greater harmonisation is necessitating similar pressures of centralisation of institutions.

The challenge is to build inclusive polities, which can accommodate nations of difference hut also create conditions for belongingness of diverse groups. From an educational perspective this can be a 'creative moment' since nations of interculturalism can be utilised to develop integrative mentalities based on nations of difference providing multiple options.

Diversities in their own right can be counterproductive if they conflict with citizenship and other liberal democratic principles. Given that there are deep divisions, and uneven development, what can be done to develop new friendships, constructive and creative imaginations? There is already a legacy of exclusive and negative phenomenon of racism, xenophobia, chauvinism and sexism.

We currently also face a dilemma because old solidarities which existed in the society based on class have been destroyed, especially as the younger generation confront greater levels of polarisation by being divided into winners and losers. Such polarisation, where the losers feel that they owe nothing to the winners poses a new challenge for intercultural education. How can the school build a set of resemblances or a stake amongst multi-divided groups in society, where groups who are losers may not share solidarities or a set of resemblances.

Intercultural education, therefore, has a complex role of addressing the sense of exclusions and loss amongst both black and white youth. The previous policies, which privileged one or the other group, may prove to be counterproductive by exacerbating differences and reducing features of commonality amongst different groups. Hence, the state, through the school, the youth service and the career guidance service, is not impartial but intervenes because both black and white groups are excluded. Schools and other institutions have an important task in turning the majority / minority issue into one of inclusiveness.

The development of inclusiveness would entail reversing the polarities of majority or minority. This necessitates the development of complex common policies and strategies, which include not only white / black groups but also bridges the gaps between all those who are considered a permanent minority and nurtures nations of common citizenship for all. Such policies and processes can instil the enduring nation of fraternity or new solidarities and develop "communities of development and hope" as Judith Green describes it. So the real challenge is how the democratic processes in society including democratic education can be guarantors of social integration in highly differentiated contexts. Encouragingly, amongst many of the young British there are already positive examples.

Many young people currently only demand their fights but do not necessarily accept that they have obligations. The public culture therefore has to be inclusive of values derived from minorities and majorities and not just the dominant groups in society. Intercultural education therefore has to have an inclusive notion, which captures the imagination and enchants the disenchanted young people. To engage young people, who are disaffected by the political process, it is useful to use constitutional and human rights principles, as well as progressive and democratic struggles within the curriculum.

## Teacher Education

In terms of teacher education and the curriculum another set of issues are raised. European higher education institutions educate and train doctors, architects and lawyers and only train hut not educate teachers. Higher education institutions cannot ignore the same broadly based rigorous education for teachers. If the Harvard Business School trains barracudas, then teacher education institutions should not merely train teachers as social workers to pick up the pieces that the barracudas leave behind.

(a) *Teaching or training?* At the first level the claim that has to be discussed is whether the issues are about teacher training or teacher education. 'Training' implies a lower order of knowledge and skill. Here the argument is that to get the best educated and professionally qualified teachers, their education should be undertaken at universities or institutions with comparable standards. Teachers therefore, as autonomous professionals should join a teacher education institution after an undergraduate degree, and have a professional autonomy similar to those in other professions. Again the differences between Sweden and Britain may be important because there may be very different focii on teacher education.

Hence, in terms of current needs of interculturally educated teachers more in-service, or continuing education of teach ers in schools may be necessary. A high level of professionally and rigorously educated teachers who have a postgraduate accredited qualification is essential to raise the profile of the teaching profession. As a part of this accreditation there is a need for intercultural dimensions of courses to be built into the teacher education process.

A highly rigorous and professional teacher education raises some complex issues. Students from smaller nationalities and minorities who have done well at university tend to join other professions and not the teaching profession. Yet to make intercultural teacher education effective both teacher education institutions and schools need to have diverse student and teaching members of staff. Not only does teaching have to be made an attractive profession but education of the underclass, minority and smaller nationalities needs to be improved, and measures instituted to ensure that a number of them do join the teaching profession.

An accredited teacher competence which is validated and includes an integral intercultural dimension is essential to ensure that what is at the core an essential educational issue is not marginalised. In this sense intercultural education for teachers should not be seen as an issue relevant to urban culturally diverse school s alone, but for all schools in Europe, including rural schools.

(b) *Need to counter racism*: The rise of racism and xenophobia with a high level of fascistic activity in all European countries requires a concerted effort to combat it and should be an essential aspect of everyone's education for Europe in the New Millennium. Legislation and legal measures at national and European level are necessary, to deal with this malaise. Institutions ought to have effective policies and action plans not only to counter incidents as they arise hut also to develop teaching strategies from which positive intercultural programmes can emerge.

The issues for teacher education in general and the intercultural dimensions of it are twofold: what do teachers need to know in terms of the knowledge dimension, and what teachers are able to do - which has a skills dimension? If teacher education is of a high quality then the expectations of a teacher's understanding of knowledge issues and skills would be of a high order. The role of teacher education institutions should be to ensure that this is the case.

*(c)* *Professional competencies:* Those who join the teaching profession ought to bring to the field a learning experience from their undergraduate education to ensure that at the postgraduate level there is a systematic study of teaching and learning, as well as planned clinical teaching experience in schools, which is closely supervised and monitored. In the British and American contexts those who study to become teachers complain that education courses fail to prepare them for teaching. If asked about intercultural dimensions they smile and shake their heads.

Teachers not only need a command of the subjects they teach, a sound grasp of the techniques of teaching their subject hut also have information on research and teaching. a grasp of children's growth and development and an understanding of the differing intercultural needs and learning styles.

*(d)* *Status of teacher education*: The status of teacher education institutions, and their structure is critical for the role and position of teacher education itself. If teacher educators are seen as consisting only of previous school teachers, whose knowledge of subject and knowledge areas or of the educational science and research in itself is of a low order, then teacher education and intercultural dimensions will not be rigorous.

Teacher education should be an integral part of the university - and should establish good links with schools in the same way as medical schools are linked with hospitals. This situation would create the possibility of a cross-fertilisation from knowledge systems, and its practice generally to educational science would benefit the development of intercultural teacher education. There is, therefore, a need for an expertise of teachers in schools, who have become teacher educators to have a good academic background and ability to work together with others to develop a sound intercultural teacher education. One of the accusations is that intercultural education 'waters down' the educational process and is not rigorous or able to raise educational standards. Hence, intercultural education needs to lake issues of quality and equality as its dual task. Equality ought not to exclude quality.

## Curriculum Issues

Centric curriculum do not serve the needs of socially diverse polities. Non-centric curriculum is needed in the European context of the new Millennium of globalisation.

(a) *Knowledge implication:* The taxonomy of societies and how those who belong to it are constructed, as well as those who are seen as not belonging has consequences of a legal nature, because of the accordance or denial of citizenship rights. From an academic perspective it also has the implication of how knowledge systems in a particular society are constructed. How knowledge of 'the others' is seen as being external to the education systems, because they are not seen to belong to society has clear implications for teacher education.

In the European context an intercultural curriculum is essential at teacher education level, to ensure that teachers not only have a non-Eurocentric knowledge hut also the skills to teach an intercultural curriculum. Samir Amin and Martin Bernal have made extremely important historiographic analysis about the reconstruction of a European history in the 18th and 19th centuries which exclude the learnings and understandings the Greeks acquired from the Egyptians and Phoenicians. With the rise of racism, and of anti-Semitism the Egyptians, and Phoenicians were excluded. Greece then becomes constructed as the pure childhood of Europe, with no links to other civilisations or their knowledge systems.

Such a construction excludes linguistic and knowledge systems of those groups who are seen as being semi- or uncivilised. Apart from the languages, histories and knowledge of subordinated nationalities in Europe, this construction excludes languages and knowledge of other group s who also live in Europe.

The development therefore of an non-centric curriculum in schools and more importantly in teacher education institutions requires pedagogues to work closely with academic historians, social scientists and other researchers in their respective cultural fields in an attempt to construct a non-centric curriculum. One problem in the implementation of intercultural education is that the languages, histories and cultures of subordinated groups in Europe are not seen as having equal value with those of dominant European nationalities. Such an entitlement to a non-centric curriculum is perhaps one of the greatest challenges to actualising the development of an intercultural teacher education. Issues of knowledge in this sense are not ones of political correctness but arise out of substantive exclusion in mainstream or dominant knowledge systems.

### *Structuring of Intercultural Teacher Education*

It follows from the above points that teacher education as it stands at the present time in many contexts is poorly placed to implement effective intercultural policies and measures. Not only do teacher education institutions need to be postgraduate and research oriented and have close links with other university faculties, they also need to have close links with schools. The structuring of intercultural dimensions would be marginalised if teacher education institutions themselves have a lower status as a university institution. A further issue is how intercultural issues are located within teacher education institutions themselves.

If intercultural dimensions are left to a few interested staff without any institutional or structural arrangements to allow for a more integrated approach within teacher education institutions, then such issues would be marginalised. Each subject area has to acquire and develop its own expertise and it may also require development of inter-disciplinary and across institutional frameworks to implement such changes. This, therefore, requires not only the involvement of a few enthusiasts but of an institutional structure, mechanisms and infrastructure to ensure that necessary changes will take place. Changes within teacher education institutions are necessary because as institutions, they would have customs, procedures and practices which either directly or indirectly discriminate.

Such discriminatory practices may not be evident at the surface level and can only be eliminated if changes in institutional structures can bring about greater openness in their operations. These discriminatory practices may not only have relevance to intercultural education, but may also have general implications for educational equality, including the issue of gender equality. Policies for intercultural teacher education cannot be effective unless they have support for all the staff, and that changes are seen to be made (a) on student admissions; (b) staff recruitment, development and promotions; (c) initiation of research and curriculum developments. Such changes require an evaluation of their effectiveness, and cannot be of a tokenistic nature. Hence, methods of monitoring the implementation of any strategies and policies is necessary. Teacher educators cannot themselves initiate changes unless there is staff development, which allows all the staff an opportunity to update their knowledge and skills.

### *Education of Interculturally Competent Teachers*

Teacher education institutions ought to ensure that the intercultural competencies of teachers include their personal and profession al development. Such competencies should include expertise in their subject but ought to have a more academic as well as practical dimension to their education. This entails a complex evaluation of values, standards and methods across a range of their activities. Intercultural education not only presents complexity in the above areas but also on issues of pedagogy and of learning how to teach, as well as classroom organisation. Teacher education therefore has theoretical as well as practical dimensions. There is a continuing tension about the balance between these conflicting demands. This has the obvious implication of how much time should be devoted to theory as opposed to practice.

### *Teacher Education and Culture of Racism*

Amongst young people the nation of being taught to be part of, and belonging to, complex localities is important. Hence, the nation of territorial belongingness, which is not exclusive but shared, is worth exploring both within schools and youth clubs. There is a need to develop inclusive schools in nonexclusionist-neighbourhoods, which are not no-go areas for others but are confederal communities. Such communities would be based on values of shared resemblances, which are neither racist nor patriarchal. This necessitates the re-vamping of the old Greek concept of "paidea" and the German notion of "Bildung" to develop an interactive and intercultural "paidea" and "Bildung" within complex schools and their communities.

If through academic and formal political and intercultural education as well as, through active citizenship engagement, this process is not undertaken, the underclass or the pauperised groups of whatever nationality or religion will activate their own separatist "politics of recognition". Such a process could heighten notions of fragmentation and divisions with potentially dangerous political consequences. Even if such group s are statistically small they cannot be written off as having no political consequence. Urban ghettos and rural blight have a way of permeating the body politic which prisons and internal security cannot contain because of their corrosive potential. The divisive aspect of the "politics of recognition" is a powerful issue in the United States as well as in many parts of Europe. The current crisis of rising racism and neo-fascism in the European Union context in response to rising Islamic fundamentalist activity is a case in point.

Intercultural Education thus does have to have a national as well as a wider focus. Hence the notion being an "Asian, Scottish, British and European" and its other national equivalents that exist in other European countries around Europe are all critical for intercultural education. This is especially important because Britain and Sweden as members of the European Union need to educate citizens who have a critical understanding and engagement so that they do not uncritically accept a "Fortress Europe". Such a narrow interpretation of Europe is in social terms strengthened by Eurocentric, Swedocentric or Anglocentric curriculum with divisive consequences.

Research and development entails not only work in schools, educational institutions but also the communities from which institutions draw their staff and students. In Britain cases of racial violence, harassment and murder do affect what goes on inside institutions. This is particularly the case because of the ensuring denial of any real educational process. Neither children nor young teachers can be educated properly if there is an overt or covert racism within institutions.

Research and action on this issue is required within communities where racism is operationalised and spill-over into the school. Likewise, there are instances, when the culture of racism within the school can spill-over into the community. Teachers unfortunately get caught in this issue, whether or not they are responsible. Their education cannot ignore this complex linkage, which in many cases teachers tend to deal by using common-sense. Yet, sometimes, children do not consider being given the correct facts (e.g. refugees, immigration) as sufficient ground to abandon racist views. Teacher educators need to play a fundamental rote in dealing with these complex issues so that teachers have the skills and understanding to deal with them. At the level of in-service and continuing education of teachers, many practising teachers have enough experience to carry out action research, which can be turned into systematic strategies of dealing with xenophobia, and racism in the classroom / playground and the school community.

### *Teacher Educators*

(a) *Diverse background of teacher educators.* As there is a need for the recruitment of teachers in schools from diverse social backgrounds, there is also similar need for the recruitment of teacher educators. At various institutions, which have equal opportunity policies, as well as policies against racism, the recruitment of teacher educators from different backgrounds is not yet a reality. This situation is not helped by the major funding problems confronted by teacher education institutions since funding is now being directed to schools for training teachers.

(b) *Linguistic diversity.* Teachers with diverse linguistic background have a major contribution to make in teaching a non-centric curriculum. Yet, from amongst the minority communities very few join the teaching profession. The obvious implication for those who speak non-European languages is that while 14.6 percent of their population attend universities, only 4.7 percent end up in the teaching profession. There are not many interculturally educated bilingual teacher educators and because of this shortage many of the linguistic repertoires could disappear from the linguistic map of Britain as perhaps Sweden. Teacher education has not taken seriously the potential of the linguistic diversity. Perhaps home language teaching in Sweden may now be encouraging more bilingual education. This development would not only enhance understanding between different cultural groups within European countries, but contribute to European understanding of the world, which it colonised at one time, but learnt very little from and about. In linguistic terms the learning of languages which all European children are exposed to in their communities would also enhance the learning of European languages, which have now become essential to membership of a multi-lingual Europe. Hence, intercultural bilingual education which builds on the first languages of children to teach second and other languages is extremely important.

(c) *Creative aspects of teacher education.* Teacher educators have an important contribution to make in teaching about the importance of knowledge and skills amongst the teachers they educate, as well as to enthuse love of learning and teaching. It is the spark which teachers ignite in their students about learning, which carries them through life and allows them to develop love for knowledge. Teachers and teacher educators generally come from backgrounds where education has a very high value. This is a commitment and value which would not go amiss in Europe, where the traditional respect for education has eroded, and the importance of education is seen in purely functional terms. We need to untangle 'education' and 'training' to re-instate the value which accrues to education in its own right.

(d) *Diverse values and secular societies.* In essentially multicultural societies with diverse value systems, teacher educators can contribute to the construction of meaningful, common and shared values for the whole of the younger generation. Yet, because there are very few teacher educators from diverse backgrounds, there is

> hardly an erudite level of discourse or even discussion on this major issue. Since secular democracies are under threat and siege in all parts of the world, the multiple effect of the role of intercultural teacher education ought to be in the forefront of such a complex issue. The contributions to the discussion and debate are mainly from the Christian, agnostic or humanitarian quarters. Yet, the need for developing a more meaningful discourse, which involved greater sections of a very diverse population with differing values, is not taking place.

In dealing with these issues teacher education institutions also ought to play an important role along with others in social sciences, humanities and cultural studies to construct a more imaginative and meaningful academic understanding of contemporary societies. Given the existence of racism and even fascism in society, there is the growth of reactive fundamentalisms. The denial of rights, both individual and social and political rights has great implications for the way in which the younger generation will refuse to accept that they have any obligations to society. With the conflation of racism with anti-Islamic feelings in Europe a new enemy is in the process of being constructed to replace communism, which is seen as dead. Teacher educators ought to engage in discussions with philosophers and those working on values education from a variety of backgrounds in order to examine this issue seriously and to inform the whole process of education. In this sense an inclusive curriculum would help to develop shared and common values for a democratic society.

The demand for separate religious schools which can act as sanctuaries against racism and postmodem dilemmas is already a reality and can be very divisive. Teacher education institutions can make a contribution to solving this issue. This is particularly the case if there are staff from another background who can negotiate the complexities involved in this process.

Most of the understandings of rights of young people in many national contexts come from the media and not the school. Young people are not taught to read these messages critically. This raises important considerations for teachers, curriculum planners, schools and other educators of what the education systems needs to do about citizenship education either in tandem with or as a response to the media.

# 6

# Understanding Social Transformation

Social change is an elusive concept. It is inevitable and yet, paradoxically, it depends on the will and the actions of ordinary individuals. We embrace change, yet something in our nature fiercely resists it. We structure social movements, political campaigns and business strategies around the need for change, yet we hardly understand how it works. These apparent contradictions may partly explain the increased attention to change today in a number of disciplines, from anthropology to quantum physics to management theory to social science.

While a great deal has been written about social change in the fields of history, sociology, organizational theory, and even psychology, much of it focuses on the recalcitrance of social systems — how and why they resist change — rather than the change process itself. This may have something to do with the ambiguous nature of the concept. First, there seems to be little consensus about what constitutes change. The causes, the processes, and the effects of change are often spoken of as if they are one and the same thing. Second, it is notoriously difficult to measure change — how do you know when a change has taken place? And third, change occurs on many levels — cultural, social, institutional, and individual — and it is often hard to draw clear distinctions between them.

Sometimes change occurs spontaneously on several levels at once. This problem is especially troublesome given the specialization of academic research today. Psychologists, physicists, and anthropologists rarely exchange notes and so the connections between, say, complexity theory and cultural change are easily missed.

## Changing Philosophy

The cyclical process of birth, growth, breakdown, and disintegration has been a perennial theme in philosophy dating back to the ancient Greeks, and perhaps further. Heraclitus, who is remembered for his maxims "there is nothing permanent except change" and "you can never step into the same river twice," compared the world order to an ever- living fire, "kindling in measures and going out in measures." His compatriot Empedocles attributed the changes in the universe to the ebb and flow of two complementary forces which he called "love" and "hate." Correspondingly, the ancient Chinese philosophers viewed reality as the dynamic interplay of two opposites — the yin and the yang. Their keen understanding of change is reflected in the term they use for "crisis" — *wei-ji* — which is composed of the characters for "danger" and "opportunity."

While the function of change preoccupied many of the great Western philosophers, it was not until the late-nineteenth and early twentieth centuries that the first comprehensive change theories were articulated. During this time social philosophers sought to make a science out of history and began more systematic analyses of social change. Among the foremost, if more conjectural, of these was Arnold Toynbee's *A Study of History*. Based on exhaustive studies of some thirty civilizations, Toynbee postulated that the genesis of a civilization consists of a transition from a static condition to one of dynamic activity. This transition may occur spontaneously, through the influence of some civilization that is already in existence, or through the disintegration of one or more civilizations of an older generation.

Toynbee saw the birth of civilizations as the result of a dynamic interplay which he called "challenge-and-response." A challenge from the natural or social environment provokes a creative response in a society, or a social group, which induces that society to enter the process of civilization. The civilization continues to grow when its successful response to the initial challenge generates cultural momentum that carries the society beyond a state of equilibrium into an overbalance that presents itself as a fresh challenge. In this way, the initial pattern of challenge-and-response is repeated in successive phases of growth, each successful response producing a disequilibrium that requires new creative adjustments.

After civilizations have reached a peak of vitality, they tend to lose their cultural momentum and decline. An essential element in this cultural breakdown, Toynbee suggested, is a loss of flexibility. When social structures and behavior patterns have become so rigid that the society can no longer adapt to changing conditions, it will be unable to carry on the creative process of cultural evolution. It will then break down and eventually disintegrate. Whereas growing civilizations display endless variety and versatility, those in the process of disintegration show uniformity and lack of inventiveness. The loss of flexibility in a disintegrating society is accompanied by a general loss of harmony among its elements which inevitably leads to the outbreak of social discord and disruption.

Toynbee noted, however, that during the painful process of disintegration, the society's creativity — its ability to respond to changes — is not completely lost. Though the cultural mainstream has become ossified by clinging to fixed ideas and rigid patterns of behavior, creative minorities will appear on the scene and carry on the process of challenge-and-response. The dominant social institutions will refuse to hand over their leading roles to these new cultural forces, but they will inevitably go on to decline and disintegrate, and the creative minorities may be able to transform some of the old elements into a new configuration. The process of cultural evolution will then continue, but under new circumstances and with new protagonists.

Toynbee's ideas echo those of Oswald Spengler, Pitirim Sorokin, and other social thinkers who viewed change as fundamentally cyclical in nature. The major alternative to this model is the linear or evolutionary view of change perhaps best articulated by Herbert Spencer, Karl Marx, and August Comte. This interpretation recalls the faith in science and the inevitability of progress which swept through the social sciences in the nineteenth century. Spencer, who coined the phrase "survival of the fittest", saw all social change as the manifestation of a natural law of progress.

The dynamic force in progress was, like that in biological evolution, the competitive struggle for existence in which the fit survive and the unfit perish. This interpretation of social change was especially popular among the so-called Social Darwinists (even though Darwin himself was no Social Darwinist and Spencer's theory of social evolution preceded Darwin's theories of biological evolution by several years.) If Spencer's evolutionary philosophy provided a philosophical justification for individualism, Karl Marx's theories did the same for collectivism. Marx's theories were based in large part on Hegel's view of history as a dialectical progression. Hegel postulated that one concept (thesis) inevitably generates its opposite (antithesis), and that their interaction leads to a new concept (synthesis), which in turn becomes the thesis of a new triad.

Marx adapted this model to his analysis of social change, asserting that all changes in society arise from the development of its internal contradictions. He saw the contradictory principles of social organization as being embodied in society's classes, and class struggle as a consequence of their dialectic interaction. Class struggle was the driving force of history for Marx. He held that all important historical progress was born in conflict, struggle, and violent revolution. Human suffering and sacrifice was a necessary price that had to be paid for social change.

### *A Scientific Paradigm*

A more recent perspective on change comes from historian of science Thomas Kuhn. In *The Structure of Scientific Revolutions,* which has been called the most important book of the twentieth century, he introduced the concept of a *paradigm* — a conceptual model or set of assumptions about reality that allows researchers to isolate data, elaborate theories, and solve problems. A scientific paradigm, as Kuhn defined it, can be as all-encompassing as Newtonian physics or as specific as the notion that life exists only on earth. The chief characteristic of a paradigm is that it has its own set of rules and illuminates its own set of facts. In this way it becomes self- validating and therefore resistant to change.

Kuhn observed that as long as a paradigm explains most observed phenomena and solves the problems most people want solved, it remains dominant. But as new phenomena begin to contradict it, the paradigm succumbs to increasing doubt. As these anomalies multiply, it is thrown into crisis. When a new paradigm is articulated — such as Einstein's theory of quantum mechanics — a broad paradigmatic shift occurs. In this way, long periods of "normal" science are followed by brief "revolutions" that involve fundamental changes in basic theoretical assumptions. In Kuhn's view, the history of science is not one of linear, rational progress moving toward ever more accurate and complete knowledge of an objective truth. Instead, it is one of radical shifts of vision in which a multitude of nonrational and nonempirical factors come into play.

While Kuhn was dealing with paradigms in the history of science and has repeatedly cautioned against overgeneralizing in applying the concept to the process of social transition, it nevertheless provides a very useful metaphor for understanding the nature of change. This is reflected in the near-universal usage of the word *paradigm* today. A good example of how the word has been applied in a more general sense is offered by physicist and philosopher Fritjof Capra. A paradigm, he says, "is a constellation of concepts, values, perceptions and practices, shared by a community that forms a particular vision of reality that is the basis of the way the community organizes itself. It's necessary for a paradigm to be shared by a community. A single person can have a worldview, but a paradigm is shared by a community."

The paradigm concept illustrates the extent to which social change can hinge on the state of mind of individuals. In *Global Mind Change*, Willis Harman observes that "throughout history, the really fundamental changes in societies have come about not from the dictates of governments and the results of battles but through vast numbers of people changing their minds — sometimes only a little bit." Because of the way these changes of mind occur, the effects can appear sudden and spontaneous. We tend to think of cultural innovation as the work of small elites, or what Toynbee called "creative minorities" — leading philosophers, religious thinkers, scientists, and artists — who infuse society with new ideas. But, as Daniel Yankelovich points out in *New Rules*, "every now and then a new way of conceiving life and its meaning arises spontaneously from the great mass of the population."

Kuhn's model also sheds light on how change operates in the natural world. For example, biologist Elisabet Sahtouris describes how the metamorphosis of a caterpillar into a butterfly follows a similar change pattern. In metamorphosis, small cells known as imaginal discs begin to appear in the body of the caterpillar. Since they are not recognized by the caterpillar's immune system, they are immediately wiped out. But as they grow in number and begin to link up, they ultimately overwhelm the caterpillar's immune system. Its body then goes into meltdown and the imaginal discs build the butterfly from the spent materials of the caterpillar.

These imaginal discs can be likened to the anomalies in Kuhn's model of paradigmatic change. The caterpillar's immune system does not recognize them, just as the dominant paradigm in Kuhn's model fails to account for anomalies. Finally they overwhelm the system and usher in a new phase. Interesting parallels can also be drawn between imaginal discs and the "creative minorities" in Toynbee's theory of the rise and fall of civilizations. As Toynbee showed, the seeds of the new civilization are contained within the old one just like the blueprint of the butterfly is contained in the cells of the caterpillar.

### *Cultural Renewal*

Another model of social change has been described by anthropologist Anthony F.C. Wallace based on his studies of both indigenous and modern societies. In his 1961 book *Culture and Personality*, he observed that the change process begins with a shift away from cultural harmony, a change that shows up first in the form of increased individual stress. A growing number of individuals find that they are unable to meet certain cultural expectations. At first this is perceived by both the individual and the society at large as an individual problem. But as the number of these individual deviations grows, it begins to weaken the social fabric, eventually to the point where the society must acknowledge that the problem is more than personal. At this stage, it is difficult for the society to return to a state of equilibrium without undergoing a process of revitalization. According to Wallace, this process depends on a number of variables:

— *The formulation of a code.* An individual or small group — typically people who have been directly affected by the stresses in question — builds a new idealized image of a "goal culture" that stands in attractive contrast to the existing situation.

— *Communication.* The formulators then communicate their vision to others, beginning with those most affected by the stresses at the root of the problem.

— *Organization.* Once the vision begins to attract converts, some form of organization is required to manage the group and implement a plan.

— *Adaptation.* As the new vision gets broader exposure, it generally grows and changes. This happens for various reasons: the initial vision is usually incomplete, especially in its practical details; certain accommodations may be made to broaden the appeal of the vision; and the original vision may include such things as predictions that fail to materialize, thus requiring re- explanation.

— *Cultural Transformation.* If the movement is able to gain enough support within the society, the thrust shifts from communications to implementation. If the "goal culture" cannot be immediately established, then a "transfer culture" is adopted as the route to get to the full vision. If this cultural shift is successful, the stress experienced by individuals declines dramatically.

— *Routinization.* Once the initial shift of cultural transformation has taken place, the next stage is to establish the new vision as the new steady state, which generally means institutionalizing it in various ways. Those in the vanguard of the transformation process may find this last stage difficult and disappointing, but the majority of the population is glad for a return to normalcy so that they can get on with their lives.

Wallace observes that this kind of revitalization can be either reactionary or innovative in its basic thrust. The reactionary mode is characterized by a belief that present problems can be resolved by "doing the old way harder," and generally tries to undo or suppress recent changes that are seen as the cause of the problem. The innovative mode, on the other hand, attempts to get "lagging" parts of the culture to catch up to recent changes that are seen by the innovators as either positive or unchangeable.

In complex societies under stress, there are usually many revitalization movements competing for attention and converts as the culture begins to disintegrate. Wallace notes that the inherent conservatism in most social systems favors reactionary movements. It is common for a culture to attempt a "let's do the old way harder" revitalization as the first response to realizing that something must be done to get society back in track. It is only after the failure of a reactionary revitalization attempt that a culture is willing to risk fundamental change.

This shift from innovation to reaction and back again is often described in common parlance in terms of a swinging pendulum. The metaphor suggests that social change follows predictable laws of motion and that movement is static in one direction or another. But, as Daniel Yankelovich points out, social change is better described as a process of "lurch and learn." In his forty years of monitoring social trends in the United States, Yankelovich had found that society tends to lurch, often mindlessly, in a new direction and it is only after a period of reaction that integration takes place.

For instance, in the 1960s young people lurched away from the prevailing notion of duty to the search for pleasure. Similarly, there was a lurch away from work to leisure. "The reaction of young people to their father's nose-to-the-grindstone way of life was to see in leisure the possibilities of genuine self-fulfillment. After that lurch, they gradually found that the kind of self-fulfillment they were seeking often could be fulfilled better through a certain kind of work than through leisure."

### *Scientific Perspectives*

Some of the most fascinating contributions to the theory of change in recent decades come not from sociology or anthropology but from an eclectic, multidisciplinary group of researchers at the frontiers of quantum physics, general systems theory, and the emerging theories of chaos and complexity. Nobel laureates such as chemist Ilya Prigogine, physicist Murray Gell-Mann, and economist Kenneth Arrow, along with of host of others engaged in the study of complex systems have pioneered a new approach to understanding the instability and fluctuations that characterize seemingly random events, be it at the level of molecules, of biological systems, or even of social systems.

The science of complexity can be loosely divided into two disciplines. The first is nonequilibrium physics which is based on the discovery of fundamental new properties of matter under far-from-equilibrium conditions. The second discipline is the modern theory of dynamical systems, which is especially relevant for our purposes here since dynamical systems include a wide range of processes including chemical reactions, individual organisms, ecosystems, economies, and social systems. The central discovery here is the prevalence of instability. In essence, instability means that small changes in initial conditions may lead to large amplifications of the effects of the changes.

Ilya Prigogine, who won the Nobel Prize in chemistry in 1977, has been at the center of the emerging science of complexity. In his book *Order Out of Chaos* he explores the nature of change in what he calls "dissipative structures." Dissipative structures are best described as open systems in the sense that they interact with the larger world around them by constantly trading energy and maintaining themselves through an endless dynamic flow. One of the chief characteristics of these systems is that they are subject to constant fluctuations or perturbations, sudden shifts that allow for novelty and unpredictable change. A river can be taken as an example of a dissipative structure: while it acts in consort with the larger environment of which it is a part, it can be seen as an independent system; like all living systems it is subject to constant, erratic and apparently random fluctuations.

According to Prigogine, a single fluctuation adding its strength to other fluctuations may become powerful enough to reorganize the whole system into a new pattern. The points at which this happens are "bifurcation points," at which deterministic description breaks down and the system follows one of several possible forks in the road. These "stochastic" (i.e., not predictable) processes demonstrate that open systems are not mechanistic but random. Prigogine uses the term randomness to denote not blind chance, but rather non-determinism, spontaneity, and novelty. Open systems can thus be thought of as dynamic and "creative."

Prigogine likens the universe to a living organism because it has room for random behavior, allowing dissipative structures to recreate themselves into unforeseeable patterns. These novel patterns are often triggered by small variables or perturbations whose presence can pull the entire system away from one kind of behavior toward a new and unexpected one. In this way, matter is not something static — inert molecules that are governed by pushes and pulls — but as something active and alive. Except for systems at equilibrium in which no further exchanges take place, open systems are constantly attuned to their environments. In these open systems, matter is not isolated and solitary, as scientists once assumed, but instead it is responsive, relational, and self-modifying in response to the activities of other matter. In these systems, the smallest change may "destabilize" the system and bring about an outcome not predicted by the logic of linear equations.

Prigogine's theory of dissipative structures and order by fluctuation echoes emerging theories in other fields, such as quantum physics and biology, which are challenging our traditional understanding of change on several fronts. There is growing evidence that systemic change is not a mechanistic, progressive, and linear phenomenon whose causes and effects can be clearly isolated. While Newtonian science has long sought to isolate the basic building-blocks of nature, recent theories suggest that nature appears more like a complicated web of relations between various parts of a unified whole. As the German quantum physicist Werner Heisenberg put it, "the world thus appears as a complicated tissue of events, in which connections of different kinds alternate or overlap or combine and thereby determine the texture of the whole."

## Theories of Social Change

The science of complex systems offers some intriguing parallels between the natural and the social world. Just as the notion of direct causation has been found to be faulty in dynamical systems, it is now widely recognized that so-called "prime movers" such as strong leadership or economic dislocation, once largely unquestioned in sociology, are impossible to isolate from the other causal factors that prompt social change. Social philosopher Alvin Toffler has expressed the emergent view this way: "I think more in terms of process, interrelationships, rhythms, non-equilibrium, and fields than individual causal vectors; more in terms of mutually interactive systems, than of one-way causality."

As sociology has adopted a less deterministic approach, one that acknowledges the inherent interdependence and reciprocity at work in social systems, the emphasis has shifted from the *causes* of change to the *conditions* that are most conducive to change. As sociologist Bruce F. Ryan put it, "if cause is to be sought for change, it is to be found through the analysis of the conditions and processes giving rise to the particular sequence of events." Conditions that tend to precipitate change include:

— A lack of cohesion among the various constituents of a social system.

— The inability of groups or individuals to adjust to their larger social or physical environment.

— Rigid and centralized social structures.

— High population densities.

— Social diversity.

— Creativity and innovation.

Each of these conditions leads to the kinds of social tensions which ultimately manifest in change. By way of comparison, it's interesting to review the characteristics of social systems which are relatively stable over time. Typically these societies have been 1) small in size, 2) isolated from contact with other cultures, 3) technologically unsophisticated, 4) unable to store or transmit knowledge through writing, 5) highly respectful of tradition, and 6) bound to a shared and consistent value system.

Another condition at the root of social change is the oft-cited theory of cultural lag developed by William Fielding Ogburn in the 1920s. He explained that when different systems within a society are out of sync with one another, different rates of change affect different social sectors in varied ways. The result is that institutions struggle to adapt to the time-pacing of other institutions. For example, in the business world innovation and renewal tend to occur very rapidly, whereas public schools and government bureaucracies typically change very slowly. These lags in adaptation create powerful tensions in society. Alvin Toffler, who has been much influenced by Ogburn's theory, attributed the condition of "future shock" in part to this phenomenon of cultural lag.

The literature on social change focuses to a large extent on the dynamics of social interaction — how groups are formed, how minorities deviate from established norms, how conflict is born and resolved, and the fluctuations in collective behavior. A growing body of research also looks at the process of "diffusion" — the process by which innovative ideas are spread and ultimately take root in society. The trouble with much of the academic research on change is that, on its own, it's not very useful. In the words of one observer, "sociologists put primary emphasis on attempting to build a body of verified theory about social behavior, including social change, rather than themselves trying to induce change. The practitioner, on the other hand, although likewise interested in understanding, is principally concerned with inducing change, rather than merely accounting for it." This shortcoming has not been entirely lost on social scientists. In fact, a subfield of sociology has emerged in the past few decades devoted to "planned change." This development is a reaction in part to the shift from the *study* of change to the *methods* of controlling and directing it.

One especially useful, if perhaps excessively academic, roundup of "General Strategies for Effecting Changes in Human Systems" is provided by Robert Chin and Kenneth Benne in their classic textbook *The Planning of Change*. In their analysis, change strategies fall into three categories: 1) rational-empirical, 2) normative- reeducative, and 3) power-coercive.

The *rational-empirical* approach assumes that men and women are rational and practical and will change on their own given the appropriate conditions. These strategies include:

— Provide the right information, education or training to allow individuals to change of their own volition.

— Ensure that the "right" people are in the right "place" to bring about needed changes.

— Invite the perspectives or expertise of outsiders.

— Engage in research and development.

— Promote utopian thinking to stimulate creativity and "best-case" scenarios.

— Clarify the issues and/or reconceptualize the situation in order to bring about greater overall understanding among members of the group.

The second category of strategies — the *normative- reeducative* — is predicated on the view that change begins from the bottom up, not the top down. That is to say, it focuses on changing the individuals that make up a social system. It is the preferred method of counselors, trainers, and therapists. Two strategies characteristic of this approach are to:

— Improve the problem-solving capacities of a system by encouraging individuals to be self-diagnosing.

— Release and foster growth in the persons who make up the system.

The *power-coercive* approach to effecting change is the one most commonly associated with political movements and social activism. In the words of Chin and Benne, "these strategies are oriented against coercive and nonreciprocal influence, both on moral and on pragmatic grounds." Strategies in this category include:

— Using political institutions to achieve change.

— Shifting the balance of power between social groups, especially ruling elites.

— Weakening or dividing the opposition through moral coercion or strategies of nonviolence.

Another taxonomy of change strategies is offered by Roland Warren, a sociologist who has devoted much attention to social change at the community level. His list of community-based change strategies include: consensus planning, bargaining, protest movements, research- demonstrations, social action, non-violence, organizations of client populations, community development, conflict, elite planning, organization of indigenous groups, and civil disobedience. He classifies these under four headings:

1) collaborative strategies,

2) campaign strategies,

3) contest strategies, and

4) a combination of strategies.

From one perspective, individuals and groups are the objects of change. They are at the receiving end, in the sense that change happens to them. From the other perspective, individuals and groups are the initiators of change and change follows from human volition. Both perspectives have their validity, of course, and they are closely interrelated. For instance, when one social group actively tries to bring about change, there are invariably other groups who feel put upon and try to resist the change.

### *Management Theory*

One field of inquiry that has taken a particularly proactive approach to the subject of change is management theory. This is not surprising, perhaps, given the competitive pressures confronting many organizations today. In a world buffeted by change, many organizations have learned that the only way to survive is by innovating, that the only stability possible is stability in motion. In the opening lines of *Managing the Future: Ten Driving Forces of Change for the 90s*, Robert Tucker writes:

> Two years after *In Search of Excellence* reported on forty-three of the "best run" companies in America, fourteen of the forty-three firms were in financial trouble. The reason, according to a *Business Week* study: "failure to react and respond to change."That "change" and "innovation" have become the bywords of organizational management in the 1990s is reflected in a myriad of business books with titles like *Mastering Change: The Key to Business Success*, *Knowledge for Action: A Guide to Overcoming Barriers to Organizational Change* and *The Change Masters*. As Common Cause founder John Gardner has said, "perhaps the most distinctive thing about innovation today is that we are beginning to pursue it systematically. The large corporation does not set up a research laboratory to solve a specific problem but to engage in continuous innovation."

One of the more influential management books to emerge in recent years is *The Fifth Discipline* by Peter Senge, director of the Systems Thinking and Organizational Learning Program at MIT's Sloan School of Management. Senge believes that the greatest challenges confronting organizations today involve fundamental cultural changes. Addressing these challenges requires what he calls collective learning. Organizations must be able to learn in order to survive.

The traditional approach to dealing with complex problems is to break them down into smaller, more easily managed problems. But this approach could be fatal to organizations, according to Senge. When we reduce complex problems and try to isolate their various parts we "can no longer see the consequences of our actions; we lose our intrinsic sense of connection to a larger whole," he writes. "As daunting as it may seem, we must destroy the illusion that the world is created of separate, unrelated forces. When we give up this illusion, we can then build learning organizations."

The learning organization is one in which five learning disciplines are continually pursued:

— Personal Mastery, "the discipline of continually clarifying and deepening our personal vision, of focusing our energies, of developing patience, and of seeing reality objectively."

— Analyzing one's mental models and envisioning alternative ways of thinking about the world. Working with mental models means exposing our own ways of thinking, as well as making that thinking more open to the influence of others.

— Building a shared vision, "unearthing shared pictures of the future that foster genuine commitment and enrollment rather than compliance."

— Learning as a team, which starts with dialogue and the skill of overcoming defensiveness and other patterns of interaction that keep members from learning — individually and as a team.

— Thinking systemically, seeing patterns and the "invisible fabrics of interrelated actions, which often take years to fully play out their effects on each other."

According to Senge, the fifth discipline — systems thinking — ties all the other disciplines together. This kind of thinking involves "a shift of mind from seeing parts to seeing wholes, from seeing people as helpless reactors to seeing them as active participants in shaping their reality." Senge notes that the really significant and enduring innovations he has observed have grown out of people from multiple constituencies working together. In education, for instance, "it's been a few committed teachers with some bright ideas, in concert with a principal who has a particular view of his or her job, in concert with a superintendent who is in line with that principal, and in concert with people in the community who are very much part of the innovation process."

Many of Senge's ideas are echoed by Rosabeth Moss Kanter and her colleagues in *The Challenge of Organizational Change*. They focus on how organizations learn to change, emphasizing "the sad fact ... that, almost universally organizations change as little as they must, rather than as much as they should." They characterize learning organizations as "self-designing," "self-renewing," and "post-entrepreneurial." They are flexible and open, and all levels of development — individual, team, work group, and organizational — occur simultaneously and synergistically.

The importance of systems thinking and creating a common vision also figures prominently in the organizational approach of Gary Frank, David Angus, and Bob Rehm. In what they call "future search conferences" or "visioning meetings," they bring together a diverse group of people to create a shared vision, innovation, and joint planning. The rationale here is that meaningful, deliberate, consensual, and preferred change must involve as many people with a stake in the issue as possible. It also recognizes that any organization is a part of a larger environment. "The relationship of the organization to its external environment, how that environment is changing, what the change either means to us or how we can influence the change are the key ingredients of the search."

### *Individual Change*

The emphasis on systems thinking is a recent development in organizational thinking and has yet to be embraced in the mainstream management literature. The same might be said about the role of individual change, or what Senge calls "personal mastery." While much has been written about the processes which help people achieve change, a more fundamental question involves whether they are willing to change in the first place. From this perspective, social change has a great deal to do with individual motivation. Effective strategies for change must build on the caring and personal commitment of all the players involved. Social philosopher Philip Slater makes this point in his book *A Dream Deferred*. "People are reluctant to change because change is uncomfortable and demands a great deal of energy," he says. "Therefore when people ask where to start working [for change], the answer is that since change makes heavy demands on motivation and energy, you should start where you *care* the most and do what you like to *do* the most — that will be where you contribute the most energy and be most effective."

Robert Theobald has spent the better part of three decades organizing communities for change. In his book *The Rapids of Change*, he notes that people often ask him whether a particular change is possible. "I respond by saying that this is the wrong question," he writes. "Instead, each of us needs to ask where our commitment is and where we shall act. Once we are committed, we will find ways to be effective."

### *Strategies for Change*

A considerable amount of research has been done on how and why change occurs and the methods people use to consciously bring it about.

#### *Build new relationships*

A crucial first step in any process of effecting change is what

David Mathews calls "banding together." It means forming relationships, organizing, and claiming collective responsibility for a given issue or situation. This can range from highly organized community town meetings to a few neighbors getting together in someone's living room to discuss their concerns. In some cases, building new relationships may only be possible by fundamentally changing relationships that are already in place. The key is to develop a sense of group identity as well as a sense of agency. Banding together generates "a sense of the possibility for change," Mathews writes. "Being associated with, and committed to, others gives people a feeling that they are equal to their problems." It is therefore an essential prerequisite to bringing about desired changes.

### *Discuss and deliberate*

All effective change strategies hinge on discussion and deliberation. At a minimum, discussion allows the issues to be named and framed. It also helps individuals develop a shared perspective. As Robert Theobald points out, "most fundamental change activities break down because those involved in them do not take the time to gain a shared model of reality." At a more fundamental level, dialogue allows for what physicist David Bohm calls a "higher social intelligence." One of the chief obstacles to change, he says, is that "we've organized our societies by algorithms — that is, by sets of rules by which we try to affect each other like parts of a machine. The result is that we can't talk with each other about things that are really important." Dialogue helps to eliminate false divisions among people, builds common ground, and allows for the emergence of a more systemic perspective.

### *Develop shared visions and goals*

Setting new directions for the future is one of the most powerful ways of effecting change. When people come together "in such a way that their individual visions can start to interact," as Peter Senge puts it, a creative tension is established that gives focus, direction, and context to changes as they occur. Some techniques for developing common visions include futures commissions, search conferences, and visioning meetings in which participants develop "best case" scenarios and articulate common goals. As Senge says, "we communicate our individual visions to one another and eventually start to create a field of shared meaning where there really is a deep level of trust and understanding — and we gradually begin to build a shared vision." This process is very different from such perfunctory strategies as writing "vision" statements. It often involves a great deal of reflection, listening, and mutual understanding.

*Foster social capital*

Robert Putnam and others have used the term "social capital" to denote the networks and norms of trust and reciprocity that characterize healthy social orders. The term suggests that capital can be measured in social as well as economic terms, that relationships have an inherent value. Scott Fosler, author of *The Public/Private Partnership*, has studied the nature of community collaboration in cities across the United States. "If you look back at what it was that was really key in the development of civic and political institutions," he says, "it was trust that was based on personal relationships." Building networks and relationships within and between individuals and groups is not something that can be done overnight, but it is no doubt one of the most effective change strategies available to communities and civic organizations.

*Participation and Diversity*

Fundamental change is impossible without the participation of everybody with a stake in the problem or issue. Without the full participation of all concerned, perspectives will be missing and there is a good chance that some of the issues involved will go unaddressed. Another aspect of this is the inherent value of diversity. Research in anthropology, sociology, and biology shows that homogeneity fosters stability, while diversity invariably produces change. It follows that planned change is best achieved by promoting diversity.

*Leadership roles*

There are many types of leaders, from presidents and mayors to teachers, neighborhood activists, and even parents. But no matter what form they take they lend cohesion to a group and act as spark-plugs for change. Their vision, drive and personal commitment can be keys to galvanizing a group into action. Leaders are also able to champion and protect those within groups who are most willing to risk change.

*Identify outside resources*

Fundamental change tends to be difficult and painful and always involves uncertainty and risk. Since most communities and organizations that embark on the journey need outside help — from foundations, consultants, civic organizations, trade associations, government departments, etc. — they need to develop linkages to outside sources of capital and information. These linkages not only facilitate the process of change they often provide opportunities for lateral learning and growth.

*Set clear boundaries*

When planning for specific kinds of change, it is important to operate within clearly defined boundaries - - for both psychological and practical reasons. Boundaries provide frameworks for measuring change and give focus and direction to one's efforts. They also provide a sense of what is feasible. On a practical level, clearly defined goals allow one to make realistic plans.

*Draw on the examples of others*

Change takes place in an infinite variety of ways and there is no single strategy that will work for every individual or group. Still, those seeking to effect change may take comfort and inspiration from the examples of others. Not only does this provide mentors from whom they can learn, it offers them conviction that their goal is attainable.

*Adopt a change mindset*

Nothing precipitates change like a crisis. Necessity, after all, is the mother of invention. The question is whether it is possible to adopt a crisis-perspective without a crisis, or at least a mindset that is constantly attuned to change. Many innovators and change agents insist that it is possible. What is required, they say, is a shift of perception from seeing change as dis-equilibrium to seeing it as a constant. Strategizing for change ultimately comes down to whether individuals are motivated to change, learn, and grow.

# 7

# Cultural Sociology of Learning

Organisational learning is central in enabling organisations to adapt to changing expectations and the forces of the global economy. The process of globalisation has, ironically, partly been responsible for the imposition of greater constraints on organisational development. Globalisation, which has been equated with market liberalisation, has also brought with it new pressures. Some argues that the 'heightened volatility, hypercompetition, demographic changes and the explosion of knowledge' have resulted in an environment made up of discontinuity, in which organisations are under pressure to continuously adapt.

Many would argue that the climate in which business operates cannot be controlled, but there is scope for influencing the internal environment of organisations. Organisational learning can achieve two outcomes:

— fostering an efficient and effective working environment, and;

— supporting and encouraging innovation and change.

Key aspects of learning include an integrated system of working practices, as well as clear and open channels for the development and dissemination of knowledge. However, there is still a mindset in many organisations that change should be treated with great caution. Learning is often resisted and difficult to achieve. Some argues that conventional forms of learning breed fear and there does seem to be an element of unease, on the part of companies, about how they can develop a management system that reflects the integration embodied in some standards. However, it is also clear that the influx of certification standards and codes of practice into organisations has often been overwhelming and disjointed.

## Management of Learning

Von Krogh and Venzin suggest that there is a move towards 'the management of knowledge' but we would suggest that this approach is counterproductive and in some ways is in direct conflict with the environment that should be fostered. The 'management of knowledge' suggest a process that is controlled, and, by its very nature, contrived. It requires a system and a framework that is often too rigid to accommodate the flexibility associated with learning, innovation and change. An approach that tells organisations what to expect, where to look, what to ignore and what should be valued defeats the object of the exercise. The expectations and beliefs shape the learning landscape and set boundaries. In such circumstances, innovation and creativity will be unable to flourish.

Knowledge is not something that is to be controlled, but is something that should be disseminated with the maximum coverage and scope. Knowledge, it has been said, is discovered, while inventions are created. Useful knowledge is discovered through the application of wisdom to information. There is therefore a progressive, cumulative hierarchy of: information, knowledge and wisdom. We are awash with information today, we scramble for knowledge to cling onto and sometimes when we take time to reflect we discover wisdom.

In a healthy learning environment, there should be time for reflection, communication and evaluation. There should be time and tolerance for mistakes. Unfortunately, pressures on time mean that these are often not areas that are considered to be an investment. Thatchenkery argues that 'In a world where action rather than reflection is valued, even the reflective learning organisation apparently has to race at a pace that leaves little room for deliberation'.

However, reflection, communication and evaluation must be at the heart of any strategy that strives towards learning, development and progression, which will ultimately lead to competitive advantage. An integrated and holistic approach that incorporates such elements is not a cheap option, as time is money. Nevertheless, in cases where organisations are willing to take a long-term approach and accept that budgets need to be attached to non-tangible aspects of the working day, the benefits can be considerable.

***Standards and Learning***

Companies are encouraged to adopt certification standards, often in the form of a checklist. Such standards are relatively easy to adopt but require little, if any, cultural change. The checklist mechanism leaves little room for learning. Again, this is a reflection of the time constraints that companies face. It indicates the realisation by organisations that certification standards do carry weight, yet it is also a reflection of the devaluation of these very same standards.

Standards that are profound in their aims yet also realistic about current pressures will need to integrate managerial theory and practice into a coherent and workable strategic entity. Organisations strive to be efficient in their processes and effective in their decision making in order to gain competitive advantage.

Most management theories would not only claim to have a predictive capacity in their ability to link cause and effect, but often generate stringent test procedures that define the precise conditions to balance cause and effect. Theoretically, the results are reproducible when using the same formula. However, in practice, there are an infinite number of determinants that will effect the outcome of any decision being made.

Therefore it is almost impossible to apply one, single, all-encompassing, prescriptive formula to a diversity of organisations and sectors. Changeable external market conditions are only a small element of that equation. A great deal of the influence will derive from the internal ethics and values of the organisation, and the individuals involved, and from the priorities of resource allocation.

The combination of such determinants is unique and more importantly context-bound. Organisations operate in environments that necessitate re-evaluation, adaptability and sometimes radical change. Therefore it is neither realistic nor desirable to expect the creation of a monolithic management system that can be slotted into any organisation with a prescribed outcome. In order to gain greater insight and understanding of the nuances, there is a need for a study that also scopes the evolution of the individual organisation's values and ethics.

## Organisational learning and cultural change

Organisational culture has been described as 'the common set of shared meanings or understandings about the group/organisation and its problems, goals and practices' and 'the taken for granted and shared meanings that people assign to their social surroundings'.

Organisational learning on the scale envisaged by sustainability criteria involves changing the culture of the organisation, not only so that it becomes orientated towards the precepts embedded in sustainability of social justice, equity and revaluing environmental resources, but also in order that the organisation can unlearn and relearn its mission, vision and values.

There are numerous interpretations of what learning entails within organisational boundaries, yet the evolutionary process is, in fact, not so much a sign of fragmentation, but an indication of the cross-fertilisation that has taken place between the disciplines. Learning is a topic that can be approached from disciplines as diverse as psychology, cultural studies, strategic management and organisational behaviour.

Learning can take place at different levels and in varying forms. C. Wright Mills highlights the interplay between different levels of analysis. According to his model, the individual is placed in the center, and is affected by, as well as affects, the family, the workplace and even the industry. A multi-directional ripple effect can take place within this model, where the learning that occurs at the individual level will have learning consequences at the family level, in the workplace and finally in the industry.

Similarly, from a top-down perspective, the learning that takes place at the industry level will have an impact in the workplace and then, in turn, will affect the individual and their families. Such a model highlights learning as a mechanism of information dissemination that feeds on interpretative processes and interpersonal communication. Individuals are not the only subject of the learning process, and it is here that many organisation fail in their understanding of the extent and breadth of the issue. Innovation, learning and change do not occur as a result of spoon-feeding information to individuals throughout the chain, in a manual or handbook format.

Some argue that learning needs to be based on the encoding of specific routines in an organisation. The bank in our sample has attempted to encode an ethical and dynamic practice within its organisation and made it part of its unique selling point. When the sector was suffering, there was a need to establish a new 'edge' to its business. Therefore, it was necessary to embed the ethical stance in all areas of its business.

The water company in our sample also pointed out that their Environmental Policy was largely driven by a need to differentiate. Although there was a certain amount of stakeholder pressure, one of the key drivers came from the desire to increase the share price.

In an era of mergers and acquisitions, it is increasingly difficult to maintain standardisation across all areas of operations. The car company in sample, which has been part of an acquisition, highlighted the difficulties they have faced. They found that there was a cultural difference as well as the differences in the terminology between the company and its parent. The company itself uses the term 'sustainability' whereas the parent company refers to 'corporate citizenship'. Furthermore, the company's perception of corporate citizenship is very different to that of its parent. For this reason, encoding specific routines in an organisation can be highly problematic and impossible in the short term.

The encoding of certain practices can also at times be uneven, and again will be determined by the dispersed or concentrated nature of power within the organisation. The car company is an example of a heavy topdown model where the Board has been proactive in driving sustainability. There has been a Sustainability Strategy Committee in place since 1995, comprising 10 Board members and the Managing Director. It is a highly structured committee that meets five times a year as well as meeting on a monthly basis with the environmental representatives of each section. The Board drives down the issues through the environmental representatives who feed the information to their teams of 20. This reflects a 'training kit' approach where innovation and learning is passed down through to all employees. In 1999, there was a substantial change at Board level, which due to the top-down nature of the model could have had an adverse effect on the sustainability drive. Fortunately, the new members of the

Board did, in fact, continue the drive, and the past year and a half have turned out to be more dynamic and signalled a real change in attitude.

Learning, innovation and cultural change, by their very nature, embody conflict, making mistakes, and, making compromises. All the organisations studied understand the value of sustainability initiatives, but that does not mean that the current approach is perfect. The water company have regarded the issues as important since their sector is energy-intensive and therefore contributes towards global warming. There is also the growing public perception of the unreliability of water resources.

Sustainability was a subject high on their agenda by the mid-1990's when there was a drought and increased public discussion about global warming. The increased focus on these two issues in the space of a five-year period of time put great pressure on the sector. However, the extremes in climate have made it difficult to plan water resources and there is a need to build more storage facilities and increase capital investment, which has effectively driven up costs significantly. This has been compounded in the UK by strengthening regulatory pressures on water quality. Ironically, they have had to become more energy intensive, therefore increasing their impact on the environment. There is a discrepancy, in other words, between the short-term and long-term pressures imposed by the regulatory bodies.

## Strategies for Learning and Innovation

Clearly, organisations are at different stages of maturity and learning on sustainability and it is difficult to draw comparisons between them. The size, sector, location, and age of the organisation are all determining factors and will affect the level of exposure to new ideas and methods of working. Therefore, caution must be exercised when attempting to examine learning, innovation and cultural change across all types of organisation. It is however possible to describe in a little more depth the characteristics that reflect a 'learning company'.

### *A learning approach to informing organisational strategy*

It requires a concerted effort to develop a strong company policy and strategy geared towards the development of a learning environment. Implementation, evaluation and improvement need to be built into the strategy to ensure that the mechanisms for learning are being monitored and regularly re-assessed.

The water company, rapidly achieved a great deal by developing an intranet which housed an electronic directory of the environmental operational procedures. The company discovered that its intranet was an efficient, effective and accessible form of information, and provided a means of crosslinking. The result is that the intranet is now a normal, integrated part of day-to-day practices, and allows employees to develop a broader understanding of the environmental drive.

An environmental policy that is electronically accessible makes it easier to understand the relevance of specific standards, the implications of those standards and what is expected of the organisation. The annual report is available to all members of the organisation, but there is also a summary version on the intranet that makes information easily accessible. Unfortunately, due to a lack of resources, the company have been unable to quantify the use of the intranet, so although there have made great attempts to disseminate information, the company cannot yet measure the access or impact.

Learning, innovation and cultural change are not easily quantified and cannot be approached scientifically. A strategy needs to be developed that allows time for reflection and promotes an environment that is conducive to reassessment and change.

***Participative Policy-making***

All members of an organisation should be able to contribute to the processes of developing policies and forming strategies. Although it is vital to have strong leadership to drive the policy, it is also equally important to engage stakeholders. There is a movement away from the idea of stakeholder consultation as it is often treated as a token gesture where stakeholders are merely asked their opinion, without their views being incorporated into strategy or any thought being given to the long tern implications of such 'conversations'. In contrast, stakeholder engagement requires a proactive partnership approach on the part of the organisation.

Many organisations, including the car company, recognise the importance and value of stakeholder engagement, but recognise that this is still one of their weaker areas. In their case, the engagement so far has taken place in an unstructured form. Therefore a successful learning environment must allow for all members of the organisation to contribute to and shape policy decisions. By opening up discussions, there is inevitably going to be resistance to and tension on many issues. However, by debating the issues widely and thoroughly, it is possible for the majority of stakeholders to reach a workable business decision. The result is that all members can claim 'ownership' and feel greater commitment. Furthermore, it is important to note that there are certain requirements in terms of the attitude and responsibilities of management:

— there needs to be a realisation and understanding at higher levels of the organisation that all members of the organisation have the right to be engaged in the policy-making process;

— if the members of the organisation are fully engaged as stakeholders, it is inevitable that there will, at times, be a degree of conflict and tension that arises during the course of the policy-building process. However, the diversity of opinions is a valuable resource and can be channelled in a manner that leads to creativity, fresh ideas and innovative solutions. Therefore, managers need to be able to develop skills that enable them to manage the process and convert conflict into creativity;

— the fostering of an inclusive environment must be viewed as an investment. The water company has developed the Eureka Scheme, which encourages employees to put forward ideas that they believe would benefit the company; if the suggestion has a successful outcome, then the employee is rewarded. The (control) bank operates a similar scheme called the Brainwave Initiative.

### *Growth of information*

Some argue that information technology needs to be used to inform and empower people rather than to disempower them. Again it involves a shift in attitude at a management level. This involves making information widely available, disseminating information in order to promote understanding about the organisation's systems and processes. Therefore, appropriate information systems need to be in place to support such initiatives.

The water company find that it is not difficult to raise awareness about sustainability issues at the operational level, and the monthly team meetings are interactive rather than one-way team briefs. On the other hand, the company reported that it can be difficult to encourage all employees to use the intranet as sometimes they are simply not interested. This helpline has been in operation for one year and the company reports initially that it is becoming increasing popular as a means for employees to have an input into decision-making processes. However, there have been some concerns raised about the degree of confidentiality, and therefore the team meetings are being used to alleviate some of the suspicions.

Employees of the water company have specialisms but will all be aware of the environmental dimension of their work. Every second month there is a team briefing which highlights the environmental issues that affect the organisation, but also focuses on ways in which the employees can improve their environmental standards within the office. There is a newsletter and the intranet is considered to be a source that will provide answers for up to 90% of employees' questions. The bank also has a strong commitment to disseminating information and regards communication as being central to its business practice. It has well-established internal magazines and an intranet, with regular articles on the environment and society.

***Formative Accounting and Control***

Formative accounting needs to ensure that the systems of accounting, budgeting and reporting are structured to assist learning and innovation. This is important in terms of internal stakeholders' morale and sense of value. Accounting and budgeting are important areas that concern the shareholders, but if tied in with learning and innovation, can have dual benefits.

***Internal exchange***

Organisations need to foster working environments where individuals, groups, departments and divisions can engage in a regular dialogue with the aim of exchanging information on expectations, negotiating and providing feedback on issues. In large organisations, departments may be in competition with each other, which may promote hoarding rather than sharing of information. This calls for the development of ways to engender a more holistic approach to develop collaboration.

The water company found that being a relatively small company, of 1500 employees, the scope for communication and constructive dialogue is greater. They have also found, since moving to new premises which were built on sustainability principles, that sustainability has, to some extent, become a part of daily conversations. The award-winning premises have been built with sustainability to the fore. The features of the building include solar panels, natural ventilation, and facilities to recycle rainwater and grey water. Recycled and local materials have been used wherever possible, and there is a community room for use by schools and community groups.

### *Enabling structures*

Roles need to be fluid and loosely structured, in order to allow for growth and development. This is important, both for the well-being of the individual and for the organisation as a whole. The overlap of skills between individuals provides a pool of resources, but also a pool of creativity and innovation that is generated through critical mass. Where individuals are operating to specific context-bound remits, there is reduced scope for sharing ideas, which, in turn, stifles innovation and creativity.

The bank has shown itself to be proactive in this area and has embodied the change in work culture through its Project Leo. A survey of staff highlighted two key issues - they were keen to have wider roles and they wanted more responsibility. In response both to the surveys and market pressures, job descriptions have been loosened to the extent that 300 job descriptions have been reduced to 26 role statements. Moreover, the whole sample group of companies argued for an integrated approach that gives priority to innovation, learning and cultural change. They stressed that the drive needs to be a 'part of the business success model, in order for it to be institutionalised'. In the case of the bank, ethical practice has been incorporated within professionalism and is given the same attention at Board level as other issues.

The (control) water company has a firm commitment from the Managing Director who appointed an Environmental Director to the Board. The appointment signalled a broadening agenda and redistribution of priorities. The environmental policy was later adopted group-wide and had to be made compatible with all subsidiaries. There are similarities to the bank, in that a decision was taken that, rather than having strict job descriptions, which constrain learning potential, there should be a move towards roles that are more generic and based on tasks and targets. Currently, the company are trying to review the method of monitoring targets, as it has caused some problems. The bank has not moved too far away from the job descriptions approach, but find that the descriptions are framed more broadly in terms of key responsibilities and personal skills. This highlights the move away from rigid competencies. The employees also tend to work in teams, which allows for dialogue and sharing of information.

The airline is also a strong proponent of the value of teams, and more broadly the idea of decentralisation in the sense that each department is encouraged to develop a mission statement with objectives to define and steer their contribution. The organisation conducts an Employee Opinion Survey in which every member of staff completes a questionnaire covering issues relating to workplace, morale, role, objectives and managers. The survey is then followed up by an action plan, which is constructed by the department itself. The survey is one of the mechanisms used to monitor change over time.

### *Intra-company Learning*

Joint training, sharing in investment, research and development, and job exchanges can be excellent ways of pooling resources and learning from each other. Rather than fostering a 'hyper-competitive' environment that is based on a win-lose situation, a collaborative approach based on benchmarking can save on resources in the long-term - especially in larger organisations where there are a number of different companies.

The car company found it useful to undertake a SWOT (Strengths, Weaknesses, Opportunities and Threats) analysis across all 32 companies within the organisation in order to compare results. Internal benchmarking has been a useful tool given that they have been subject to acquisition in recent years. They have been able to learn from their parent company, though there have been differences in the terms used reflecting different entry points, a difference in culture and variations in language and connotation: for example, as mentioned earlier, the research company uses 'sustainability' to describe its current drive, whereas the parent company refers to it as 'corporate citizenship'.

### *Learning Climate*

Learning involves making mistakes, unlearning and relearning and this is a view that needs to be made clear throughout the organisation. Mistakes can take many forms, but Pedler, Burgoyne and Boydell argue that 'there's no such thing as a failed experiment - as long as we learn from it'. Learning, innovation, change and creativity are to some extent based on trial and error. There are certain processes that can create a more conducive environment, but to tailor the learning to a specific company there needs to be a degree of experimentation.

### *Personal self-development opportunities*

All stakeholders need to be encouraged to take responsibility for their own learning and development. However, it is the responsibility of management to provide guidance as well as the opportunity for selfdevelopment. The bank showed that it has made great progress in this direction and actively encourages employees to take ownership for their self-development. Pay rewards are also offered for external learning, which is considered to increase the capability of the individual as well as the organisation.

The bank maintained that learning is a valued part of its organisation and has even created a Corporate University, which supports e-learning and e-training, in addition to more formal methods. For example, in the year 2000, the bank invested £70 million in training across the entire organisation, equivalent to £890 per person. It stressed that all funded training must be specific to the employee's job. Professional exams are particularly encouraged.

***Some Lessons of Change***

There is a wealth of literature and research on organisational change and it is worth reflecting on some of the conclusions either before embarking on the process of embedding sustainability in organisations or to allay some of the frustrations of those already seeking to do so. Some suggests the following strategies for significant organisational change. Given the results of this and other research on sustainability in organisations it is clear that we may not be thinking strategically enough. The key points to emerge from the investigation are that organisations should:

— Expect a 3-5 year time frame;

— stress the importance of choice and symbolism for senior decision-makers, and therefore ownership at all levels;

— design outcome oriented working groups;

— vision to produce real-time strategic change;

— organisation development activities;

— coaching and monitoring;

— encourage and recognise 'Champions';

— set in place reward structures and systems;

— provide training & development;

— allocate budgets for innovation and adequate resource allocation;

— make identifiable links to core business;

— accept the grand strategy, but, remember 'local' flexibility.

### *Language of Sustainability*

The multitude of acronyms and codes relating to sustainability often places a barrier between management and the wider organisation maintaining the exclusive nature of debate. An increase in the flow of accessible knowledge will require a move away from the jargon that corporate social responsibility has been associated with. The subject is not, in fact, as inaccessible and unapproachable as it first seems, then the issues themselves may not be as complex as they appear.

At the same time, the discourse of sustainability conceals more than it reveals. Some argue that 'sustainable development' is ill-defined from the perspective of the individual corporation. No individual company can be 'sustainable' within an unsustainable economic system - so how are business people to interpret the far-reaching ideals of definitions of sustainable development such as that of the Brundtland Commission?'. Yet the terms are attributed boundaries, though these are as blurred as the terms themselves. However, this does not mean that such words do not carry specific meanings.

The use of language can be a means by which the subject area can be protected and therefore the larger organisations that have units dedicated to the issues are able to stay ahead. The fact that there is little public debate about the definition of these words means that individual companies may attribute their own unique interpretation.

The bank does not use the term 'sustainable development', but instead talks about 'environment and the society'. It has internalised many of the issues and does not actively seek certification to many of the recognised standards. It has decided that its preference is to deal with the environment and the society from its own resources, and it produces an environmental report part verified by the accountants Price Waterhouse Coopers. It also has internally set targets.

Qualitative change is more of a priority than quantitative measurement-focused strategies. Rather than focusing on standards, many of which are checklist in form, it puts greater emphasis on engaging employees in making cultural changes. Although the airline has taken on board a number of certification standards, there are also a number of international initiatives employed by the organisation that promote innovation. Discourse analysis highlights the fact that there is always the potential for diversity of meaning even in the case of the simplest word.

Similarly, sustainability can be, and often is, symbolic of a policy that is either perceived as an added obstacle in the path of business or as a means of contributing to positive change. To the newcomer, or the non-expert, the ambiguity surrounding sustainability means that the term is loaded with meanings.

## Home Versus Work Values

For any individual there may not be a constant set of values that feed into different areas of their lives. That is to say their approach to social and environmental responsibility is often embedded in a subconscious way in their activities at home, but they do not necessarily transfer these values into the workplace. The answer sometimes lies in the lack of empowerment in the workplace, or in the fact that values may not be explicit. If sustainability requires significant cultural change in organisations then organisations themselves have to focus on mechanisms to empower employees. These in turn may not have always felt that they have had a substantial stake in the organisation, its decision-making processes and the development of strategy.

Therefore in order to embed values that are compatible with sustainability, it is necessary to make employees feel that they have an element of ownership. The bank has been very keen to develop and promote shared ownership of its sustainability values. It considers small teams are pivotal in the building of partnerships within the organisation, so employees work in teams that are made up of clusters of three. The partnerships are not only seen to promote ownership, but also provide a manageable number to embed cultural change.

In addition to empowering employees, it is also necessary to consider the development of a process that makes sustainability values automatic rather than burden. It is useful to look to the socio-cognitive model of organisational culture advanced by Silvester, Anderson and Patterson who argue that culture and cultural change takes the form of a process whereby people understand events in terms of cause and effect relationships. It is believed that this is because they are motivated to understand why such events occur, predict when they might occur again and thus render their environment more controllable. Unless there is an element of control on the part of the employee, thought processes that determine reaction to circumstances will take a conscious form. When addressing the links between sustainability and innovation, learning and cultural change in organisations it is necessary to reinforce the codification.

Communication and cultural change Communication does, however, form one of the most critical dynamics in the process of cultural change. Philipsen regards culture as being a conversation and this is reinforced by Duck's view that culture is developed through the generation of shared meanings which comes about through communication between individuals. For this reason, the internal communication systems of organisations are crucial to the development of a culture based on sustainability.

The airline has a department with over 50 employees dealing with internal and external communications. The department operates a 'multi-level and multi-media' approach. Although sustainability appears at times to be a new and innovative concept, it is perhaps not radically different from the dilemmas faced by organisations in the past and therefore it is often the case that sustainability needs to be framed within different types of discourse. It may appear threatening because of the manner in which it is presented.

The water company have found that they are having to make a conscious change in the discourse according to the audience, and that the language used for those at a senior management level will be radically different to that used at the operational level. Sustainability has effectively to be normalised in order to become a daytoday issue.

## Realisation of the Business Value of Sustainable Development

The accountants, surveyed 481 environmental, health and safety, and other business executives in North America and Europe. In an attempt to gauge the views companies have of sustainable development, they sought to examine how widespread the concept actually was, and also the extent to which it was recognised as a 'route to creating business value'.

Ninety-five per cent of respondents agreed that sustainable development was important to their companies and 80% believed that their companies could derive real business value by implementing a strategy which was underpinned by sustainable development. However, there appeared to be an element of contradiction between the commitment of companies to sustainability and their commitment to make available resources for these processes. So there is a rhetoric of sustainability that is not always linked with the allocation time and money to the issue.

The same survey showed very different perceptions of what business values were to be gained from being 'sustainable'. In an open-ended question, over half of the respondents pinpointed eco-efficiency as the greatest benefit, and smaller numbers quoted improved external relations and competitive advantage.

Since it is difficult for companies to agree on what is to be gained from such an approach, it becomes problematic to develop a strategy for its promotion. Sustainability issues can most commonly be found under the banner of 'environmental concerns' and one of the greatest challenges is how to push it up the hierarchy to make it an integrated part of corporate strategy.

It is often the case that companies are willing to consider an approach to sustainable development, but search for immediate benefits that are both visible and provide financial gain. Yet the true benefit of sustainable development may not be seen in the lifetime of the majority of managers. Thus, one can begin to understand why it is difficult to promote such issues to senior management, who may feel direct pressure from shareholders to account for every aspect of an organisation's operation. The vast majority considered themselves to be at the stage of making some progress, but since the question was subjective it calls into question the validity of the interpretation.

Therefore it is no real surprise to find that the majority of companies responding felt that sustainable development was important, but this was as much based on the framing of the question as the issue itself. It has become politically incorrect to say that one is not in favour of sustainable development.

However, even the companies who considered themselves to be at the forefront of the sustainability movement sometimes confined their activities to the more traditional areas of action, such as pollution prevention, environmental auditing and energy efficiency. In contrast, full-cost accounting, industrial ecology and closed-loop systems received little exposure. Certainly, it is a great deal easier to manage a programme of pollution prevention, but the gains are limited. Dedicated strategies to foster organisational learning are not so easy to manage and quantify. If 'the crunch' may be 50 years off, companies ask themselves, why make space on today's already crowded agenda?.

Therefore, there needs to be a paradigm shift and reassessment of business priorities. This may require an element of visioning, in order to anticipate future scenarios - there needs to be some degree of long-term goal setting or projection that the entire organisation can be part of. Seventy five per cent of those questioned felt that their company's overall vision and strategy was in need of improvement. Where will a company have to make the most changes in order to implement a sustainable development approach throughout its organisation?'

If 75% of respondents pinpointed the company vision, then this response highlights the fact that a great deal of progress can be made with very little cost. Only 17% responded that their company should 'get out of a certain business'. The company vision serves a number of purposes, including being a driving force and a unifier. However, in organisations where sustainable development is driven by an individual, or a small group of members of the Board, there tends to be a gap between those with the vision and those who are working at the operational level or even within the middle management decision-making strata. The extent of the gap reveals the lack of integration of the concept of sustainability within organisations.

## Strategies for Incorporating Sustainable Development into Business Practice

### *Understanding the context of sustainable development*

It is necessary to develop an in-depth understanding of the broader context of sustainable development that goes beyond merely the organisation's impact on the local environment to a realisation of the impact of the industry at large and communities around the world. This can entail the organisation taking a disinterested view of itself, and reassessing what sustainable development means for the individual company.

### *The role of Strategy*

There needs to be a clear strategy that gives direction to the overall organisation and offers an inclusive and working vision, rather than a vague mission statement. This will not involve the imposition of radical new ideas, which are in fact a rarity, but existing strengths and strategies need to be harnessed and merely reshaped. There is no definitive system that can provide a single solution for organisations in their quest towards a more sustainable business practice, as the system needs to be tailored around internal strengths and weaknesses. Management consultants Arthur D. Little argued that, 'The path forward to sustainable development is likely to be different for different industries. Even industries such as chemicals and energy, which appear to share similar issues and experiences, treat the sustainable development challenge in quite different ways.

Furthermore, it is crucial to stress the fact that the internal dynamics of an organisation are always paramount, and that for cultural change to have longevity, one must work with the organisational personality. Change is best achieved when employees can relate to the processes at hand, while maintaining elements of familiarity is an important part of changing the culture.

### *Integrating Sustainable Development into Core Business Activities*

Sustainable development should be made part of the core business practice that builds on an organisation's strengths and reinforces the commitment of the movers and shakers. The process of learning, innovating and changing culture needs to be fairly fluid, since the strengths and values can change over time. Therefore it is imperative that flexibility is maintained and the vision is constantly reassessed. All employees, from the Board to operational level, should be fully aware of how the business value of sustainable development relates to their own concerns, responsibilities and sphere of influence.

One of the members of the control group and one of the SIGMA group make a concerted effort to focus on the tailoring of language to suit the audience. In the case of the control member, the management has made a conscious effort to avoid the sustainability discourse since they believe that it would alienate more than it would motivate. The issues of sustainable development are high on the agenda, but are couched in familiar terms.

### *Triggering Action*

Sustainable development must ultimately be about taking action rather than falling back on rhetoric. Action needs to be discussed through a process of stakeholder engagement and there needs to be mechanisms in place to monitor those actions.

## Sustainability and Innovation

Sustainable development will not happen without innovation. Furthermore, organisations can make a great deal of progress with minimal cost. New technologies and product design can certainly be an important part of striving towards sustainability, but these are only part of the solution. Rather, the alignment and motivation of staff towards a common goal can be achieved through less tangible means that address employees' attitude to their work, understanding of its impact and contribution to sustainability. This again reinforces the importance of employees having a sense of ownership of ideas. So if employees are given an opportunity to mould the sustainable development process, rather than having it forced on them, there is a greater possibility of being able to move the organisation as a more unified entity towards creating positive change in society an the environment.

The research conducted by Arthur D. Little suggest the following:

— Sustainable development provides an opportunity, and focus, to resuscitate or even re-think vision and strategy with a view to greater prosperity for all;

— Sustainable development also provides a driver for innovation - in processes, technologies and products to enhance competitiveness and business growth;

— Communication of sustainable development goals and activities is a powerful way to strengthen relationships with customers and suppliers.'

Clearly, innovation is not just about new products, but needs to be considered as a central part of business strategy and processes. Edwards highlights the fact that it is now more common to think of innovation as a 'dynamic, on-going process. Innovation and creativity can have a dramatic effect on the dynamics of an organisation and transform patterns of growth, income and competitive advantage. In addition to the working environment being conducive to innovation, there needs to be genuine commitment at all levels of the organisation.

## Theory and Adult Learning

A consideration of intertextuality and of reception theory can help to illuminate understanding of the adult student's relationships with reading. Theories of intertextuality insist that texts are not selfcontained systems. They incorporate other texts -those the writer has read and those the reader has read. Such theories may concern themselves with a text's relationship with other written texts; they may also define texts more widely, suggesting that, "at the very least - the 'textual' and the 'extra-textual' inhabit each other, or that - more radically - the 'extra- textual' is another kind of text".

Reception theory takes up a range of positions from the extreme subjectivity of Holland's argument, that reading is primarily a recreation of the reader's own identity, to those which admit the rhetorical and affective properties of texts. Iser distinguishes between the artistic text, that created by the author, and the aesthetic text, its realisation by the reader. He draws attention to the fact that texts are never complete in themselves but consist of pauses, spaces and gaps which require completion by the reader who must make connections and bring aspects of her/his own experience to the act of reading. For Iser a literary text is a "gestalt" produced by the reader's active striving to make something coherent from the words. Some introduces the importance of context, which always restricts the possibilities for reading without absolutely determining them. He identifies the existence of shared, but not monolithic or stable rules for interpretation and this allows for the influence of history and culture in shaping interpretation.

The literary repertoire of the text consists of factors such as form, plot and characterisation; its structural and rhetorical properties in effect. Its general repertoire is composed of the morals, ideas, values and beliefs to which it refers and which help to construct it. The text's repertoires are not static, but shift in relation to the reading context. Readers also have repertoires and are "inhabitants of particular sociocultural formations, with particular literary and general ideologies, who appropriate from their society, both consciously and unconsciously, their own particular repertoires".

These theoretical frameworks suggest, therefore, that students' relationships with reading will be shaped by their cultural, social and personal experiences, inseparable from their sense of subjectivity and social belonging. The constructivist approach taken by reception critics and by explorations of intertextuality is compatible with Freire's writings on liberatory education. Reception criticism insists that reading is a creative process. Freire promotes a pedagogy which encourages learners to create their own worlds rather than to receive them ready made.

This is precisely what happens when students are encouraged to recognise their active roles as readers, rather than to absorb a static and idealised text supposedly representing the author's consciousness. Moreover, Freire sees people's engagement with popular culture as "an integral part of the culture of resistance" and emphases on the active reader are particularly significant when thinking about popular culture, so often presented as a powerful, brainwashing phenomenon. Freire's ideas about the use of "generative themes" in education lend themselves readily to a reflexive, intertextual engagement with popular texts. If teachers and students can identify the "generative themes" which permeate students' lives, then these can be studied through the concrete examples of cultural products.

Those explorations can be used to develop a critical and creative consciousness. Similarly, it is possible to connect adult education work on transformative learning with intertextual approaches to textual study. Once the reflexive nature of the reading process is accepted, the potential of literature as a transformative educational medium is clarified. It has the capacity to introduce the reader to "disorienting dilemmas" in the form of concrete literary examples. These dilemmas are understood intertextually, are interpreted reflexively in terms of the students' own life experiences and consequently the exploration has the potential to challenge existing meaning perspectives and promote transformation.

### *Broad Societal Changes and a Shift to the Right*

Notwithstanding the undeniable importance, and perhaps inevitability of this shift, there were also losses in the move toward system building from the era of the Great Society to that of the neoliberalism of the Clinton era, with the Reagan

"Revolution" of the 1980s serving the role of midwife. As part of this ideological movement to the right among Republicans and Democrats, the conceptual shift from campaign to system paralleled the rise of ABE as a distinctive field linked to human capital development. This, in turn, exacerbated the marginalization of adult literacy as a separate entity, never securely grounded in federal policy, based on an ethos of localism, community development, and an instructional program geared to the self-identified needs of students, themselves, whether as community members or individuals.

This shift was part of the cost and an aspect of broader historical trends in moving from campaign to system during the last four decades of the twentieth century. "Global economic restructuring," or the transition from manufacturing to information in the emergence of the post-industrial society is the predominant socio-economic transformation that accompanied the shift from campaign to system. The need to retool a largely unprepared workforce for the informational era "required a level of literacy which had never before been demanded of the blue collar workforce". Reports like Workforce 2000 and Jump Start depicted the new need cast in dire forecast through an aura of demographic inevitability.

The articulation of such problems served as the impetus that galvanized the business community to focus on adult literacy as a way of meeting their human resource needs, if not of the immediate present, than of the near future, to an almost certainty. However, "[a]s concerns about the skills of the workforce grew, preparation for employment became ever more explicitly the primary purpose of education" at all levels. As Merrifield put it, "[t]he customers of adult education began to be defined as employers, interested in the 'product' of skilled employees".

Merrifield identified related social changes from the 60s to the 90s in the increase of rural and inner-city poverty, a widening gap between the wealthy and the poor, and a new wave of immigration, largely from Southeast Asia and Central

America. In response to these socio-economic trends, policymakers began to focus on whether "participating in adult education help[s] people get a job, get off welfare, get off crime".

This narrowing of focus linked largely to human capital development, fighting crime, and welfare reform, is part of the historical shift from the so-called campaigns of the 60s to the system building of the 90s. Within such a context, "accountability" became linked with what government could obtain for its "investment" in ABE/adult literacy in reducing "social problems like unemployment, crime, drug abuse".

## Reinventing Government

The emphasis on "performance accountability" was also a product of "reinventing government" initiatives largely through the appropriation of business metaphors. Thus, through the Government Performance and Results Act of 1993 performance accountability terminology became couched in such language as "'customer,' 'results,' 'efficiency,' 'return on investment'" , with requirements for "federal agencies to clearly define their missions and to establish long-term strategic goals, as well as annual goals". Meanwhile, budget deficits and taxpayers revolts shifted the focus "to downsize government, and also to end the social support system created in the Great Society legislation of the 1960s.

Amendments in federal adult education legislation in the 1980s and 1990s emphasized job training and welfare reform and "de facto have established new purposes and rationales for adult literacy education, dominated by preparing low-income adults for work". In short, as part of the shift from campaign to system, the federal government has significantly cut its proportion of per capita spending for adult education compared to state spending. It has also tightened procedures for accountability, drawing on business language and concepts for its modeling of good programming, and narrowed the focus on what is defined as legitimate purposes for adult education, drawing largely on the "deficiency" model of adult literacy.

The political culture, including the Democratic Party, has moved considerably to the right since the social reform era of the New Frontier and the Great Society. However, the technocratic persuasion of the "best and the brightest", clearly in the ascendancy in our current, post-industrial era, was also a critical feature of political life in the 1960s.

### *A Nation at Risk*

Merrifield points to similar changes in the educational system. The 1983 Nation at Risk policy document linked public education, and the concept of "excellence" to "employers needs for skilled workers" in the emerging post-industrial economy. This was accompanied by a 'back to basics' movement in K-12 education" and reform initiatives stemming not from educators, but from state legislators and governors. The impetus was the perceived informational needs of preparing future employees to meet the challenges of the new economic order. The importance of "accountability" and a renewed emphasis on standardized testing was a central part of this reform initiative.

Although not specifically stated in "Contested Ground," the recognition within the political culture of a broad-based attack on progressive education is clearly present in Merrifield's policy report as subtext. This was led not only by conservative and moderate Republicans, but by "new" Democrats, too, who began to stress "competence over ideology" for the sake of linking education to the perceived needs of the national interest. As put by Shapiro, neoliberal Democrats like their Republican counterparts, emphasized "high technology, economic competitiveness, and human capital formation through education," though, like their liberal predecessors, also remained committed "to redress the deepening problems of poverty and inequity in American society". However, the extent to which they could balance these two tendencies particularly over such issues as NAFTA, welfare reform, reinventing government, and "investment" in education was not always clear.

Merrifield does not quite come out and say this in "Contested Ground," but it is evident from Life at the Margins that any 21st century policy on adult literacy needs to be premised on the theoretical assumptions and best practices of what she refers to as the New Literacy Studies. The core tension between current policy and Merrifield's vision is partially manifested in the policy requirement of standardized and quantifiable forms of measurement, juxtaposed against the quest of grounding "performance accountability" in qualitative terms based on the actual needs of adult learners as defined by them. What concerns Merrifield is the static understanding of adult literacy upon which standardized tests are based.

The Comprehensive Adult Student Assessment System (CASAS) and the 1975 Adult Performance level (APL) study upon which it was based, do focus on perceived "functional" needs of adults with low levels of literacy mastery and are therefore linked in certain ways with "real-life" learning. Yet they are premised on the mastery of discrete "tasks" that often ignore the more dynamic interaction between the world of print and the lives of adults that a more complex understanding of literacy as practices would illuminate.

Merrifield is also concerned about the deficit model of literacy upon which the APL and CASAS are based though she ruefully acknowledges the widespread use of CASAS, of which she is critical, to buttress state-wide competency-based assessment systems in several states. As she puts it, "competing concepts of literacy -as skills or competencies and as social practices [which she favors] -are at the heart of what performance means". What is troubling about this conflict for Merrifield is that the more complex understanding of adult literacy upon which the New Literacy Studies are premised has little current standing in contemporary policy initiatives.

What Merrified critiques is public policy based upon a "view of literacy, as a discrete and fixed set of skills, transferable to one context to another, from which economic and social development automatically follow." From this perspective, "[t]he social impacts of literacy appear to be the guiding purpose for public investment in literacy education" that from Merrifield's view is not a direct outcome of such work.

While a sophisticated understanding of literacy has emerged with the New Literacy Studies, dominant social, economic and political trends from the 1960s to the 1990s mitigate against any broad-based policy orientation premised on such a framework. At stake is not merely "contested ground" in the uneven struggle for power, knowledge, and influence, but whether or not a dynamic consensus linking sound theory and practice to policy can at all emerge in the current political, social, and economic climate.

## Unpacking Terms

Accountability and Performance, deals with the thorny issue of mediating the expectations of the various stakeholders of adult literacy education. Central to this discussion is the issue of "value" in that accountability inevitably points to the purpose of adult education as articulated by the various stakeholders. Acknowledging conflicting views and purposes among them, Merrifield calls for the differences over accountability to be "negotiated," notwithstanding significant differentials of power and epistemological assumptions among the various groups that comprise the constituency of adult literacy education.

### *Dilemmas of Mutual Accountability*

Notwithstanding her praxeological quest for an emergent consensus based upon inclusiveness and "mutual accountability," Merrifield's critique of the politics of literacy that drives the current adult basic education system is somewhat muted. However, she does critically point to the difference in terminology between "stakeholder" in referring to funders, taxpayers, employers, and state agencies while "[d]escribing learners as participants or customers" in effect, as "clients."

In addition, she points out that "different groups of stakeholders may have different interests and informational needs" that require negotiation through dialogue in the development of any comprehensive accountability system. She seeks a framework for accountability that both supports student learning goals on an individual basis as well as the interests of the financial supporters of adult literacy to demonstrate more system-wide efficacy.

As she puts it, "[f]or performance accountability, responsibility to students for learning achievement needs to be combined with clarity and rigor in establishing goals and outcomes, documenting achievements, and reporting". However, the issue is not only the need for additional rigor. It is as she elsewhere points out, different value systems that ground the motivation and expectations of individual students and practitioners often against those representing corporate and governmental interests of elites, who shape policy mandates by providing the basic financial support to the system.

Moreover, despite her critique of top-down perspectives, the stakeholders upon whom she concentrates, "leaders, policymakers and researchers" carry considerable weight in "Contested Ground." In fact the actual voices of students and front line program staff are marginal to "Contested Ground," though at least the voices of students permeate Life at the Margins. This in itself is an interesting peculiarity of the policy study genre, a far from neutral literary artifact. Merrifield identifies the capitalist metaphor of "return on investment" in reporting to funders, "clearly the primary purpose on the minds of state directors right now" as the most important rational for "performance accountability."

Such investment is framed on "what difference adult education makes in society" largely based on the deficit model of adult literacy that Merrifield clearly rejects though she does not powerfully level as immanent critique at this juncture in the text. In addition to "investment," although clearly related, these groups also draw at least on the imagery of "performance accountability" as a "[t]ool to sort out 'good' programs from 'bad,' -...particularly important for state directors, who often find they have less power than they would like to weed out bad programs from good, when state political relations are at stake".

Despite her use of scare quotes there is no discussion or analysis at this point of what state directors meant by "good" or "bad" programming. However, one suspects that what is valued among the top-down groups upon whom Merrifield focuses is programming that conforms to policy mandates which often conflict as she well knows, with other perceptions of effective programming identified by other stakeholders. As Merrifield wryly puts it, though, "[n]ot all purposes can be met at once, and not all require the same measurement, data, or reporting".

More importantly, not all purposes for "performance accountability" among all the groups of stakeholders that comprise the adult literacy constituency can be epistemologically or politically squared. This is the more fundamental issue that is muted at this point in Merrifield's discussion, though it can be elsewhere teased out in "Contested Ground" and is surely evident in Life at the Margins. While not explicitly critiquing the views expressed above, Merrifield does level an implicit criticism in the paragraph that follows the discussion of the views of the literacy policy elite. As she puts it:

A focus on educational improvement challenges a powerful, but outmoded metaphor for performance accountability borrowed from industry: the production line. The dominant metaphor in measuring results portrays adult education as a production process, with adult learners rolling off the end of the line, equipped with certain skills and knowledge which can be tested and reported in the same way that businesses make sure that widgets coming off the production line meet specifications.

Logically, this perspective challenges positivistic assumptions such as those that comprise the Workforce Investment Act and the National Reporting System which assume that direct and quantifiable relationships can be made for example, between hours of instruction and "measurable" learning gains. Such a view could be read as a fundamental critique of the dominant policy perspective, though Merrifield does not directly connect the analysis to the expressed views of the policy elite. She does not do so, one suspects, because the literary genre of her "report," requires a guise of neutrality which belies the view and tone assumed in Life at the Margins.

Critique of the dominant view is subliminally expressed within "Contested Ground," but not in a frontal criticism against current policy perspectives. Rather, her critical subtext grounded in the perspective of the New Literacy Studies, seeps through the pages of this NCSALL report, but it is subtle and needs to be carefully teased out.

## Total Quality Management

One of the key areas that Merrifield draws on to forge a consensus is humanistic management thought, particularly Total Quality Management (TQM) which, though far from neglectful of outcome assessment "is much more comprehensive and process oriented". TQM focuses more on development, which is largely missing in the current quantitative outcome driven adult education system. In TQM the primary emphasis is on "continuous improvement where workers themselves monitor "inputs and outputs, how a process is working, assessing quality, and evaluating production". Merrifield points out that "TQM is concerned with accountability, but above all with quality". She quotes Sondra Stein, currently National Institute for Literacy (NIFL) Director for the Equipped for the Future (EFF) project, for further support on the potential importance of TQM for the field of adult literacy.

TQM's approach to quality is based on the recognition that achieving quality is not magic: rather, it is a direct result of the conditions, the processes and structures that make up the "production process." Therefore, by paying careful attention to each step of the process, and analyzing it to see how it facilitates or impedes the process, contributes to or interferes with quality, an organization can have a powerful impact on increasing quality.

Merrifield also points to the burgeoning literature on the "learning organization" which "facilitates the learning of all its members and continuously transforms itself. As Merrifield puts it, in the learning organization, "learning, not just by individuals, but by the organization as a whole, is a way of responding to changing environments and multiple demands". Such learning is the antithesis of bureaucracy and requires a high level of trust and commitment among all the stakeholders in pursuit of a common vision. It is anything but squared with top-down policy mandates like the NRS supported by the State Directors of Adult Education.

Rather, for consensus to emerge based upon the precepts of TQM and literature grounded in the "learning organization," federal and state government will require a shift in its role from enforcer to that of participant in the development of an ABE/adult literacy system based on mutual accountability and negotiation. Obviously policy only receives its legal status through government, but the manner by which it emerges and mechanisms of evaluation, in principle, are open to a wide array of developments that may prove more, rather than less, democratic in the participatory sense. The extent to which current policy mandates circumscribe further development of the ABE/adult literacy system is a large issue that receives little direct examination in "Contested Ground," though the subtext bristles with critical commentary.

## Impact of the Workforce Investment Act

Although "Contested Ground" was written before the enactment of the Workforce Investment Act and the accompanying National Reporting System, in her discussion of performance accountability initiatives, Merrifield traces back to the National Literacy Act of 1991, key steps that led up to its passage in 1997. She identifies the program quality indicators developed by the U.S. Department of Education in 1992 in which by 1996, they had "become the guiding framework for states in their efforts to define program quality and to hold programs accountable".

The quality indicators, which guided policy throughout the mid-90s, became increasingly diminished with the passage of the WIA, which has its own set of "uniform" criteria. Merrifield points out that "there are no requirements for states to report their indicator measures or standards to the federal government" and therefore, little power of enforcement.

Also, given the importance of performance outcomes, the quality indicators were limited, on her interpretation, because they focused primarily on process. Yet, in such a marginal system as ABE with scant resources, the quality indicators point to important aspects of program development such as educational gains, program planning, curriculum development and instruction, staff development, support services, recruitment, and retention that could provide a broad framework for coherent system reconstruction. Such would be particularly the case if the emphasis were more on the framework the quality indicators provide rather on enforcement and legal sanctions as pervasive within the WIA legislation.

Merrifield states that "[p]rogram quality efforts are just a first step toward performance accountability". The concern, though, is that with the current emphasis on "performance accountability" based upon the "standardized, measurable, and objective" criteria set by the NRS, any emphasis on programs struggling with quality indicators or other complex form of measurement, will be marginalized. This is so due to the effort required to adhere to the new standards that have emerged through a top-down process and mandated upon the system rather than worked out in dialogue with the broad constituency that comprises the field of adult literacy education. In short, talk of quality indicators has gone out of fashion with the increased focus on performance outcomes.

A similar dilemma faces programs seeking to develop performance accountability measurements based on the National Institute for Literacy's Equipped for the Future (EFF) project while also building capacity to meet the requirements of the NRS if they desire to qualify for federal funding. The WIA allows EFF standards to count as "secondary measures." However these do not meet the requirements of the reporting system for "a uniform set of quantitative measures" designed to illuminate direct correlations between certain inputs of instructional hours and direct learning gains based upon standardized criteria of objective measurement upon which Merrifield puts little stock.

Finally Merrifield points to the "seven categories of outcome measures" that the state directors of adult education agreed upon as the criteria for evaluating a program's effectiveness: "economic impact, credentials, learning gains, family impact, further education and training, community impact, customer satisfaction. Depending on the construction of the evaluation framework, such categories could correlate with the EFF standards, for example.

The latter focus more on process or how adults learn, though closely linked to the specific "role maps" of worker, citizen and family member. However, given the normative assumptions of assessment for "uniform" measurement based upon the positivistic assumption of "objectivity," neither the Office of Vocational and Adult Education nor the state directors of adult education were inclined to move toward any complex qualitative design as implied in the EFF standards. In any event, the NRS train was well underway by then with the emphasis on quantifiable, measurable standards that directly link the inputs of education to the desired social outcomes.

## Conflicting Perspectives on Literacy

Merrifield concludes different view of literacy through which she levels her immanent critique against the dominant system, though in a somewhat muted way. Specifically, she contrasts the concept of "literacy as competency" that dominates policy perspectives with the concept of "literacy as social and cultural practices," the position she favors.

She points to the Adult Performance Level (APL) study and to the Comprehensive Adult Student Assessment System (CASAS), as prime examples of the literacy as competency perspective. These complementary frameworks laid the groundwork for the competencybased movement in adult basic education and made an important contribution in shifting focus away from a school-based approach that defined literacy as merely the mastery of decontextual reading skills to the attainment of "tasks related to everyday life".

The more recently developed National Adult Literacy Survey (NALS) also draws on the literacy as competency thesis. From this perspective "literacy is [viewed as] a technical skill which is transferable to multiple contexts, and that a single set of competencies can be defined". These various approaches assume: that competencies can be measured in formal tests, and that there is an equivalence between how well a person completes the pencil and paper test and his or her ability to perform a task in real life. And finally, it assumes that the tasks chosen for the test are both important to everyone and can be accomplished in only one way.

The competency-based approach also "assume[s] that knowing how well someone reads tells us something about how they carry on the rest of their lives", in short, they point to a one-to-one correspondence between their mastery and adult functioning, a position rejected by Merrifield. As she puts it, "[p]erhaps the central issue is who decides what is competence, and who chooses the tasks".

For Merrifield, it is clear that such activity lay with the adult literacy learners rather than the specialists who developed the various competency-based assessment formats. While she assumes this position, she does not strenuously advocate for it in "Contested Ground." Yet it is clear in Literacy at the Margins that what is particularly troubling for Merrifield is the linkage of competency-based adult basic education to the deficit model of adult literacy in which the fundamental problem is that learners are lacking in certain cognitive ability or "survival" skills.

As she and her colleagues put it, "many people who perform below targeted levels for 'functional literacy' may nevertheless be functioning adequately, or to their own satisfaction in their everyday lives". Commenting further they state that: Proponents of the idea of functional literacy assume a direct connection between the ability to interpret text in a life-skill task and the ability to perform that task in real life. Our profiles suggest that equating literacy with everyday life may be too simple. Although we are a print-based society, there are many ways of accomplishing life tasks effectively. The people we profile are very 'functional.' They pay taxes, hold jobs, may own homes, pay rent on time, shop, raise children, and are generally good citizens (though they seldom vote. Their literacy and learning strategies demonstrate how they function with limited literacy.

This hard-hitting critique against the epistemological assumptions of competency-based education that there is a direct correlation between literacy development and social functioning is present though muted in "Contested Ground." A probing of the NCSALL policy report requires a coming to terms with Merrifield's critical subtext expressed more fully in Literacy at the Margins.

Merrifield's views are most explicitly presented through her discussion of "literacy as social and cultural practices." The core assumption of the New Literacy Studies is that the role of literacy in facilitating social and personal goals is contextual to the specific individual or group of individual involved. Central from this perspective, are the social contexts in which literacy and language are embedded and their specific roles in mediating those contexts, in which the impact of literacy may be central or peripheral.

On this interpretation, literacy is a contextually grounded intervening variable rather than a "technical skill, which once acquired can be applied to many different tasks". The advocates of the New Literacy Studies identify many "literacies" rather than a singular literacy that apply to the various social contexts wherein individuals mediate print in relationship to various social behavior and attitudes.

As Merrifield puts it, "[r]eading has no meaning unless we say who is reading in what setting, and for what purpose -we have to separate the medium from the message (meaning)" as well as to discern their relationship. In her discussion of the New Literacy Studies, Merrifield distinguishes between "literacy practices," "literacy events," and "domains." Literacy practices refer to the "'[g]eneral cultural ways of utilizing literacy' that people draw upon in the varied contexts in which they live their lives-s c hool, work, home, social groups, neighborhoods" Literacy practices are linked to power relationships and to values as well as behavior. They are the practices where the text meets the world that people engage in during their everyday lives and they are quite varied. Literacy events refer to the specific reading tasks in which individuals engage during the course of their everyday lives such as a job manual, a newspaper, a food package, a note from school, or a magazine article.

Domains refer to "the broad contexts of life in which we operate", the key social environments that give shape to our lives, whether the home, the workplace, or a neighborhood or community setting. Each of these domains are "shaped by the broader culture and by class, gender, ethnicity, and regional variations". It is from these broad cultural environments that the notion of "multi-literacies" arises to help explain the relationship between the realm of print within them and the social contexts in which they are embedded.

# 8

# Challenges of Global Cultural Differences

The reality of global cultural difference challenges the goal of creating an integrated world trading system based on common rules and norms. For advocates of trade liberalization, as represented by the expansive, post-Uruguay Round trade agenda, global cultural diversity represents an irritating distraction on the road to a rationally organized world economy. For opponents of globalization, the perceived threat to the global diversity of values and practices represents one of the great dangers of the policies animating the World Trade Organization (WTO).

The potential conflict of culture and trade takes numerous forms. The principle of non-discrimination, fundamental to WTO procedures, is challenged by the problem of maintaining "a common set of rules among countries with quite different cultural, social, and political systems". As trade policy expands from rules governing goods to a broader agenda, it increasingly intrudes on domestic policy and values. Rules governing labor mobility, market access, intellectual property rights, and corporate governance are four areas with important implications for domestic cultural principles and preferences.

Trade practices are increasingly contested on ethical grounds, often reflecting the clash of cultural principles.

Examples include controversies over animal rights, child labor, and environmental protection. Moreover, "culture" and similar terms are invoked with increasing frequency to justify departures from liberal trade: as in Japanese rules limiting practice by foreign attorneys; in French defense of farm subsidies as a means of preserving rural social life; or in Saudi opposition to foreign investment in the insurance sector.

Trade theory has considered many causes for resistance to trade liberalization. Much of this literature has examined why trade liberalization efforts proceed gradually rather than all at once. Some of these papers focus on adjustment costs in the form of reduced wages, and increases in sectoral unemployment. Yet the economic analysis of trade liberalization has largely ignored formal modeling of cultural factors, despite the fact that national cultural differences form an inescapable aspect of the global economic system. Some exceptions have begun to appear in print.

Asserting cultural difference has become an increasingly common vehicle for challenging dominant policies and institutions, including a liberal international trading system. Such claims reflect our assumptions regarding the nature of culture, notoriously one of the most complex concepts in the lexicon of social theory. In the most abstract sense culture describes a system of understandings through which social life is transacted. But culture exists in and through distinctive contexts-particular places, times, and social groupings-producing "bounded and localized system[s] of meanings". In western Europe and North America, such local systems of meaning dictate that traffic proceeds on the right; that employment opportunities should be gender-blind; and that consumption should be maximized.

This usage, broadly representative of anthropological theory, contrasts with another: culture as a society's intellectual and artistic achievements, a usage alive and well in economics. In the latter sense, culture involves "activities drawing upon the enlightenment and education of the mind rather than the acquisition of purely technical or vocational skills". Relative to the broader, anthropological usage, this is both highly restrictive and highly commodified. From this follows the notion of cultural industries, including cinema, ballet, book and magazine publishing, and the like.

Operating within a cultural system thus constitutes a type of bounded rationality. Choice under cultural constraint remains nonetheless a rational procedure: "the realism injected by bounded rationality does not alter the essentially rational nature of Homo Economicus; it merely redefines the boundaries of rationality".

Thus a religiously observant Muslim banker acts rationally in avoiding transactions involving payments of interest, given the prohibition on interest in Islamic law. He maximizes utility within what is possible, usually by having the lender share in the risk of a borrower's investment, so that the rate of return is not fixed in advance. Similarly, because it is prohibited in the Torah, an Orthodox Jew will not shift her diet choices from beef to pork, regardless of how low the price of pork may fall. Her marginal rate of substitution of pork for beef remains zero.

The decision of a Muslim to refuse interest-based transactions, or for a Jew to observe kosher diet rules, reflects social norms, rather than individual preferences. Each decision is derived from publicly recognized principles that define the scope of permissible action. A cultural system is not merely constraining, but also constitutive, akin to the system of rules that establishes an exercise in game theory. Without such rules, there is no game.

## A Trade Model

This model will later be altered in two distinct ways to incorporate cultural aspects. The model is a factor-proportions trade model in a small open economy producing two goods using two factors of production. Production exhibits constant returns to scale in capital and labor and can be described with a Cobb-Douglas production function.

$$S_A\ (L_{A'}\ K_A)\ L_A^{\ a}\ K_A^{\ 1-a}$$

$$S_B\ S_B\ (L_{B'}\ K_B)\ L_B^{\ \beta}\ K_B^{\ 1-\alpha}$$

Here $S_A$ is the supply of good A, $L_A$ and $K_A$ are labor and capital used in A, and a is the share of labor used in A production. Similarly $S_{B'}$ $L_{B'}$ $K_B$ and b are the counterparts in good B production. That $\alpha < \beta$ which will make good A capital- intensive and good B labor-intensive. Full employment of capital and labor is maintained throughout. The world price of good A, in terms of the numeraire good B is given by $p_w$ and that the world price is such that the country would import good A in free trade. It will be useful to describe the model as a sequence of events in two stages. The first stage is a historical period establishing initial conditions. The second stage is a period of trade reform.

In the historical stage, a protective, non-prohibitive tariff, t, is in place on imports of good A. Profit maximization by all perfectly competitive firms in each industry assures that labor and capital is allocated to its most efficient usage between A and B production based on the domestic price $P_D = (1 + t)P_w$. All workers and capital owners are paid the value of their marginal products. The exogenous world price also assures that outputs are uniquely determined with the above information.

Demand for goods A and B is represented by a community-wide utility function that is Cobb-Douglas in form, given by,

$$U(C_{A'}\ C_B) = C_A^{\ a}\ C_B^{\ 1-a}$$

where U is the utility, $C_A$ and $C_B$ are total demands for goods A and B respectively, and $\gamma$ is the share of income spent on good A. In the aggregate, utility maximization implies that the marginal rate of substitution in consumption must equal the domestic price ratio. Finally the assumption of balanced trade completes the equilibrium conditions. All workers and capital are homogeneous and that an interior trading equilibrium is achieved. Therefore in equilibrium, workers receive the same wage and capital owners receive the same rents in both industries. We'll assume parameters such that an interior solution is achieved with positive production of both goods occurring with capital and labor allocated between the two industries.

### *Model Variation 1: Cultural Affinity of Work*

#### *a) Non-Pecuniary Cultural Benefits*

The existence of a non-pecuniary cultural benefit for workers in the import-competing sector of the labor market, and examine its effect on worker mobility when a decrease in trade protection yields falling wages. Labor economics has long recognized that a decision to accept employment or to remain employed is determined by more than the respective wages offered by alternative firms and industries in a worker's job choice set.

Because employment information and worker mobility are neither perfect nor costless, short-run labor markets may diverge from long-run equilibrium conditions. Beyond these factors lies a range of intangible influences on job choice, conventionally termed psychic or non-pecuniary benefits.

Monastic labor, as seen in Catholicism's Benedictine Order, offers an extreme example of the importance of non-pecuniary benefits. The very considerable labor that is entailed in monastic life is not directly compensated: material simplicity is the norm. From the perspective of monastic culture, work itself has positive utility, one element in a mode of life intended to bring an individual closer to God. In the words of an early monastic text, "I go to the place where labour is, and labour becometh unto me a pleasure".

It is not the activity per se that generates the psychic benefit found in monastic labor-otherwise, all farming, book binding, and teaching would be compensated at the minimal levels of food and shelter found in monastic households. Rather, the non-pecuniary benefits accrue from the work performed in the cultural context of monastic life: the utility of labor is at least in part culturally mediated. This is not a new idea. As Lester Thurow noted, "In a society where many people place a high premium on 'machismo,' a job with high physical risks may be considered a better job than a job with low physical risks".

The types of cultural values suggested by Thurow can be expected to influence job choice in all relevant occupations across the labor market. But because such effects are not sector-specific, they are unlikely to affect the patterns of economic adjustment that would be encountered by import-competing industries facing trade liberalization. Cultural effect on job choice, one that reflects the intrinsic attributes of a particular economic sector, which the term non-pecuniary cultural benefits (NPCBs).

NPCBs can originate in at least two ways. First, following the analyses of Keat and MacIntyre, work may provide psychic benefit directly by the opportunity to achieve excellence in a culturally salient activity: scientific discovery in biomedical research; athletic achievement in baseball; artistic accomplishment in jazz piano. Second, work may generate psychic benefit indirectly, by involvement in a valued, culturally distinctive social system integrating work and community. Under the rubric of "the multifunctional character of agriculture," the European Union now asserts the importance of a range of public goods agriculture provides: distinctive rural landscapes, biodiversity, and the viability of rural social life. Similarly, American timber workers discuss the value of their work not so much in terms of the intrinsic satisfaction of their dangerous and physically demanding jobs, but the benefits they experience from living in rural, forestry-based communities. The two sets of benefits are not mutually exclusive. Both types of sector-specific cultural benefits affect the demand for employment in such sectors, and thereby the impacts of changing wages in import competing sectors produced through trade liberalization.

*b) Cultural Affinity Model*

To model this effect assume that the NPCB is exogenous and fixed in value. Without loss in generality, also assume that the cultural benefit arises only for workers in the import-competing industry. With the NPCB included, the utility function for workers in the import-competing sector is rewritten as,

$$C_{LA}\,(C_B^{\,LA}, C_B^{\,LA}) = C_B^{\,LA})^a(C_B^{\,LA})^{1-a}+N_A$$

where $U_{LA}$ is the utility of a representative worker in industry A, and $N_A$ is the nonpecuniary cultural benefit that accrues to this worker when he or she works in industry A. This benefit disappears if the worker switches employment to the B industry. The effect of the cultural benefit is to raise utility of workers above the level attained by workers in industry B. Even though workers in each industry make the same wage, the benefit $N_A$ accrues to A workers but not to B workers. Furthermore, workers in B have no incentive to switch to A, since, having no history working in A, they would not receive the cultural benefit. This implies that the development of cultural sentiments in A, i.e., an increase in the value of $N_A$ over time, will not upset the initial equilibrium. Since in the historical period, workers in both industries received the same wage, an escalating cultural benefit over time raises worker A utility above that of workers in B. This extra benefit corresponds to a non-pecuniary rent.

*Trade Liberalization with Cultural Resistance*

Next imagine that trade liberalization is achieved with a

reduction in the tariff on good A imports. The tariff reduction will lower the domestic price of good A. The immediate effect, before any adjustment occurs, is to lower revenue and thus profit in industry A while raising profit in B. Higher profit in B will result in an increase in wages and rents, whereas in industry A, factor prices will begin to fall. These differences will inspire a shift of capital from A to B, but not labor. Although a worker in A can now receive a higher wage in B, this wage initially will not be sufficient to compensate for the non-pecuniary cultural benefit received by staying in industry A.

This means that in the early stages of trade liberalization, capital will adjust between industries but labor will remain fixed. This is identical to a specific factors model with labor as the specific factor and capital the freely mobile factor. As is well-known from that model, trade liberalization will raise the real return to the factor specific to the expanding industry and lower the returns to the factor specific to the contracting industry.

The real effects on the mobile factor, capital, will be ambiguous. However, the country is labor abundant, the nominal return to capital will fall as adjustment occurs. As the tariff on imports is reduced further, workers will remain in industry A until the utility of working in B at a higher wage finally equals the utility of remaining in industry A.

*National Welfare Effects*

This model is to compare the overall national gains from trade that accrue with and without a cultural affinity effect. The increase in national welfare from trade liberalization within the simulation, with the cultural affinity and without, is shown in In the absence of a NPCB, it is well known that free trade results in an improvement in national welfare, despite the fact that the country's relatively scarce factor will suffer real losses. When workers receive a non-pecuniary cultural benefit as a result of work in industry A however, the adjustment of capital and labor is no t as complete as would occur without the cultural benefit.

This is because in free trade a wage differential is maintained between workers in the two industries, which represents a market distortion. However, since the distortion acts to maintain the cultural benefits of industry A workers, national welfare does rise with free trade in this version of the model compared with protection. Figure 1 shows, however, that the percentage increase in national welfare is lower in the presence of the cultural benefit. Thus, the presence of cultural benefits and the willingness of agents to act on them by resisting the switch to expanding export sectors, reduces the overall benefits from trade liberalization.

A further implication is that estimates of the benefits that countries will attain from trade liberalization may be overestimates of the effects because these studies do not explicitly incorporate cultural effects into their models.

### *Political Economy Effects*

When the liberalizing country is labor abundant, trade liberalization initially benefits only the workers in the expanding export sector. Workers in the import sector and all capitalists are hurt initially. If the proportion of workers in industry A together with capitalists form a majority of voters in the country, then there may not be support for moderate trade liberalization in a capital abundant country. However, in free trade, and for very small tariffs, the utility of workers in A may exceed their utility in the original protected economy.

This result is demonstrated for the particular parameters chosen in the simulation. Thus, if tariff reductions are substantial, and if workers form a majority in the country, then there may be sufficient support for trade liberalization. This suggests that under conditions of labor abundance a more severe trade liberalization package may actually engender greater support than a moderate package. If the liberalizing country were capital abundant, however, trade liberalization would initially benefit both the workers in the export sector and the capital owners.

This implies that moderate liberalization might gain the support of a larger group of individuals and if the majority of voters are capitalists and industry B workers then there will be political support for moderate trade liberalization. However, once the adjustment of workers from industry A to B begins, wages of all workers will fall, although rents to capital will continue to rise. For sufficiently large trade liberalization, utility of all workers may be below the original level with protection. Under conditions of capital abundance, a more ambitious trade liberalization package may not generate sufficient political support to be enacted.

### *Cultural Effects of Trade Liberalization with NPCB*

A common criticism of trade liberalization is its contribution to global cultural homogenization. In the cultural affinity model, moderate trade liberalization need not lead to declining employment in the industry with NPCB. Insofar as work directly or indirectly contributes to cultural transmission, although wages decline, non-pecuniary cultural benefits remain.

In effect, falling wages eliminates the non-pecuniary rents that were obtained with protection but need not have an effect upon the work culture or the number of workers who enjoy these benefits. In addition, the larger the cultural affinity of workers, the stronger is the resistance to adjustment. When the cultural affinity is very large, even a movement to free trade may not sufficiently reduce wages to induce a shift of workers between industries.

Thus, the stronger the cultural affinity in an industry, the less likely that trade liberalization will result in a loss of the cultural understandings with which it is associated. Also, in

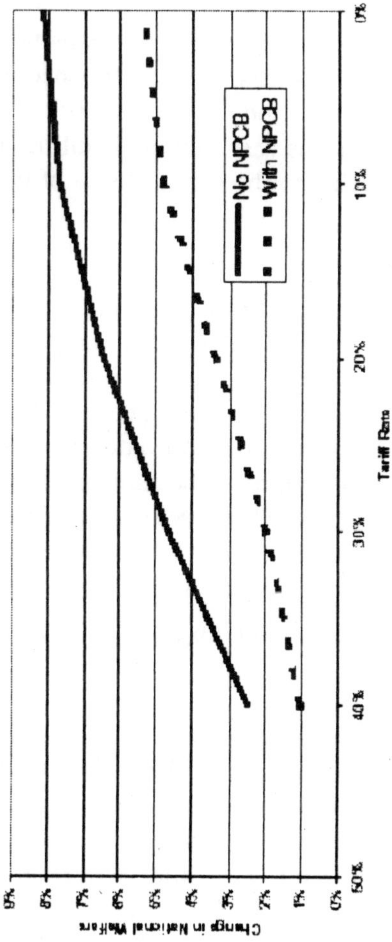
No NPCB
With NPCB
0%
10%
20%
30%
40%
50%
Tariff Rate
Change in National Welfare

*Figure 1*

cases in which trade liberalization does result in the shift of some, but not all, workers, there will be a rebound of wages for those who remain in the declining industry, if the country is labor abundant. This occurs because once some workers do begin to move between sectors, the wages for all workers rise. Thus those workers who can endure the transition, may enjoy wages in free trade comparable to those obtained with protection and will enjoy the non-pecuniary cultural benefits as well. Of course, in this case, national cultural benefits will have been reduced due to the reduced size of the industry.

### *Cultural Evolution*

Consider briefly the model in a dynamic context, in which, over time, older workers retire from the workforce while young workers enter. To model a dynamic system, hypothesize that younger workers have a smaller affinity for work in the import sector than do older workers. This may reflect a lack of appreciation for the community life associated with that particular production sector, or exposure to a more modern system of values during their childhood.

Once trade liberalization has begun, because of the cultural aversion to job switching by the veteran workers, a wage differential between industries develops. However, when workers retire, it will lower the supply of workers to the domestic import competing industry, which in turn will begin to raise the wage of remaining workers. New workers entering the workforce will not be attracted to the import sector because of the lower wage and because they have no cultural attachments to the sector. Thus they will seek work only in the high wage export sector. The increase supply of labor to this sector, over time, will bid down their wage rate. Eventually, wages in the import sector will rise up to meet the declining wages in the export sector and all workers will again be paid the same wage.

In the long-run equilibrium, all workers with a cultural affinity for the old sector will retire and eventually die off.

These cultural effects will disappear from society. However, presumably they will be displaced by new values among the younger generation. These workers will likely develop their own affinity for working in the new sectors and will display the same aversion to potential adjustment in their future.

### *Model Variation 2: The Presence of a Cultural Externality*

While the first model variation considers non-pecuniary cultural benefits resulting from participation in production (the cultural affinity model), the variation developed here considers non-pecuniary cultural benefits resulting from consumption of certain goods and services: the cultural externality model.

#### *Cultural Externalities*

Film, television, newspapers, and magazines provide a picture of the society in which they are produced. In this way media can be powerful determinants of national identity. The protection of domestic information and entertainment media from the dominant market power of foreign competitors constitutes the most widely recognized example of cultural constraints on trade. Exempting information and entertainment media from the normal WTO principle of national treatment (treating goods or services in a uniform manner regardless of the country of origin) defines for many scholars the "cultural exception" in trade policy. For advocates of these protections, visual media such as film and television, and print media such as books, newspapers, and magazines should not be understood as conventional goods or services, but as "cultural products" created by "cultural industries."

The protection of a nation's cultural products, argues French foreign minister Hubert Vedrine, is justified "by their impact on the language, the mentality, and the deep identity of the country," as well as by the quasi- monopolistic position of American media. Canadian efforts to protect domestic media have been among the most widely discussed examples of culturally protectionist trade policies. The United States is not only Canada's largest trading partner, but increasingly the source of its news, its entertainment, its political commentary, and-many Canadians fear-its values. Some statistics: 95 percent of feature films screened in Canada are foreign; and 83 percent of newsstand magazine sales are for foreign periodicals. Whether the predominance of foreign media should be a matter for concern depends on one's understanding of the appropriate role of media and the value of market competition.

Opponents of protections for domestic media hold that success or failure of media enterprises should reflect consumer preferences, in a manner comparable to other goods and services. If Canadian consumers did not prefer foreign films, television programs, newspapers, or magazines to their domestic counterparts, they would not dominate local markets. Proponents of protections approach the problem with fundamentally different assumptions.

### *A Cultural Externality Model*

To model such a cultural public good, assume that all individuals in Country A receive benefits from the presence of a locally produced "cultural" good. Consumption of the cultural good by other residents of A is assumed to raise each individual's utility. In this way cons umption by each person has a positive external effect on all others, i.e., there is a consumption externality, and thus the good has public good characteristics. The utility function of a representative individual, i, is given by,

$$U^i (C^i_A, C^i_B, S_A) - C^i_A)^a (C^i_B)^{1-a} + i^i S_B$$

where $C^i_A$ is the individual's consumption of the cultural good, $C^i_B$ is the individual's consumption of good B, and $S_A$ is the total amount of the domestic cultural good produced. The final part of the expression incorporates the additional utility each consumer receives from aggregate consumption of the domestic cultural good, where $\mu_i$ represents the individual's marginal utility from additional production of the cultural good.

Each individual's consumption of the cultural good A is so small relative to the aggregate production $S_A$, that each person maximizes his own utility assuming there is no effect upon the aggregate production level. However, the presence of the externality effect in consumption implies that the government can raise national welfare using a trade policy. In this case the national welfare function can be written as,

$$U(C_A, C_B, S_A) = (C_A)^a (C_B)^{1-a} + i S_A$$

where $C_A$ and $C_B$ are the aggregate consumption levels of goods A and B, and m is the summation of the mis across all individuals. Consider the use of a trade policy implemented by the government to try to enhance the value of the cultural externality. Suppose the government imposes an ad valorem tariff given by *t*. In this case the domestic price will differ from the fixed world price by the formula $P_D = (1 + t)P_W$.

First, in the presence of the cultural consumption externality, the optimal tariff is positive for the small importing country. The size of the optimal tariff depends upon the strength of the externa lity effect. The greater the marginal impact of total consumption on each individual, the larger will be the optimal tariff. This result implies that protectionism in the form of a tariff is a national welfare improving policy when it protects against imports that compete with a culturally important domestic product. It also means that trade liberalization that encourages greater imports of a foreign good, which competes with a domestic good that has cultural value, may result in a reduction in well being for the country rather than an improvement. This argument can be used to argue for a cultural exception in trade policy, that is, that countries should be allowed to protect against imports of goods, or should be allowed some exceptions in trade liberalization for goods that compete with culturally important domestic products.

But trade protectionism is not the first-best policy option in this case. Instead, a policy directed at the heart of the imperfection will correct for the distortion at lowest possible cost. Since the imperfection is a positive consumption externality in the use of the domestically produced product, the first-best policy option is a consumption subsidy on the domestic good alone. In this case however, a consumption subsidy applied only to the domestic good is equivalent to a production subsidy. If domestic consumers receive a rebate on purchases of the home good, then domestic producers will be able to raise their own prices while still undercutting the foreign price.

If the domestic firms raise the price only a little though, the local consumer's price for their good will be lower than the world price and all consumers would demand only the local product, creating excess demand. This means that domestic firms can raise their price and output until the new producer price minus the subsidy is equal to the world price for the good. At this point consumers are indifferent between the home and foreign good.

Domestic producers will be able to sell more of their product while imports of the substitute product will fall. Consumers, ultimately, will pay the original price for the subsidized product and thus their choices will not be affected. This result is equivalent to a domestic production subsidy, which will raise the producer's price but not the consumer's price of the product. Consider the use of a domestic ad valorem production subsidy (s) implemented by the government to enhance the value of the cultural externality. In this case the domestic producer price will differ from the fixed world price by the formula $P_{prod}=(1 + s)P_w$. The new producer price affects domestic production decisions, but since the consumer's price remains equal to the world price, there is no effect upon consumer choices.

Table 1 compares the results of this simple simulation. Notice that optimal protection, either using a tariff or a production subsidy, results in substantially fewer imports and greater domestic production of good A. The cultural utility effect of protection is small relative to total utility but the increase relative to free trade is substantial.

*Table 1*

| | *Free Trade* | *Optimal Tariff* $t = 19.2\%$ | *Optimal Subsidy* $s = 26.8\%$ |
|---|---|---|---|
| Good A Imports | 78.5 | 50.1 | 51.0 |
| Good A Production | 4.9 | 25.2 | 30.8 |
| Total Utility | 65.1 | 66.1 | 66.5 |
| Cultural Utility | 0.5 | 2.5 | 3.1 |

These results are expected since it is consistent with the theory of the second-best. Although a trade policy could improve national welfare in the presence of this type of cultural externality, a purely domestic policy, the production subsidy, could do so at lower cost. If a state believes it is imperative to protect a part of its national culture when foreign imports appear to threaten it, subsidizing the local activity is a better policy than implementing restrictive trade measures.

Of course, it is true that tariffs are often easier to implement since they generate government revenue rather than obligating government expenditures. In addition, despite the opportunity for cultural conservation through the use of trade or domestic policy, optimal implementation assumes good knowledge about the nature and magnitude of the cultural effect. In the case of cultural externalities, m would be difficult to measure accurately. If $\mu$ is relatively small for a country and if that country places a very high protective tariff or production subsidy into place, then the cost of cultural conservation may result in a reduction in national and individual welfare. In other words, in the case of inaccurate measurement, a government will not be able to assure that the protection provided will result in a national improvement. Just because an optimal tariff or subsidy exists, does not imply that the appropriate level is easy to identify. In other words, it is not true that any tariff or subsidy will be better when there exists a cultural externality, only that properly chosen tariffs or subsidies can lead to an improvement.

## Sociology of Healthcare

In 2002, In US, the Health Development Agency (HDA) organised three seminars that aimed to explore how government policy gets, or does not get, translated into practice. It aimed to identify the factors that help or hinder implementation, as well as the criteria that lead to success or failure. The seminars brought together an invited audience of policy makers, managers and practitioners from healthcare organisations, local government, central government departments and academic researchers. Graham points out that national policy shows a range of interpretations of what is meant by tackling health inequalities. At one end of the continuum, addressing the health disadvantage of poor groups and communities is the focus. The focus widens at the mid-point to narrowing the health gap between those in the poorest groups and those who are better off.

### *Policy Development and Implementation*

The process of policy development and implementation for tackling health inequalities. The arena of health inequalities demands recognition of the complex nature of the system, and the interdependence of factors operating to influence health and efforts to improve health. There needs to be a better balance between the top-down, command-and-control style of policy making and a local, bottom-up approach based more on lateral partnerships and networks. Policy delivery is more likely if local stakeholders are fully engaged. The experiences of local stakeholders are explored.

*Complexity and interdependence*

Implementing policy and delivering improved health is difficult work, especially in complex political and organisational settings. Some argues that while 'whole systems models are useful in recognising the interdependence of parts of the system of governance, they are less helpful in deciding precisely where to intervene ... Holism is desirable in principle, difficult to achieve in practice'. Some observers consider policy implementation to be a problem that seems to be getting worse. The ability to get policies and decisions implemented is becoming increasingly rare.

But in order to look afresh at how traditional approaches to policy and implementation might be modified or replaced, a new intellectual underpinning for policy is required. In addition to a reformulation of the intellectual basis of policy, the organisational systems used to deliver policy on the ground also need to be rethought. As many commentators have argued, if progressive policies are to succeed in complex arenas, then moving from hierarchical and command-and-control modes of operating to more lateral network models is a prerequisite. In particular, mechanistic command-andcontrol systems are unsuited to the complex, unpredictable demands of contemporary organisational life. There can be few areas where this is more true than in tackling health inequalities and improving health.

Policy failure can result from bad execution, bad luck, or bad policy. It may also result from too much policy that simply overwhelms those charged with its execution. Ineffective implementation tends to be viewed by policy makers as an example of bad execution. Or external circumstances may be so adverse that bad luck is identified as the reason for failure.

A reason that is less commonly advanced to explain policy failure is that the policy itself may be defective, in the sense of being based on inadequate information, poor reasoning, or hopelessly unrealistic assumptions about what is possible with the human and financial resources available.

The point about policy failure is that it suggests there can be no sharp distinction between formulating a policy and implementing it. But studies show that the likelihood of a successful outcome will be increased if thought is given to potential problems of implementation at the policy design stage. For instance, policy failure can result from policy being imposed from the centre, with no thought given to how it might be perceived or received at local level. It is not a case of bottom-up approaches to policy and action being preferable to top-down ones. An optimal balance between the two is necessary. Problems can arise when there is evidence of an imbalance.

Only those who subscribe to a model of perfect rationality in policy making would consider that perfect implementation was possible. In fact, implementation involves trade-offs, compromises, and operating with often poor or no information. Understanding implementation, as well as securing its effectiveness, is likely to entail a number of approaches - structural, procedural/managerial, and behavioural. The seminars considered all of these.

A fourth approach, and perhaps the most fundamental, though often ignored or understated, is political. If implementation of a policy takes insufficient account of the realities of power, then the policy is unlikely to succeed. A political approach may also challenge the assumptions on which other approaches are based, eg those of behavioural analysts or management consultants.

Implementation failure often results in regrets about the absence of leadership. But it could be that problems of implementation are, in many instances, problems in developing political will and expertise. Problems of performance and effectiveness are problems of power and politics - power imbalances, powerlessness, and the inability of some groups or causes to get their ideas or policies taken seriously.

Therefore a political strategy for implementation is as important as a strategy for agreeing more technical factors, such as targets or performance indicators. 'Unless and until we are willing to come to terms with organisational power and influence, and admit that the skills of getting things done are as important as the skills of figuring out what to do, our organisations will fall further and further behind'.

The complexity and breadth of the health inequalities agenda at both national and local levels are not in doubt. They are reflected in a wide range of decision-making processes and complex partnerships spanning different decision-making and performance-management systems. As noted, the various moves to tackle inequalities resemble a complex adaptive system. Such a system has been described as 'a collection of individual agents with freedom to act in ways that are not always totally predictable, and whose actions are interconnected so that one agent's actions changes the context for other agents'. In complex systems, unpredictability and paradox are everpresent and some things will remain unknowable.

Furthermore, the interactions within a complex adaptive system are often more important than the discrete actions of the individual parts. A principal theme to emerge from studies of the policy process is that policy formulation and implementation are interdependent activities, and policy initiators should consider them in combination. If policy is to be successfully implemented, then those stakeholders who have responsibility for its implementation should be involved in its design from the outset.

### *Stakeholder views of the local system*

Stakeholder views of implementation and tackling health inequalities at local level are critical to the success or otherwise of policy, and have a clear impact on how policy implementation might be conceptualised. In their exploratory study of the perspectives of various stakeholders, were concerned to investigate the nature and dynamics of local systems within which policies aimed at reducing health inequalities are being implemented. Stakeholders' views are shaped by their different conceptions of the local system. For some stakeholders, the local system is geographically bounded, with particular emphasis placed on neighbourhood renewal and area-based initiatives such as the New Deal for Communities and Health Action Zones, which target the worst areas nationally and locally.

The emphasis is placed on a developmental approach characterised by learning, evidence and technical support, promoting experimentation and innovation to inform and influence mainstream change. In such a context, a commandand-control approach to policy and its delivery, pursued through vertically organised performance management and inspection arrangements, may be wholly inappropriate and run counter to the developmental ethos.

For other stakeholders, the local system is depicted as a network of relationships. Partnerships are seen as a defining feature and the key delivery vehicle, with local strategic partnerships (LSPs) and neighbourhood management models variously highlighted as having a pivotal role. Issues of governance, politics and accountability are important in this conception of the local system, as well as the power imbalances between the various stakeholders engaged in the process.

Local strategic partnerships are not only bringing together the health and regeneration agendas, but also bringing the democratic decision-making structures of local authorities together with different models in business and health organisations. Research into understanding LSPs is needed in order to discover how to render them more effective, or to disseminate more widely the successes of some and the constraints operating on others. Critical to such a view of the local system is a belief that devolution and democratisation are fundamental to establishing genuine relationships with local people, which could allow effective solutions to complex problems to be explored. Again, such a view of the local system based on horizontal or lateral linkages and networks is at odds with a system of policy and implementation that is vertically organised in hierarchies.

Finally, and related to the notion of governance, is the importance attached to the various levels of policy and implementation - national, regional and local. Some accounts present policy implementation as a rational process of local delivery within national frameworks of strategy and accountability. The system is portrayed as a command-andcontrol one, but with increasing degrees of devolution permitted and more promised. As noted earlier, this is in keeping with the recent thrust of government policy that seeks to emphasise local choice and diversity, with services becoming people-centred and responsibility for them devolved to enable local communities to influence the shape and impact of policies and services. Within this context of stakeholders' overlapping understandings of the local system for delivery and implementation, a number of barriers to implementation may be identified, operating at macro- and micro-levels. At a macro-level, eight themes were identified:

— Questioning of the emphasis on local delivery, eg through area-based initiatives, when there was more visible national action on issues such as income redistribution

— Tension generated by a top-down emphasis on performance management conflicting with local autonomy

— Turbulence and continuing instability in the local system arising from modernisation and organisational change

— Conflicting timeframes at national and local levels to build sustainable relationships between agencies and local people

— Tension between the focus on, and priority attached to, a downstream as distinct from an upstream health agenda, and their respective contributions to tackling inequalities

- Different perceptions of leadership roles, commitment and accountability of various government departments, eg perceived lack of connectivity between Department of Health priorities and other central departments' commitment to neighbourhood renewal
- Confusion about accountability and responsibilities in exercising a leadership role in inequalities
- Lack of understanding of public health and a preoccupation with acute hospital services among the public.

At a micro-level, other tensions were identified that had an impact on implementation:

- Emphasis on partnership working in a context where capacity is limited
- Emphasis on planning where capacity was also limited and community planning in particular underdeveloped, eg evidence from health action zones and New Deal for Communities showed that plans were generally 'hopelessly unrealistic, badly set out and unspecified'
- Emphasis on need for evidence in a context where it was difficult to 'prove' that change was happening at a community level, especially within a short timescale
- Concern with structural change versus the importance of people as drivers of change - too much focus on structural fixes, and neglect of developing and rewarding people
- Fundamental difficulties in influencing or 'bending' the mainstream, and a preponderance of short-term initiatives and/or projects.

These stakeholders perspectives are derived from a small exploratory study; other sources of evidence about stakeholders' experiences of the policy process may provide contrary views. Nonetheless, the stakeholder interviewees were selected to provide diversity in terms of their views and roles and location within the system. While it may be possible to challenge some statements, the study indicated how these stakeholders perceive their working environment and challenges to tackling health inequalities. Other studies suggest the views expressed by the respondents do not appear untypical or exceptional.

The place of evidence in decision making Partly as a result of a preoccupation with evidence-based medicine, there is a tendency to overstate the importance of evidence as a driver in decision making. Evidence on effective interventions forms part of the decision-making process for addressing inequalities in health. But it is rarely a starting point at local level. Priorities for implementation more often emerge out of the planning process, and in response to funding opportunities. The evidence base is itself the product of decision making in relation to methods for synthesis and criteria for inclusion of research studies. It informs part of the decision-making process for addressing inequalities in health, but is inadequate in meeting an agenda which is also driven by values of social welfare and equity, and where effectiveness may lie in how decisions are reached as well as an assessment of the evidence which underpins them.

### *The evidence base for tackling health inequalities*

Those seeking to prioritise initiatives to address health inequalities on the basis of the evidence face a number of challenges.

First, the intended policy outcome and focus of interventions need to be defined precisely. As pointed out above, there are different understandings of what health inequalities can mean. In particular, interventions that focus exclusively on the most deprived groups and areas will not necessarily reduce the health gap between those who are more deprived and more affluent. Unless such interventions improve the health status of those living in poor socioeconomic circumstances at a faster rate than improvements in health of the better-off, the gap will not be narrowed. Such interventions are unlikely to reduce the overall health gradient across socio-economic groups.

Second, the evidence base for tackling health inequalities is scanty. Evidence-based medicine has traditionally been based on systematic reviews of controlled intervention studies. This approach does not always fit well with appropriate research strategies to evaluate measures to address the social and economic determinants of health. Consequently there is limited evidence about interventions designed to improve the health of particular disadvantaged communities; to assess the effectiveness of health service interventions; or in relation to specific topics associated with inequalities in health. There are strong arguments for a more inclusive approach to the evidence base. The importance has also been demonstrated of drawing on decision-making models that reflect different notions of evidence, and different approaches to weighing up evidence in order to reach judgements in situations of extreme uncertainty. These include impact assessments, forecasting, scenario-building, public inquiries and the legal process.

Third, it is argued that focusing on the evidence base and the individualised interventions that typically populate it has the effect of ignoring the more important macro-level determinants of health, and the degrees to which inequity is tolerated and sustained through policies at national and local levels. Inequalities in health reflect wider inequalities. At a micro-level, too, reliance on the evidence base works against a recognition or assessment of the effects of synergy, and also underestimates context-specific aspects of achieving change within local communities.

Fourth, interventions need to reflect theoretical approaches to understanding social and environmental sources of structural inequalities in health status, how they interrelate, how they are mediated, and how they are constructed over an individual's life history. Just as inequalities in health emerge from an accumulation of different forms of disadvantage across the life course, so interventions that are appropriate for tackling these inequalities are often complex, operating on a number of different levels over a long period, and involving multiple professions and organisations each with their own values, cultures and priorities. Following a social-ecological model of health, some argue that for maximum effectiveness interventions need to be carried out simultaneously across a wide range of sectors. They state that research is needed into multi-level intervention approaches 'to contribute to our understanding of how best to create linkages between levels of influence and how to sequence or co-ordinate interventions across levels', as well as on the increased cost effectiveness of intervening at additional levels. Such an approach to generating evidence implies challenging the prevailing orthodoxy in favour of randomised controlled trials and an essentially biomedical view of what constitutes credible evidence.

It is important to appreciate that the type of evidence useful in tackling health inequalities and change management is likely to differ significantly from that which can guide clinical practice. When investigating such areas, research methods are needed that allow for the process of change to be explored and understood, rather than those that concentrate on measuring the outcome. It is not a case of opting for one or the other - both types of evaluative research are needed. A better balance between them is also needed.

Fifth, a focus on identifying new and effective interventions for addressing health inequalities may divert attention away from a critical analysis of the ways in which current policies, priorities and ways of working contribute to disadvantage, or from developing ways of ensuring new policies are critically and prospectively assessed for their effects on health inequalities. The so-called 'inverse care law' remains much in evidence.

### *A Development Focus*

While the overall evidence base is limited, in some cases more could be achieved by applying what is already known. There is a need for a greater focus on development, rather than on acquiring additional knowledge. There is a case for shifting the focus to understanding and evaluating the process of change, and how it occurs, as well as its outcomes. A sharper focus on action research might assist in bringing the two activities closer together in ways that enable research to influence practice. As Fulop et al. state, 'those undertaking action research suggest that the inevitable effect a researcher will have on an organisation or individuals while undertaking research should be harnessed for positive benefits within the organisation. In action research, implementation and research occur iteratively, and the researcher is part of the change process'. Some suggests that action research can also be used in a number of ways to generate different types of knowledge:

— When no evidence exists to support or refute current practice, or when poor knowledge, skills and attitudes exist to carry out evidence-based practice

— When gaps have been identified in service provision, or services are under-used or deemed inappropriate

— When new roles are being developed and evaluated and there is a need to work across traditionally conflicting boundaries.

### *Health Inequalities at Neighbourhood Level*

The evidence is well established that inequalities in health have a strong spatial dimension. Research indicates increased polarisation, with growing contrasts between poorer and better-off areas. The Social Exclusion Unit identified 4,000 neighbourhoods that are 'pockets of intense deprivation where the problems of unemployment and crime are acute and hopelessly tangled up with health, housing and education'.

The National Strategy for Neighbourhood Renewal is viewed by the government as an important part of its response to deprivation and inequalities. There is growing understanding of the role that 'place' plays in influencing individuals' and families' levels of exposure to health risks, as well as their chances and opportunities for being healthy.

Poorer people may have poor health in part because they have to live in places that are health damaging. People have higher exposure to physical hazards such as environmental pollution, traffic volume and rates of road accidents. People have poorer access to public services, including primary care, public transport, shops and recreation facilities. Macintyre and colleagues studied the influence of home - and specifically tenure - on health. They confirm that renters are both poorer, and in poorer health, than owners; and suggest plausible physical and psychosocial mechanisms through which features of the home and the area in which it is located might have health-promoting or health-damaging effects on physical and mental health. They also suggest that influences of housing and area on health are likely to be more direct than the more generalised effects of income and social class.

The notion of social capital has growing currency in helping to explain how psychosocial pathways could operate to influence the health of individuals and families. Lupton and Power's work on social exclusion and neighbourhoods goes some way to positioning such health risks and opportunities within a cycle of neighbourhood change, decline and potential renewal. There are thus good reasons why an area-based approach to tackling health inequalities, that is part of a wider policy for community regeneration, is an appropriate and important part of a national response to the health gap between rich and poor. But reviews of the evidence indicate that few evaluation studies of interventions have focused on economically disadvantaged areas as the unit of analysis, so there is very little robust UK evidence on how effectively to improve the health of such communities.

The focus on deprived communities will not necessarily close the health gap unless the health of those in poorer areas improves at a faster rate than in more well-off areas. The overall health gradient across socio-economic groups is unlikely to reduce without wider, population-based policies. Interventions addressing the root causes of ill health Curtis and colleagues draw on structured reviews of the evidence to identify the health impact of particular types of interventions: where the primary aim has been to change the economic, social and physical environment in neighbourhoods, with the potential of improving the health of socially disadvantaged groups and communities. They show that regeneration can make a positive contribution to improving the health of those in poorer socioeconomic circumstances.

But there is also some potential for negative impacts on the health of these groups, and a worsening of health inequalities. It is important that assessment of the health consequences of such schemes is an integral part of their planning and design. Various tools for health impact assessment are being employed at a number of levels. Health-related interventions for reducing health inequalities Bauld et al. mapped the range of evidence concerned with the effectiveness of health-related interventions for reducing health inequalities in the context of neighbourhood renewal. While, overall, the evidence base is underdeveloped, their review draws attention to a range of sources that can inform practice.

Arblaster and colleagues' systematic review of the literature identifies a number of intervention characteristics that contribute to successful outcomes in improving the health of disadvantaged groups. Petticrew and Macintyre specify a number of intervention areas shown to be effective in reducing inequalities. Systematic reviews of the evidence in the main intervention categories relevant to neighbourhood renewal are being assembled by HDA. Petticrew and Macintyre make the point that interventions can be considered successful only when they are at least as effective for the lowest socioeconomic group as for the highest. Interventions that are effective in general terms may be ineffective in reducing health inequalities.

Well established evidence on the role of access to health services demonstrates the inverse care law: in areas where the need is greatest, there is often the poorest supply or quality of provision. This pattern of inequity of access is clearest with respect to primary care and prevention services. For example, there are fewer GPs per head of population in more deprived areas compared with more affluent areas. Recruitment and retention of staff is problematic, particularly in inner cities. There is less take-up of all types of preventive care in deprived communities, and among black and minority ethnic populations. Primary care is at the centre of the government's NHS modernisation project. One of the core functions vested in PCTs is to improve population health and address inequalities.

Some notes that, 'the very breadth of activities involved - from individual health advice to organisational forms of primary care organisation to complex community interventions - is itself a stumbling block'. They also point to a variant of the inverse care law - the inverse prevention law - whereby communities most at risk of ill health tend to experience the least satisfactory access to preventive services. Lack of evidence on effective interventions is not the only factor that influences the potential for tackling health inequalities in the primary care setting.

Research has highlighted a range of factors that operate as barriers to implementation of interventions that have proven effectiveness. These barriers include lack of commitment, experience and incentives among some practitioners, as well as organisational prioritisation, and the resources and capacity to implement effective programmes. Nevertheless national tracker studies of 75 PCTs have reported progress by PCTs in establishing an infrastructure for health improvement. Emphasis has focused on addressing inequalities in access to services. Many PCTs have implemented health improvement initiatives in line with the national service frameworks.

Perhaps the most troublesome issue for PCTs is that health improvement drops down the agenda when set against the 'must-dos' related to the acute sector. A contributing factor, as a survey carried out for the HDA of PCTs and their public health roles discovered, is the paucity of work on the public health role in primary care. There is a need to look systematically at ways of building human resource capacity in public health at the primary care level. Among the themes identified in the survey, and affecting progress, are:

- Pace of change/organisational uncertainty
- Multi-disciplinary working and inter-professional relationships
- Developing guidelines on approaches to public health in primary care
- Developing the public health workforce
- Public health: everybody's business but nobody's priority?

The concept of social capital has increasingly been viewed as relevant to helping explain patterns of health inequalities in communities. It is also informing policy and intervention options aimed at reducing health inequalities, particularly through efforts and investment in building social capital in ways that can generate health benefits in socially disadvantaged communities. More broadly, policy makers increasingly view the potential of social capital for generating economic, social and health outcomes as a reason why working with communities and building social cohesion is a prerequisite to tackling deprivation and inequalities. Social cohesion and community engagement therefore become central for turning policy into practice.

The theory of social capital derives from the work of Putnum, Coleman and others. It is concerned with the production and use of resources that are embedded in social structures and networks, rather than in individuals. Putnum views social capital as the features of social life - networks, norms and trust - that enable participants to act more effectively to pursue shared objectives. The theory remains subject to debate and development. There is an increasing amount of empirical work that tests the relationship between health and measures of social capital. Although positive effects of social capital on health have been identified, there are many questions to be addressed, including the relationship to health inequalities.

There is a significant research agenda for understanding and applying the idea of social capital to benefit the health of deprived neighbourhoods. Specific intervention studies may provide a way forward that allows for more precise testing of how health benefits might flow from specific elements of social capital. For example, the spread of information, and the presence of mutual support within networks, can provide levels of protection against infectious disease and HIV/AIDS, and may enable take-up and maintenance of healthpromoting behaviours.

Strengthening community involvement in decision making, governance and democratic renewal are also viewed as ways of building social capital to improve the health and wellbeing of socially disadvantaged communities and groups. It is argued that there are opportunities provided within current policies for encouraging and supporting civic engagement and democratic performance. For example, support to voluntary and community groups, and local people's participation in policy processes, could promote social capital formation in neighbourhoods. Community leadership provides a further focus, and changed practices among elected representatives could mediate improved levels of trust between communities and institutions.

Overall, although the literature identifies various ways of building social capital, there has been very little work examining the relative effectiveness of such interventions, including the impact on health inequalities. Work to refine definitions and instruments should support the opportunities for evaluation and strengthen the evidence base. Complex interventions and the challenges for evaluation Local strategies for community regeneration and reducing health inequalities are multi-faceted and operate at a variety of levels. 'Complex community interventions' are viewed as offering the best prospects for tackling the problems of deprived neighbourhoods. Technical and methodological difficulties abound for evaluation, and there is considerable debate about the most appropriate evaluation approach. Judge and colleagues point out that such interventions do not lend themselves to traditional evaluation methods such as randomised controlled trials. A more flexible evaluation framework is needed if evidence for effectiveness and learning is to be secured. Rigorous evaluation is critical to ensuring that any potential detrimental implications of policies and programmes for health are understood, and harm avoided.

Curtis et al. highlight the types of evidence required to determine the health impacts of programmes and interventions that focus on improving the social and economic circumstances of poorer communities. The strongest evidence, it could be argued, would be derived from studies that collect similar data for large samples of individuals chosen from a variety of different places, and follow them over time, with complementary qualitative studies to collect more in-depth information.

Ideally, quasicase control methods should be used to compare populations not affected. Cost, practical and ethical reasons have hindered such research in the UK context, but there are examples of such trials in other countries. In the UK, researchers have adapted ideas of 'realistic evaluation'; and a 'theory of change' perspective developed by the Aspen

Institute in the USA. These approaches acknowledge social programmes as complex, open systems. The potential for traditional evaluation methods, including quasi-experimental designs, to explain how or why the programme works is viewed as weak, particularly given that the variety of variables cannot be controlled. Essentially, these approaches are concerned with defining and testing the logic that underpins the relationship between problems, planned interventions and outcomes.

It is evident that there are many obstacles to achieving successful change. While some may have their roots in the policies themselves, others arise from the challenge of bringing about change in complex settings, where there are multiple stakeholders in the shape of professions and organisations each with its own values, cultures and standard operating procedures. Much of the complexity is the product of compartmentalised thinking that is not joined-up, seen in the wide range of projects and initiatives that not only reinforce a fragmented approach to delivery, but also divert managers from taking a strategic, long-term view.

## Managing System Change

A recurring theme throughout the seminars was the persistence of disjointed government, despite much rhetoric extolling the virtues of joined-up policy, organisation and management, and the importance of networks and lateral forms of organisation and management. The problem can best be understood with reference to three strands of literature: central-local relations; implementation; and organisational political sociology.

The history of public policy and management is marked by cyclical shifts between central and local control, and between vertical hierarchies and horizontal partnerships or networks. Finding an optimum balance between these various conflicting pressures has proved illusive. Ferlie notes that the new PCTs are being encouraged to organise themselves in a different way from traditional, vertically organised NHS organisations centred on command-andcontrol concepts. The changes 'suggest the need to develop a more subtle and indirect leadership style, often associated with the leadership behaviours contained within the model of the learning organisation' associated with Senge. Here the focus is on the local health system or community as a whole, rather than on discrete NHS agencies. Yet, for all the rhetoric surrounding joined-up policy, organisation and management, the reality is that obstacles to moving away from a silo-based approach remain.

There remains a strong and embedded 'new public management' approach that manifests itself in imposing ever more elaborate targets, performance management systems and audits on local agencies that are required to modernise and deliver on targets. This mode of organisation is vertically structured with a strong commandand-control emphasis and style. This leads to an uneasy coexistence of two apparently distinct modes of organisation, or intellectual approaches. The outcome is confusion, stress, and greater uncertainty among local organisations. The key question is: will a governancebased mode of lateral organisation reach its potential, or will it remain marginalised by a still powerful new public management movement?

The shift from vertical silos to horizontal, joined-up arrangements is not without historical precedents. There is a long history of joint working in respect of health and social care. A lesson from this is the 'long-lasting nature of the key obstacles', including ministerial ambition, departmental survival, rigid boundaries, and inflexibility in public expenditure. There is a substantial evidence base testifying to 'decades of disjointed working'. Countering the tendencies to fragmentation and disjointedness requires shifts in both the vertical relationships between centre, region, locality and neighbourhood; and the horizontal links between organisations at different levels of the governance system. For such a wholesystems approach, complex systems need to be understood in terms of the interactions between the different parts of a system and its environment. But while whole-systems models may be useful in acknowledging the interdependence of the various parts of the system of governance, they are inherently liable to failure as disequilibrium sets in. They are as robust as their weakest link, and what may start as virtuous circles can easily become vicious circles.

Securing effective joined-up policy and organisation requires effective leadership and management. If this is absent, for whatever reason, including a culture of systems compliance and poor motivation, it is unlikely that the modernisation of policy and implementation will be realised. According to Senge's model of a learning organisation, future leaders and managers will increasingly need to think and act systematically by:

— Seeing interrelationships rather than static structures

— Understanding how systems evolve through time

— Focusing on areas of high leverage

— Avoiding symptomatic 'solutions' such as short-term fixes.

Hambleton et al. devised a threefold view of leadership:

— Designed and focused leadership - provides a clear vision of future direction, a firm manifesto, a dedicated budget, a high-profile leader

— Implied and fragmented leadership - provides a consensual view of direction, operates on an implicit rather than explicit forward plan, puts together packages of resources through joint funding arrangements, invisible leadership

— Emergent and formative leadership - relies on implementation to shape policy, reflects pragmatism in guiding future direction, uses ad hoc resources to make progress.

Designed and focused leadership can offer a more autonomous leadership, depending on style and representational legitimacy. The fragmented, multiorganisational model, which implies a collaborative approach to leadership, may offer weak leadership that is subservient to external policy influence. Formative leadership reaffirms the fragility of partnership structures and processes to achieve desired ends. Less is known about 'good ways to manage initiatives which cross boundaries between public, voluntary and private sectors, about initiatives which are based in communities and involve networks of different agencies, or about management outside the rules'.

Equipping managers with the skills needed to operate in this challenging environment - one marked by the need to balance stakeholders' interests, understand complex accountabilities, and manage for social outcomes - is being addressed by the NHS Modernisation Agency, the NHS Leadership Centre, and the NHS University, among others. The leadership modernisation programme is informed by three key components: successful care delivery systems; successful improvement science practitioners; and successful leaders. But the focus of activity is still on the primary and secondary care delivery system, rather than on public health. The notion of public health management as a topic meriting dedicated attention is beginning to attract attention, not only in the UK but globally. Public health goals cannot be achieved without a serious partnership across the disciplines of public health and management. Studies of managing change in health systems can provide useful insights for managing change in public health. In their study of strategic change in the NHS, for example, Pettigrew et al. identified eight factors accounting for receptivity and change, derived inductively from their studies of change at district level:

— Quality and coherence of policy generated locally
— Availability of key people leading change
— Long-term environmental pressure
— Supportive organisational culture
— Effective managerial-professional relations
— Cooperative inter-organisational networks
— Simplicity and clarity of goals and priorities
— Fit between district's change agenda and its locale.

The factors offer 'a linked set of conditions which provide high energy around change'. Importantly, 'this energy and the capabilities which underpin it cannot be conjured up over a short period of time through the pulling of a single lever'. Receptive contexts for change are dynamic, and can be created by attention to the factors listed above. They are also reversible, by the removal of key individuals or by some other act which serves to create disequilibrium in the local setting. Arguably, those engaged in improving population health have not been exposed to such ways of thinking and bringing about change. Experience of implementing the National Strategy for Neighbourhood Renewal illustrates a number of the points made above. Commenting on previous programmes and the lessons to be learned, Fordham suggests that 'inadequacies in programme implementation' were responsible for many of the weaknesses identified. These include:

— Failure of local partnerships to exert significant influence over partner behaviour
— Lack of inter- and intra-agency coordination
— Project-driven mode of operation which focuses on spending special funding rather than influencing main programme budgets

— Inadequate project development and appraisal technology.

The Neighbourhood Renewal Unit identified some further important weaknesses, including:

— Lack of relevant skills and experience on the part of those involved in programme implementation

— Frequently faulty analysis of the relationship between problem diagnosis, underlying cause and proposed remedy

— Failure to take sufficient account of what has worked, or not worked, elsewhere.

Drawing on early evidence of the operation of the Neighbourhood Renewal Strategy introduced in early 2001, Fordham observes that 'implementing the national strategy will prove challenging'. Among the critical issues to be considered are:

— *Securing cultural change* - the Neighbourhood Renewal Strategy's insistence on joint working and a more focused use of main programme resources requires a process of cultural change within all the implementing agencies

— *Skills development* - new ways of working are called for, within and across disciplines, in ways few staff have experienced - but the promised national skills strategy is still being developed, and in any event it will count for little if local agencies do not respond to it, as seems likely; LSPs have yet to produce local learning action plans that indicate how skills gaps are to be dealt with

— *Project-based culture* - the focus on projects remains, rather than influencing main programme budgets, which could prove dysfunctional if the long-term aim is to become mainstream

— *Using evidence* - the reluctance to seek or use evidence survives, as those recruited to the Neighbourhood

Renewal Strategy tend to subscribe to an experiential view - 's/he who does, knows'.

In a study of 88 areas prioritised for neighbourhood renewal, the Audit Commission was concerned with identifying barriers to change, and strategies that appear to be overcoming the barriers. Departments still adopt a vertical, silo-based mentality, each setting targets for local agencies that reflect their particular priorities. Greater consistency would provide local agencies with a coherent central steer, and remove some of the confusion which is evident. On the other hand, if local commitment to change things is weak, progress will remain poor regardless of how the centre responds.

The Commission's research also discovered a strong desire on the part of local agencies for fewer initiatives and projects. These detract from the message that mainstream budgets and services are the keys to change. In such a fragmented context, learning the lessons in order to encourage mainstream approaches becomes a hit-or-miss affair. Fewer initiatives would encourage the use of mainstream programmes. The research explored the workings of LSPs, and discovered considerable variation in the ways they function. Numerous problems were identified, including the absence of communication strategies in half the sample, and the absence of monitoring arrangements in half the sample. The ways in which meetings of LSPs are run can reduce efficiency and effectiveness.

The Audit Commission research examined the skills and culture in local agencies to determine their fitness for purpose with respect to neighbourhood renewal. The absence of organisational capacity to realise the strategy is an issue for many agencies. It was also apparent that many senior managers and frontline practitioners lack understanding of the aims of the Neighbourhood Renewal Strategy. Lack of 'ownership' of the policy is therefore a serious issue for many. Slow culture change in respect of partnership working was identified.

The rhetoric of partnership is evident - but not its practice. The prevalence of 'initiativitis', and the fatigue resulting from it, may be a factor as it can create a style of management and delivery focused on the short rather than the long term. A 'bidding' mindset can divert attention from the need to bring activities and resources into the mainstream. Professional boundaries could also militate against effective partnership working and reduce the possibility of encouraging flexibility around roles. However, many local agencies recognise these problems, and many are working to find solutions.

## Cultural Sociology and Conflict Prevention

The idea of cultural determinism is generally suspected, and it came out to be particularly controversial when applied to the explanation of the causes of war and peace in the Balkans. Cultures, as much as communities, are not compact and devoid of internal contradictions and changes, nor their members are committed to a single belief-system. This makes the analysis of culture contingent to varied assumptions of cultural elites, esp. their positions toward political elites, and to historical circumstances, rather than assimilating the essentialist assumption of persistent "traits" of particular cultures.

In fact, the essentialist assumption constitute the discourse of some cultural elites. Their discourse, nevertheless, predominates the public mind, and its ideas are conducive to intolerant and conflicting relationships toward the others. However, other cultural elites exist, which discourses are convenient to tolerance and peace and congruent to similar propensities among the mainstream population. Finally, some cultural elites exist which discourses are neutral or opportunistic both to conflict and peace perspectives.

The assumptions of culture implicated by the intergovernmental agencies operating in the post-conflict situations in the former Yugoslavia is another perplexity. To my knowledge no culturally informed approaches to conflict & peace processes have been demonstrated in this area so far in parallel to ordinary "track one third parties" mediation on the macro-level.

On a micro-level, the examples of good practice of the use of arts & culture in the postconflict situation are growing in number, mainly due to NGOs and informal activities of interested artists, scientists and cultural industries entrepreneurs. Yet, although the examples of bad practice in the terms of intolerance, notably the incidences of hate-speech, in the mainstream cultural institutions, including media, have declined in number; a new language of peace and reconciliation has not been created in place of the old language. Instead, the mainstreamers have resorted to an utterly pragmatic and shapeless style of talk, mainly avoiding the sensitive issues of ethnic relations.

On the other hand, when a public discuss is occasionally arranged around hot issues, such as the Croatian national television did these months with introducing the topic of the war-crimes in its prime-time broadcasting, the whole venture seemed to resumed the symbolic clashes that preceded the war in the 1990s. Namely, speakers in the discuss who admitted that the war crimes were committed on the Croatian side too, despite of the fact that Croatia originally, in the 1990s, was an object of aggression - were condemned by the "patriotic" opponents as "traitors"; besides, the condemnation has been supported by a relative majority of the population. This reveals the actual setback of the language of peace and reconciliation in the public sphere.

Of course, the introduction of public debates about the issue which has until recently been prevented to enter into the mainstream audience, is a brave move and represents a step forward in facilitating the expansion of the language of peace and reconciliation outside the confines of the NGO-sector.

But, if taken alone, the advocacy of peace and reconciliation may create a counter-effect. This problem brings us to a more complex understanding of the peace process. Rational persuasion on the basis of universalistic principles of human rights is not a trump-card for defeating the discourse of intolerance and hatred.

Peace and war are the parts of different institutional and development strategies serving to back up one or the other fundamental orientation. This includes the achievements of the economic strategies as well, which do or do not sustain collective hopes for a better future. Accordingly, dark economic future is not a friend of peace, but of intolerance and conflict that easily converts into ethnic/national identity politics of exclusion.

Hence a reliable and a more permanent peace can only be a product of concerted policies and actions of governments, civil society sector and private economy in all fields of development, aimed to expand the implementation of human rights, the balance of economic benefits and cultural sensibility and social empathy toward the others. Although the holistic approach to peace is saluted by many, notably by intergovernmental bodies working with UNESCO's "culture of peace" programmes, its operation seems to dissipate or being limited to the niches of education and media which apparently do not contradict dominant rules and practices.

Dominant rules and practices are exercised in a more or less conflicting way by conservatives entrenched in national institutions, by proponents of the notorious international policy of the "Concert of Powers", and by proponents of the freemarket orthodoxy. In such constellation a form of peace can be improvised, indeed, as it used to be many times in the Balkan history. But, the costs of the breakdowns of such a peace arrangement far exceed the costs of all activities in favour of peace undertaken by intergovernmental and other agencies.

Culture provides spiritual energies that nourish the strategies of collective survival at different levels. At the lower level, which includes conflicts and wars, culture supports the collective cause and emulates the arsenal of symbolic warfare. At the medium level culture legitimises political or economic changes that require the abandoning of the old habits and values in political culture or economic behaviour. At a higher level culture is understood as autonomous source of a wide spectrum of creativity.

This vision, other than being just a portrait of a workshop in arts or sciences, features a host of religious movements, artistic vanguards and political utopias yearning after a different worldorder, based on peace, creativity, co-operation and solidarity. The UNESCO´s "culture of peace" programme, although dwelling the context of power and development which assume the role of culture at the medium level, has inherited some tenets of the grand narratives of peace, but primarily their holistic format. Yet, the question is whether our knowledge about the roles of culture in conflict and peace processes is systematised enough and whether supportive political and economic mechanisms are being ensured for to sustain the holistic vision of peace.

Well, the reasons are many as much as the examples of non-prevention that may be instructive, including former Yugoslavia. For example, it took several years in between the warning signals sent by several social scientists in former Yugoslavia at the end of the 1980s/beginning of the 1990s and the UN and NATO interventions. Nevertheless, it is difficult to argue that the war in this case, at last its beginning, could have been prevented. There was no strong political will among the leading actors, primarily the Serbian political leadership at that time, to avoid the conflict.

Most importantly, the war was the mode of bringing the new nation-states into existence, whereby some segments of national cultural elites did participate in that venture. War and peace are very complex enterprises. They involve participation and collaboration of virtually all sectors of a society, including cultural which provides a general mind-set for one or the other enterprise. However, the contributions of each sector are not unique, but are many-sided and ambiguous. Ambiguities within culture, in particular, include options and alliances that cultural elites establish with political and economic elites.

Of course, synergies created in violent conflicts and in peace activities differ. First, the language of peace and non-violence lacks a "mythical focus", unlike the language of violence which is preoccupied with past times, which meanings are more or less (re)invented and accompanied with ideas of conspiracy and revenge.

Another important distinction is the assumption of the others. The language of peace minimises differences or takes them as the element of diversity which motivates curiosity and expands communication. The language of violence "inflates minor differences into huge issues", bringing them to the level of non-relatedness and exclusion from the outer world. To this image, the social world is divided into ultimate and self-referential categories of people(s).

Also, the alarms are installed and they happen to whine up moral panic as soon as the borderlines are blurred. Finally, the language of violence is typically derived from a groupmind and a group support. The intellectual proponents of nationalism, racism and similar ideologies, that endorse clashes between the categories, take their group attitudes correspondingly. They cannot function outside relatively firm group ties or established institutions. This aspect might explain the massive "conversions" of communists in former Yugoslavia into fierce nationalists in the new nation-states.

On the other hand, peace activists and intellectual proponents of plural identities and inter-ethnic reconciliation, although obtaining some group support and networking, take their attitudes mostly on individual basis. This is why peace culture is relatively weakly founded in the social milieu, unlike the groupminds and institutional settings of the proponents of conflict and violence, and why more intellectual and institutional reinforcement of the germs of milieus of peace culture in the area of the former Yugoslavia is needed.

### *Cultural discourses*

Cultural discourses are relatively consistent narratives produced by cultural elites, which provide a symbolic meaning to a collective strategy of survival. As such, intellectual, linguistic, artistic and religious skills and competencies are related to other forms of collective power. Nationalistic discourse, for example, pleads that all sources of power need to be tightly intertwined and eventually mobilised for the sake of national cause. This and other types of discourses that are schematised bellow will serve as a framework for the interpretation of the roles of culture in conflict and peace processes in the former Yugoslavia.

#### *Type 1: Culture in the Service of Political Power*

— Boundary and conflict-making interests (e.g., nationalism) that used to be superseded by a counter-power which is ideologically transcendent, but non-democratic

— Statist nationalism, "Ersatz"(surrogate)-nationalism/ statism (e.g., the Communist Sovietism or Yugoslavism)

— (Neo)racism (e.g., the "clash of civilisations")

— Historicism (deductive and analogy-driven thinking focused on grand historical narratives or particular events or episodes of the past), monumentalism/celebratory/ spectacular

— Focusing on ethnicity as the only reliable form of collective social life, whereby language and/or religion are marked as distinctive features of a nation.

— Group-mind predominates
— Cultural pessimism, cultural optimism pretended This discourse is essentialist and mostly prone to draw the definite borders & boundaries between ethnic/national groups and to assume conflicts between them as inevitable. It is strongly connected with a central power. If repressed, it accepts the imposition of the mono-culture as a tactical solution, i.e., as a means to achieve the nationalistic goals other way around.

Some variations within this type occur, for example the evolution of liberal nationalism in Slovenia and Macedonia in the 1990s and in Croatia and Federal Republic of Yugoslavia in the 2000, or distancing from the rightist nationalism on a part of clergy in the Roman Catholic Church in Bosnia and Herzegovina and in Croatia. Such an evolution depends on personal choices in career as well. If an artist or scientist makes a political career, as it used to happen relatively often, it may give rise to authoritarian, narcissistic and destructive traits of his/her personality, which happened to be absorbed or sublimated in his/her professional career.

Individual conversions from this discourse to other discourses are rare. Marriage between culture and political power is at the very core of this discourse and cannot be exchanged with other discourses that lack the substance of political power. This is why, for example, the bulk of the intellectuals who belonged to the Communist Party in the second Yugoslavia and who prophesised Marxist internationalism have substituted their discourse with nationalism in the 1990s: they always choose the modalities close to the political power. In general, having highly conformist attitude, this discourse is vulnerable to loosing a strong institutional support.

***Type 2- Art-for-art's sake***

— Pure aesthetic interest

— Elitism sometimes combined with (neo)culturalism / (neo)racism

— Cultural pessimism

Withdrawal from politics and broader public engagement; occasionally addressing the public for the sake of the professional interests Sceptical or hesitant toward cultural-industry business, or it depends on his/her estimation as to how much his/her personality and authorship could be preserved in such an enterprise

The opportunism predominates in this case, that is to wait for to see which political tendency is going to prevail so that the coexistence may be re-established and his/her internal peace & harmony be restored. The occurrence of ethnic and similar conflicts is interpreted as a natural disaster which human intervention by the means of political or public engagement is incapable to prevent. In the case of the second Yugoslavia, some former Marxist intellectuals have converted to this type.

***Type 3- Entangling culture and market economy***

— Interests are focused on cultural industries, competitive markets and mass culture

— Cautiously oriented across the boundaries & borders in searching for wider audience

Apolitical attitudes or pragmatically/ambiguously politically oriented

— Easier to merging culture with other sectors

— Economic rather than specifically cultural optimism

Prone to abandon the links with the Type 1, but also eager to keep the clientelist ties with the political regime for to obtain funds from the state financial budgets for culture. Basically profit-making oriented. Staying in peace with all important others is seen as a precondition for a good climate in cultural industry business. Reasons for conversions are basically utilitarian and realistic rather than idealistic. This discourse is still underdeveloped in the area of the former Yugoslavia. The bulk of private producers in the book industry, for example, heavily depend on state co-financing of their programmes.

***Type 4 - Alternative***

Transboundary and pluralistic oriented, multiple identity, prone to take the part in consultation, dialogue and training in conflict resolution on all sides of the ethnic conflict - Uses experimental and syncretistic forms of expression by merging arts with other genres that is occasionally dedicated to peace initiatives

— Non-institutional and event-culture displays, no permanent programmes or repertoires

— Anarchic assumptions and short-term activities devoid of generalising organisations & networks and long-term activities

Individualism predominates, sometimes combined with egocentric attitudes, that discourage other people to join, primarily people from the mainstream who take similar attitudes but who are accustomed to obtain collective support and approval on the basis of permanent ties and reciprocity

— Preferring sustainable forms of industrial and economic development, an interest in postmaterialism and the "life politics"

This is not an entirely new discourse, for some vanguard styles and experiments in arts have been launched in the former Yugoslavia in the 1960s already with a remarkable international success. However, the NGOs appeared only in the 1990s. Mostly dedicated to conflict prevention and peace process, but with limited resources and a little impact on social mainstreams. Occasionally converts to other types and then mostly to the Type 3. It is also questionable, as the third sector activities in general, which ways would this discourse develop if some larger amounts of financial funds or decision-making power would be poured into the sector. My experiences with the cases that approached to such an opportunity indicate the appearance of the tendencies toward monopolist attitude and closure, which is an evidence for that civil society and peace culture cannot be completely secluded from the characteristics of the mainstream society and culture nor the former can maturate in a self-containment.

## Cultural Patterns

Cultural patterns are beliefs and values that are not rationally systematised into a set of propositions and arguments in the terms of cultural discourses, but represent relatively incoherent descriptions of the common sense which constitutes everyday views and practices of a social majority. The evidence for that is given in numerous cross-cultural surveys based on the analytic model of "national culture". The model describes differences between cultures in the terms of hierarchy vs. egalitarianism, collectivism vs. individualism, masculinity vs. femininity, and anxiety vs. relaxed attitudes. Empirically, great dispersions of the attitudes among people in each country exist. Also, the patterns are suspect to environmental changes that have taken place in the last decades.

The same applies to the case of contemporary Croatia, for example. The profile of the "national culture", based on samples of high school students and their parents and teachers, indicates a slight preponderance of beliefs and values in terms of egalitarianism, femininity, collectivism and anxiety. Other surveys, based on different analytical models, indicate that a considerable majority of people in Croatia supports the principles of democracy, including the equality between men and women and between national or ethnic groups.

Finally, social distance scale in Croatia toward Serbs, when compared with the year 1993, has significantly been reduced in 1998. This result can be ascribed to the armistice and a peace process that followed the end of 1995. These developments illustrate certain plasticity of the attitudes among mainstream people, including their views of the others. This may possibly be taken as the case for cultural optimism of peace, as "enemies" from yesterday have gradually been re-framed into neighbours and other socially closer categories.

Unfortunately, the process of lessening the social distance cannot be generalised so far. The mainstream opinions are strongly influenced by the opinion leaders in media, governments, political parties, churches, war-veterans associations, etc., whose biases are more rigid and persistent. The opinion-leaders are embedded in the settings which discourse essentially depends on the likelihood of periodical conflicts on the basis of ethnic and similar categories. That agenda-setting reinforces raison d´etre of such leaders.

Finally, an enormous research literature about the role of cultural patterns in conflict & peace processes exist that cannot be commented here, but only with reference to the use of the terms "culture" and "cultural differences". The attempts at defining permanent traits of a culture are delicate as they bring the language of research into area of the Type 1 discourse. This is the case with the former Yugoslavia too, since some of the political leaders insisted upon racial/civilisation differences between Balkan peoples in the terms of Huntigton´s "clash of civilisations". Nevertheless, Huntington himself was unable to construct the concept of "civilisations", least the premise of "inevitability" of their clashes, without conceding that only by interference of the actual political discourses and power strategies into traditional vocabulary of the meanings of a particular culture or religion the notions of "civilisations" and their "clashes" become instrumental.

Thus, cultural divisions are often made-up by politically motivated indoctrination, where the Type 1 discourse is projected into whole arrray of cultural patterns of a collective. As a consequence of such homogenising, differences within a culture are neglected or concealed.

# Bibliography


Barry Schwartz, "Social Change and Collective Memory: The Democratization of George Washington." American Sociological Review 56: 221-36, 1991.

Bennett M. Berger, *An Essay on Culture: Symbolic Structure and Social Structure*. Berkeley: University of California Press, 1995.

David Strang and John Meyer, "Institutional Conditions for Diffusion." *Theory and Society* 22: 487-512, 1993.

Diana Crane (ed.), *The Sociology of Culture*. Oxford: Blackwell Publishers, 1994.

Jeffrey C. Alexander and Steve Seidman (eds.), *Culture and Society: Contemporary Debates*. New York: Cambridge University Press, 1990.

Lyn Spillman (ed.), *Cultural Sociology*. London: Blackwell Publishers, 2002.

Margaret Archer, *Culture and Agency: The Place of Culture in Social Theory*. New York: Cambridge University Press, 1988.

_____________, "The Myth of Cultural Unity." *British Journal of Sociology* 36: 333-353, 1985.

Michael Schudson, "How Culture Works: Perspectives from Media Studies on the Efficacy of Symbols." *Theory and Society* 18: 153-80, 1989.

Richard A. Peterson, "Revitalizing the Culture Concept." *Annual Review of Sociology* 8:137-166, 1979.

Robert Wuthnow and Marsha Witten, "New Directions in the Study of Culture." *Annual Review of Sociology* 14: 49-67, 1988.

Wendy Griswold, "A Methodological Approach for the Sociology of Culture." *Sociological Methodology* 14: 1-35, 1988.

William A. Gamson and A. Modigliani, "Media Discourse and Public Opinion: A Constructionist Approach." *American Journal of Sociology* 95: 1-37, 1989.

# Index